POLICING
A CLASS SOCIETY

A Volume in the CRIME, LAW, AND DEVIANCE *Series*

Policing
a Class Society

The Experience of
American Cities, 1865–1915

SIDNEY L. HARRING

RUTGERS UNIVERSITY PRESS
NEW BRUNSWICK, NEW JERSEY

Parts of Chapters 1 and 2 are taken from "Policing a Class Society: The Expansion of the Urban Police in the Late Nineteenth and Early Twentieth Centuries," by Sidney Harring, in Crime and Capitalism: Readings in Marxist Criminology, *edited by David Greenberg. Reprinted by permission of Mayfield Publishing Company, Palo Alto, California.*

Parts of Chapter 4 are taken from "The Buffalo Police: Labor, Unrest, Political Power and the Creation of the Police Institution," by Sid Harring, Crime and Social Justice 4 *(1975). Reprinted by permission of Crime and Social Justice Associates, San Francisco.*

Chapter 5 was previously published as "The Police Institution as a Class Question: Milwaukee Socialists and the Police, 1900–1915," by Sid Harring, Science and Society *46 (Summer 1982). Reprinted by permission.*

Parts of Chapter 9 are taken from "Class Conflict and the Suppression of Tramps in Buffalo, 1892–1894," by Sidney Harring, Law and Society Review 11 *(Summer 1977):873–911. Reprinted by permission of Law and Society Association.*

Library of Congress Cataloging in Publication Data
Harring, Sidney, 1947–
Policing a class society.
(Crime, law, and deviance)
Bibliography: p.
Includes index.
1. Police—United States—History—19th century.
2. Social classes—United States—History—19th century.
3. Social conflict—United States—History—19th century.
4. Cities and towns—United States—History—19th
century. I. Title. II. Series.
HV8138.H38   1983   363.2′0977   82-20406
ISBN 0-8135-1000-7

For my mother and father
Georgene O. Harring and Sidney A. Harring
For my wife
Michelle
and our son
Malek

CONTENTS

LIST OF TABLES   ix

ACKNOWLEDGMENTS   xi

CHAPTER ONE   Introduction   3

CHAPTER TWO   The Urban Police Institution in the
                   Trans-Appalachian West, 1865–1890   22

CHAPTER THREE   The Patrol Wagon and Signal System,
                   1880–1900   49

CHAPTER FOUR   The Buffalo Police, 1865–1900   61

CHAPTER FIVE   The Police as a Class Question in
                   Milwaukee, 1865–1912   81

CHAPTER SIX   Cops as Strikebreakers   101

CHAPTER SEVEN   Liquor and the Saloon Question   149

CHAPTER EIGHT   The Crusade Against Dance Halls,
                   Gambling, Spitting, and Other
                   Recreational Behavior   183

CHAPTER NINE   The Tramp Acts and Repression of
                   Unemployed Workers   201

CHAPTER TEN   Policing Felony Crime   224

CHAPTER ELEVEN   Conclusion   247

NOTES   259

SELECTED BIBLIOGRAPHY   289

INDEX   297

LIST OF TABLES

1. 1860–1910 POPULATION OF GREAT LAKES/OHIO VALLEY
CITIES WITH OVER 100,000 INHABITANTS IN 1910   24

2. GROWTH OF POLICE FORCES IN GREAT LAKES/OHIO VALLEY
CITIES IN RELATION TO POPULATION, 1880–1915   35

3. RELATIVE STRENGTH OF POLICE FORCES IN GREAT LAKES/OHIO
VALLEY CITIES, 1890   37

4. POLICE CHIEFS' AND PATROLMEN'S SALARIES IN MAJOR
AMERICAN CITIES, 1899   43

5. OPERATION OF BUFFALO'S PATROL WAGON AND SIGNAL
SYSTEM, 1887–1896   54

6. ETHNICITY OF BUFFALO PATROLMEN AND CAPTAINS, BY
PRECINCT, 1890   79

7. STRIKES IN MAJOR GREAT LAKES/OHIO VALLEY CITIES,
JANUARY 1, 1881–DECEMBER 31, 1900   102

8. ARRESTS FOR MAJOR PUBLIC ORDER CRIMES BY SPECIFIC
OFFENSE IN BUFFALO, 1886–1900   207

ACKNOWLEDGMENTS

ALTHOUGH THE ACADEMIC WORLD tends toward individualism, especially perhaps, in the writing process, the present work would not have come into existence without a cooperative, even at times collective, effort. Hence no acknowledgment can adequately reflect the contribution that others have made to my work, not merely in the form of support, but also in the social creation of whatever skills I have and in the form of my analysis. In no particular order and without describing their special contributions I want to acknowledge and thank Howard Erlanger, Marshall Clinard, Bill Martinson, Doug Gurak, Mary Kritz, Doug Klegon, Bob Peterson, Bill Minter, George Dowdall, Jean Dowdall, Roz Lindner, Virginia Grabiner, Doris Goggins, Ray Waxmonsky, Barry Cohen, Lorraine McMullin, Gerda Ray, Paula Mollin, Stratton Rawson, Howard Kling, Susan O'Leary, Eric Swanson, Devon Hodges, Rick Abel, David Greenberg, Steve Spitzer, Jerry Markowitz, Paul Takagi, Sam Walker, John Schneider, Ken Kann, Theodore Ferdinand, David Montgomery, Donal MacNamara, Barbara Price, Natalie Sokoloff, Chris Suggs, Andy Karmen, Bob Panzerella, Edward Sagarin, Mildred Shannon, Marlie Wasserman, Helen Goral, Karilyn Konesky, Michelle Harring, Malek Harring.

This research was supported, in part, by grants from the Research Foundation of the State University of New York; the

Research Foundation of the City University of New York; and a Fellowship for College Teachers from the National Endowment for the Humanities. A State University of New York/Moscow State University Faculty Exchange Fellowship provided one semester at the Faculty of Law of Moscow State University, where I had both the opportunity to study socialist law and the time to read much of the early work of Marx, Engels, and Lenin.

I want to emphasize that I do not read the study of the police or of any other social institution as subsumed under a single academic discipline; rather, it is part of a long political process. We need to remake our society in order to provide justice, equality, and human fulfillment and to end injustice and oppression—a process that I see in class terms. We cannot remain blind to the kind of history in which Viet Nam and Watergate are simply two more sordid chapters in a history that we are continuing to write. The "cop on the beat" is an integral part in the making of this history, as are the named and unnamed people arrested on countless charges, real and fictitious.

POLICING
A CLASS SOCIETY

CHAPTER ONE

Introduction

AMERICAN SOCIAL SCIENTISTS are now in the second decade of major concern with the police institution in America, a concern born during the black rebellions of the 1965–1968 period and the antiwar movement of the 1967–1973 period. Public opinion polarized on the police issue, often along simplistic pro and con lines. Most social scientists concerned with the police as a public issue take a neutral stance, conceding that the police institution has been guilty of serious errors and shortcomings (not to mention a great deal of illegal activity) and generally pointing in the direction of orderly reform.

This study is grounded in the work of such social scientists. However, following a cue from British sociologist Maureen Cain, who criticized sociologists of the police for failing to "attempt a definition of the object of analysis," my concern is not to analyze or describe the "police problem" but to define what the American police institution is and to show how it developed.[1] Rather than take the functioning of the police institution for granted, I shall argue that its modern form emerged from class struggle under industrial capitalism and that, in spite of reform movements and professionalization, we now have essentially the same police institution that evolved in the intense class conflict of the 1870s, 1880s, and 1890s. In the conclusion I shall examine current problems in the police institution and how they can be traced to this formative process.

My focus on the concept of social class separates this work from most American research on the police institution. The prevailing view either holds that there is no relationship among class, the police, and social problems or, if it finds such a relationship, downplays its significance.[2] Research on the police has focused instead on concepts such as legality, professionalization, reform, political influence, crime control, police-community relations, and the like.[3] The resulting studies all make the assumption that the police institution is either above or outside the class struggle or that the concepts of social class and of class struggle are not particularly important in the United States.

What questions about the American police institution are most important? Scholars usually answer this question by selecting some aspect of police behavior inherent in the police role. For a Marxist scholar, however, the conduct of individual police officers and the contradictions inherent in the police role are secondary. The major question turns on the role of the police institution in maintaining the existing class system. In terms of understanding the evolution and structure of American policing, the question is: How has class society shaped the American police system? In the remainder of this chapter I shall define my terms and concepts and outline the framework for my analysis of the development and the role of the police institution in America.

CLASS

As Karl Marx saw it, the division of society into antagonistic classes determined the original need for the state and its various institutions of mediation in the class struggle, including the police.[4] Thus, in a very real sense, class struggle is at the core of the police function. A class society is one in which the population can be ordered hierarchically into distinct groupings based on their relationship to the means of production. Individuals in these groupings have some general sense of their position within the class structure, although they need not *all* by any means have this sense, nor do they have to see their position in specifically class terms. Following E. P. Thompson, I see class as a process and as a relationship, not as a static either/or variable.[5]

This outline of class structure will be the foundation for the class analysis throughout this study. Of course, debates continue about the meaning of class and about the appropriateness of individual categories. I have tried to stay as close as possible to Marx's own work in order to minimize their impact on this analysis, but in doing even that, I have already taken a position in these debates. I take my definition of class from Marx's outline of the issues in *Das Kapital*. In the American context, I consider the central issue of class society to be a struggle for power over the means of production, primarily between two classes: the bourgeoisie, the owners of the means of production, and the proletariat, those who work for wages. Other classes exist as well, most importantly, a large petty bourgeoisie, or middle class, composed of professionals, small businessmen, and a growing class of salaried, white-collared functionaries in business and government. Small farmers, in my view, constitute a distinct agrarian class, but they are for all practical purposes irrelevant in this study, except as they provided a steady supply of new wage workers for the cities.

It is not inconsistent to use a class analysis and at the same time to recognize that important divisions existed within these classes. The bourgeoisie were thrown into great disarray by the incredible speed of America's industrial revolution. The interests of the commercial bourgeoisie—those primarily involved with small-scale manufacture and trade—were undermined by the full unleashing of industrialization, and the industrial capitalists' interests won out in the long run. Similarly, locally owned (often family-owned) industries gave way beginning in the 1890s to monopoly capital with nationwide interests, and there were often important tactical differences between these two groups.[6]

On the next level down, the old petty bourgeoisie—established merchants who did not control production—had often been displaced by the bourgeoisie. A new petty bourgeoisie, composed of the growing group of professionals, had no such history. The various groups of small businessmen consisted of a wide range of people of all income levels, many of whom had close ties to working-class communities. Indeed, the saloon-keeper and corner grocer are traditional examples of petty bourgeoisie entrepreneurs solidly rooted in working-class communities, though not necessarily in working-class values. Marxists usually consider the petty bourgeoisie to be allied with the bourgeoisie because their position is dependent on the bourgeoisie's control of the means of production and because they benefit from the stability of the class society that the bourgeoisie promote.

Divisions within the proletarian class have been the subject of more research—much of it designed to refute the idea of classes by showing many other kinds of divisions. Four major divisions within the American working class have been widely analyzed. Of greatest importance during the late nineteenth century in the cities of the Great Lakes/Ohio Valley region were ethnic divisions and divisions based on the work process. Both divisions were closely related. Native-born Americans and "old" immigrants, such as natives of Great Britain and Germany, were often at odds with "new" immigrants—first the Irish, later Polish, Italian, and Slavic workers. Often the old immigrants held skilled craft jobs, as opposed to the unskilled or semiskilled industrial jobs that the new immigrants held. Two remaining differences are significant. First, race has always been an important division within the working class. In the cities of the Great Lakes/Ohio Valley region the black population was very small prior to the First World War, usually less than 5 percent; hence, race is of less importance for my research. Second, religious divisions within the working class have had some historical importance, particularly on the eastern seaboard before the Civil War, when there were widespread anti-Catholic riots. Again, religion is less important in my study than ethnic origin or level of skill.

Two concepts have great importance for the remainder of my analysis: class consciousness and class struggle. Those who do not accept the Marxist notion of class consciousness will argue that there is no such thing as a working-class view of the police institution. My argument that the police served an important role in the making of a class society requires demonstration that both those who create that role and those who acted in it had some consciousness of their collective action. Consciousness does not mean that the actors expressed themselves in Karl Marx's terminology, as some sociologists appear to demand as evidence. The terminology is unimportant. The question is whether the workers acted in a class-conscious manner in a given social situation and, likewise, whether the police were used to advance the interests of one class. Studies in late-nineteenth-century labor history have shown that the working class was highly class conscious, and there can be no question that the bourgeoisie were acutely aware of their social position and of what was required to defend it.[7] Although American historians and sociologists recognize the existence of social conflict in the United States, few deal with it in terms of Marx's view of human history as the struggle of classes and of modern Western history as the class struggle between proletariat and bourgeoisie. This does not mean, as some mistakenly believe, that all nineteenth-century social conflict must be analyzed in the context of the class structure; yet we must recognize that it was class conflict.[8]

THE STATE

The role of the state in mediating the class struggle is a central tenet of the Marxist analysis of the capitalist state, and any analysis of the police must address this issue head-on. Marxists conceptualize the capitalist state in several ways, all of which take as their starting point Lenin's famous observation that the capitalist state is an instrument of capitalist domination of other classes. Although Marxists differ sharply over exactly how to interpret this formulation in the current period, all analyses reject the pluralist notion that the state is neutral. One key element in the state's domination is its monopoly on the use of legitimate violence and coercion, a function concentrated domestically in the police institution. This capacity to employ violence if other social control mechanisms fail is more important than the actual violence because it is fully understood by all as a component of the state's power.[9]

The creation and expansion of the police force was part of a broader development of capitalist social institutions. Among the first of these developments was the trend toward the socialization of the expense of the reproduction of capital, begun shortly after the capitalist mode of production became dominant. A number of heretofore private social functions, including education, welfare, public health, and police protection, were passed to the public sector. This resulted in lower costs to the capitalist (especially with a tax system that placed a disproportionate share of the burden on other classes), as well as in greatly improved and expanded services.[10]

This transformation was more than an economic measure: it was part of a larger, qualitative process known as the rationalization of social relations. Simply put, as capitalism developed, individual capitalists' adaptations to the class struggle needed to be rationally organized and disciplined, a function beyond any individual capitalist but appropriate for the capitalist state. Sociologist Steven Spitzer has defined this process of rationalization as the depersonalization of the mechanisms through which behavior is regulated and their replacement by "rational-legal" forms. The latter rely on bureaucratic social institutions, coordinated by some kind of centralized state authority. Thus, the processes of bureaucratization, centralization, and rationalization are integrally intertwined and are major historical tendencies of capitalism, especially since the mid-nineteenth century.[11]

These processes guided the transformation of the urban police in the late nineteenth and early twentieth centuries. Every urban force was reorganized with discipline, centralization, bureaucratization, and an increased division of labor. Moreover, these changes were reflected in greater police activity in structuring urban social life. Sociologists and historians of the police have noted this process, but many have failed to analyze it in its social context and to make the connection between this process of rationalization and capitalist expansion generally.

One of the major problems in analyzing the progression of these central historical tendencies of capitalism is that no single, uninterrupted line of development can be traced. Rather, these processes tended to produce their own counterparts—that is, elements that undermined them. Bureaucratization, for example, carries with it a depersonalization that becomes an organizational problem. Centralization also creates control and coordination problems, especially if some members of the organization perceive it to be in their interest to undermine the structure. The increased division of labor in police institutions similarly created an alienation that undermined efficiency.[12]

THE CAPITALIST CITY

What was the nature of the nineteenth-century capitalist city?[13] Several answers point to issues that encompass social functions for which the city would take responsibility. The scope of national government had been roughly spelled out in the Constitution 100 years before, but the scope of municipal government was not so clearly understood. Initially, the bourgeoisie took the view that the less municipal government the better—low budgets meant low taxes. With the exception of education, most social functions that are now public responsibilities—charities, street construction, transportation, policing—were private matters long before they were taken over by municipal governments.[14]

The expansion of the scope of municipal government—in effect, a redefinition of the traditional distinction between public and private—cannot be understood outside the context of the class struggle and the labor process. As the location of work moved increasingly from small craft shops to large-scale industrial workplaces, the reproduction of the labor force became a problem far beyond the scope of the shop. Municipal government's entry into the realm of heretofore private services repre-

sents nothing less than the socialization of the task of reproducing the labor force. In effect, the capitalists turned over a
portion of that function to municipal government because government could accomplish the same result, at public expense,
far more efficiently and more legitimately than could the capitalists themselves.

This is not to suggest that all capitalists reached simultaneous
agreement on the question of new functions for the city government. It was a lengthy process marked by numerous experiments. Most capitalists, in fact, may have preferred to maintain
direct control over such a wide range of functions. But the requirements for the reproduction of the labor force overwhelmed
this reluctance.

The second characteristic of the late-nineteenth-century capitalist city was its importance as a center of plentiful and cheap
labor. The late-nineteenth- and early-twentieth-century American economy experienced sharp economic surges and declines,
resulting in complementary cycles of employment and unemployment. The city emerged as a great reservoir of workers. Aggressive recruitment overseas had produced a work force sufficiently large to allow rapid expansion of capital and to keep
wage levels low.

This reservoir of workers not only became a demographic factor in the growth of cities but also determined the cities' physical
shape. American cities became great slums as immigrants
crowded into cheaply built apartment houses and tract housing.
Whole families lived in one room, even taking in boarders. The
buildings were inadequately ventilated, and lacked proper sanitation facilities. Slums radiated outward from the factory districts, forcing workers to commute long distances to work and
providing huge profits to private streetcar companies.[15]

Cities came to embody the physical shape of a class society.
Contrasted to blocks of filthy slums were neat rows of skilled
workers' homes, quarters of middle-class homes, and boulevards of castlelike mansions.[16] The boundaries of such neighborhoods were clearly understood by all, and their meaning was not
simply geographic. Manufacturers could not walk far around

their city without passing poorly dressed workers, often carrying on an animated conversation in languages unintelligible to their employers. Whole sections of the city were off limits to members of some classes, either informally through fear, or semiofficially, as police picked up and questioned strangers. Notions about class society that may seem abstract now were concrete and obvious in the late-nineteenth-century industrial city.

Class distinctions within the city were not static but grew progressively sharper as more immigrants arrived, as factories expanded, as the boundaries of cities moved outward. Increasingly, the bourgeois and petty-bourgeois residents of the city were forced to rethink their social viewpoints and look for solutions to the growing discomfort that city living presented. Some evidence suggests that it was the petty bourgeoisie who were most affected by these tensions; they could not afford the isolation from the problems of class society that the bourgeoisie could. Richard Sennett's graphic portrayal of Chicago's Near West Side shows clearly how the class-divided city afflicted the middle class with a growing sense of isolation and fear, a sharp restriction of movement, and a tendency toward overprotection of their children.[17]

These sharpened class distinctions provided the city with easily the most democratic politics anywhere in America. The working class organized to take electoral power, especially in the Irish-dominated cities in the East. Nevertheless, it is clear that workers did not control urban government. Class-conscious attempts to seize city governments were "flashes in the pan," according to historian David Montgomery, and no working-class party managed to be re-elected until the 1890s. The machine dominated local politics, and probably more is known about machine governments than about any other aspect of the late-nineteenth-century city.[18] However, no one can seriously analyze the urban political machine and argue that it served working-class political interests. First of all, the petty bourgeoisie, small businessmen, lawyers, and other professionals tended to dominate, rather than the working class. Second, what the working class generally got out of these machines was jobs that no other class wanted. The number of city jobs expanded rapidly as cities moved into new areas of public works and public service. Not only did cities need police officers, firemen, garbagemen, drivers, janitors, and the like; they also needed ditch diggers, construction workers, and street cleaners. Third, the working class rarely won pro-working-class political decisions from these machines. This failure can be seen especially in the area of strike control policies, where class lines were clearly drawn. Time after time, the political machines ordered the police to break the strikes, often using the guise of a value-free legal order that required the police to keep streets open and to protect property.

What, then, was the urban political machine? It is best conceptualized as a mechanism for the mediation of class conflict, a power broker that effectively strengthened the power, and certainly the legitimacy, of the bourgeoisie, even though the bourgeoisie paid for it in the form of concessions to both the machine and the working class. Direct rule by the bourgeoisie in a local urban setting was a liability by the late nineteenth century. The growing complexity of urban government meant that the "hobby" mayoralties of the mid-nineteenth century were no longer convenient to local capitalists. Furthermore, the increasing rate of commercial and manufacturing activity made it economically risky to leave a business for full-time service in city government. Even if particular businessmen relished the role for one reason or another, it was a political liability for the bourgeoisie to rule directly. The petty-bourgeois machines did the job adequately, even if the bourgeoisie were often outraged by their crude methods and lack of efficiency. These excesses provoked periodic reform campaigns, which were highly successful in pressuring political machines to keep their chicanery within bounds.

This focus on the impact of the class struggle on urban society is quite different from the view of conventional historians, who describe the urbanization of this period in terms of rapid city growth and the increasing complexity of urban social relationships—and thus obscure the class dynamics of the process. It is only within the context of a class society and a class city that we can understand both the development of the police and the shaping of the police institution as we know it today.

POLICING

What does it mean to "police" a society? A Marxist analysis must begin with Karl Marx's statement that the capitalist state "employed the police to accelerate the accumulation of capital by increasing the degree of exploitation of labor." This fully testable hypothesis, together with his more political denunciation of the "bloody discipline" that turned men and women into wage laborers, shows that Marx clearly understood the police to perform a critical function in the reproduction of capital; namely, the repression and disciplining of the working class. Friedrich Engels fully shared this understanding. For example, he saw a constant relationship between the number of arrests in Manchester and the number of bales of cotton consumed in the city's mills.[19] These observations were made with reference to eighteenth- and nineteenth-century Britain, but the processes described are evident in the United States as well. "Increasing the degree of exploitation of labor" means that the police institution provides a measure of discipline and control over the working class that permits a wider measure of exploitation through the labor process—that is, more work with less resistance. The capitalist can then reinvest a larger proportion of his wealth, ensuring more rapid expansion of capital generally. Hence, the police reproduce class society daily through routine law enforcement, supervision of community life, intelligence gathering, and the like.[20]

More important, although the police institution commands a good portion of the state's domestic capacity for violence, it, along with other institutions, focuses primarily on nonviolent forms of class domination. Ultimately, the capitalist class is backed by high levels of violence, but on a day-to-day basis the capitalist system emphasizes nonviolent cooperation, induced from all classes through a variety of means. Among the other institutions involved in the reproduction of capital, the educational system, the welfare system, the public health apparatus, public recreational programs, and public works projects have all been important nonviolent weapons in the class struggle. These public institutions are supported by even more private institutions: the church, the family, the mass media, private clubs and associations, banks, insurance companies, and other capitalist institutions, all of which carry out social functions. The capitalist state itself dominates through its propaganda and media network, the pronouncements of powerful public officials, and a huge bureaucracy. These instruments are fully backed by important ideological weapons, including legal symbolism, the language of democracy, and an endless capacity for sloganeering. The capitalist class itself ultimately controls the most important single weapon in the class struggle: the organization of work—paychecks, promotions, demotions and dismissals, and work discipline. Workers who do not cooperate frequently find themselves unable to support their families, a fact lost on no American worker.[21]

Nevertheless, the division of society into classes by definition entails an immense amount of class violence. But under capitalism the capabilities of opposing classes have never been equal, except at the actual point of the overthrow of the capitalist class by workers and peasants. Spontaneous workers' movements directed against capital in the United States have repeatedly been pitted against trained, disciplined, and well-armed local police forces, the private police of employers, the militia, and even, rarely, the army. This "hired-gun" role of the local police is well documented. Although this is not their only role, it is important to state this function here, because many historians of the police ignore it, arguing that the American police were either too inept or too tightly controlled by working-class machines to serve the bourgeoisie effectively.[22] The opposite conclusion is more than attested to by the immense scale of violence directed against workers by municipal police.[23]

One of the major sources of confusion in analyzing the police institution is a failure to comprehend fully the dialectic between this violent, repressive function and the institution's other social control functions, which require lower levels of violence. Part of the key to understanding this contradiction is to examine the full meaning of the term *police*. Any society, regardless of its mode of production, can be "policed." In a capitalist society the rise of full-time, permanent forces capable of continuously asserting the power of the capitalist state up and down every street in every city represents an enormous extension of the power of the bourgeoisie and one that is absolutely necessary.[24] Although it is theoretically possible to have a class society without also making it a "policed society," this presumes the existence of sufficient social control mechanisms to stabilize the society without police surveillance and violence. Modern capitalist societies have never possessed such mechanisms. Instead, the supervision and regulation of the social relations of the subordinant class by the dominant class have emerged as prerequisites for class society.[25]

Policing assumes double importance when we remember that it is not simply a matter of the dominant class exercising political control over the subordinant class in a static society. Rather, the unfettered capitalism of late-nineteenth-century America produced staggering urban decay and disorder and with them the criminal violence so characteristic of America today; hence, the need to police a growing range of social problems unknown or of much lesser scope before the rise of capitalism.

Ironically, it is this latter function that historians of the police seize on as the "cause" for the rise of the police institution.[26] On the contrary, however, crime and disorder is an effect rather than a cause. As anthropologist Stanley Diamond cogently notes, the ruling class institutes disorder when it imposes its power over others.[27] In the case of capitalism (not Diamond's example), the imposition of a chaotic and disorderly economic and class system gives rise to serious problems in social order, to which the bourgeoisie respond by creating new social institutions. These institutions, in effect, help to legitimate the new social order by rendering a valued "service" to all classes in the society.

It is important here not to be abstract about this "policed society." The lives of ordinary people came daily under some measure of state supervision and regulation—supervision in the sense that it was important that some capitalist institution "keep an eye" on burgeoning workers' communities, regulation in that some measure of control, however minimal, was necessary both to maintain stability in the community and to provide socialization of workers to the factory system and to the requirements of urban society. When we note that rank-and-file police officers averaged only about one arrest a week, we must remember that this core regulation, supervision, and socialization function was often best performed with few arrests: the police institution gains legitimacy when it makes some accommodation to the communities being policed and an officer's effectiveness is measured by far more than his number of arrests.

This supervision, regulation, and socialization function varied from neighborhood to neighborhood. In well-to-do neighborhoods, for example, the police mainly acted as watchmen, supervising community activity and guarding against "disreputable" elements. Thus, the social class of the neighborhood being policed determined to a great extent the nature of police work. If the community was divided into district neighborhoods along class lines, a strong police presence was necessary to maintain that geographical segmentation.

As Egon Bittner has pointed out, the social services performed by the police in enforcing and legitimating the class society, though violent only a small proportion of the time, are fairly characterized as violent because the *potential* for violence is always present and gives the police their most powerful tool. An officer's suggestion that a potential troublemaker "move on" is more than a friendly piece of advice: it is a command, and the officer has a gun to back it up.[28]

The American municipal police have always had a major problem in establishing and maintaining their own legitimacy and have tended to take by force what control the population would not willingly grant. Wilbur Miller traces this tarnished legitimacy to the police institution's political role in American cities and its identification with the rough-and-tumble of urban politics. Miller is undoubtedly right, but he fails to locate this political role of the police in its class context.[29] Workers often refused to accord legitimacy to the police because much police activity was reprehensible to them, especially antistrike activity.

A full understanding of the legitimation function of the police is necessary in order to comprehend otherwise inexplicable limitations on the police. If the bourgeoisie controlled the police institution, why was police suppression of workers not even more violent? The answer is that this repression had to be accomplished *legitimately,* or at least arguably legitimately.[30] Here it is useful to locate the police within the context of the legal system, for the police are a legal institution. I fully agree with Mark Haller that the police institution was not overly concerned with any notion of legality, and police practices were designed not to conform to law but to maintain a certain degree of order in a class society.[31] This is perhaps just as well, given that the criminal courts were not overly concerned with legality, either, and did not go to great lengths to correct police abuse.

The emphasis here must be on the word *overly,* for there was adherence to standards of justice, if not to the letter of the law or to procedural niceties. A defendant had a chance to "tell his story" and to attempt to persuade the judge to dismiss the case. Given that most arrests were for public-order violations and that the defendant had already spent time in the lockup, dismissal was not especially generous. Still, the police often accused judges of being too lenient and of letting serious offenses against order go unpunished. A key to this apparent contradiction is suggested in Douglas Hay's analysis of the frequent imposition of the death penalty in eighteenth-century England, followed by commutation: this quality of mercy served to preserve the stability of and to legitimate a harsh, repressive, class-biased legal order.[32]

Capitalists' criticism of the police for being weak and ineffective in the class struggle is cited by many historians as evidence that the police were on the side of the workers.[33] In fact, the capitalists desired a degree of control over the workers that no violent force could deliver. It is important to remember that the police acted in the constraining context of a class society. Just as the police shaped working-class communities, the contingencies of the class struggle shaped the police institution. For example, the violence of the late-nineteenth-century class struggle and the difficulties of intervening in it forced constant reorganizations, including the introduction of paramilitary discipline and a hierarchical structure. Similarly, technological innovations, especially the patrol wagon and the signal system, were adopted to meet the resistance of the class struggle. The increasing isolation of the police institution from other public institutions put police officers outside the normal measures of public control that might have restrained them. These processes, common in the entire public sector but carried to the extreme with the police, reflect the special importance of the police in the class struggle.

The very composition of the police institution, however, threatened its ability to perform its primary function in the class struggle. For the police institution is not a one-class agency, even if it serves the interests of a dominant class. Internally, it reflects the class struggle. Thus the loyalties of individual officers had to be reinforced continually. Here again the legitimation function is important, for it had an internal effect as well as an external one. The value-neutral language of law and order sustained officers' self-images and their images of their departments. The opening of career channels within police departments was another important means of mitigating the effects of the class struggle. Finally, strong measures in all police forces maintained a level of work discipline equal to the level of coercion that manufacturers could use in their factories.

A class-free image of the police institution was always difficult to maintain, given the ever-present class contradictions. It was doubly difficult when the police function itself became an object of class struggle, specifically when the police came under attack for strikebreaking activities. Such attacks could be made through political assaults on the institution itself or through efforts to win the loyalty of individual officers on a one-to-one basis. Class struggle within the police institution, then, resulted not only from the internal class contradictions of the police institution but also from the institution's external role in the class struggle.

David Montgomery argues that the American working class fully recognized the importance of influencing police measures through political action. Although some working-class political actions achieved success, the overall pattern is one of failure and defeat of working-class political movements in this country. The same is true of workers' efforts to control the police: even when they were successful, they usually managed only to restrict the scope of anti-working-class police activity, never to redirect the police against the bourgeoisie.[34]

How, then, should a Marxist summarize the development of the police system and its expansion and transformation? All of the characteristics discussed above in formulating a conception of the police are based on class struggle as the key force in shaping the police institution. Clearly, the police serve as an instrument of the bourgeoisie in the class struggle. Moreover, the general evolution of capitalist institutions as a result of the class struggle fundamentally shaped the police institution through such processes as bureaucratization, centralization, division of labor, and rationalization. But the class struggle itself sharply limited the potential of the police institution, just as it determined the limits of rationalization and related processes. Using the notion of class struggle as an approach to a Marxist theory of the state and of the police can serve to correct the "crude instrumentalist" Marxist theory of the state. It is mistaken to assume that because the state is an instrument of the capitalist class, capitalists can do anything they wish with any state agency. This kind of simplistic analysis negates the role of any other class in the process of class struggle and denies the true nature of that process: it is a *struggle,* with continual victories and losses and with continual adjustments to keep the capitalist system functioning in the face of these changes.[35]

As long as intensive class conflict characterizes capitalist society, it is impossible not to take account of the central state function in the class struggle and the place of the police in this struggle. But we should not oversimplify this police function: police control of working-class communities and active repression in the class struggle is absolutely uncompromisable from the standpoint of the capitalist, but the police had other functions, too. One was the mediation of class struggle in working-class communities, that is, helping to diffuse many problems before their resolution became too difficult and threatened a fragile urban social order. Another function was the legitimation of both the police institution and other social institutions, a continual process as periods of intense class struggle undermined the neutrality claimed by those institutions.[36]

THE SCOPE OF THIS STUDY

This chapter has set forth a framework of analysis for the remainder of this study. Employing the Marxist concept of class and class struggle, I shall consider the role of the police institution in the industrial revolution in major cities of the United States west of the Appalachian Mountains in the period between the Civil War and 1915. I shall focus primarily on the cities of Buffalo, Milwaukee, and Chicago but also discuss Pittsburgh, Cleveland, Detroit, and smaller cities of the region. Within this framework, some of the most important questions are: What impact did the police have on the class struggle? Did that impact change over time? How did the class struggle, in turn, shape the police institution? What forms did capitalist domination of the police institution take?

Changes in the police institution during the post–Civil War period will be briefly outlined on a regional basis. I shall then focus on the impact of these newly formed and later restructured police departments on the balance of class forces in their communities and the effect, in turn, of class struggle within industrial cities on police evolution. In order to develop this kind of argument in the clearest possible way, I shall examine four common police functions. First, the policing of strikes and other forms of militant action will provide the clearest examples of anti-working-class police activity. Second is the policing of working-class leisure activities and the socialization of immigrant workers through police activity. The police engaged in a constant series of actions to regulate liquor-related working-class recreational activities—drinking, dancing, and gatherings of all sorts.

Closely related is a wide range of police-regulated vice activity—saloons and halls where gambling and prostitution occurred openly or with little attempt at concealment. Third, I shall look at police efforts to control tramps and tramping, the practice of traveling about the country in search of work. Fourth, crime patterns and crime waves will be examined in order to determine the class basis of crime-fighting efforts in the late nineteenth and early twentieth centuries.

This analysis, then, differs from most previous studies of the police in that it focuses on the day-to-day functions of the police institution and its impact on working-class communities rather than on the organization and change of the police institution. Because the scope of the analysis is regional, the relationships between the police and city hall, local reformers, or local manufacturers in any single city are much less important than the class nature of the police institution as a whole. Political disputes about the police in individual cities will be analyzed as part of a larger, complex pattern of class domination.

By grounding my study in both sociology and history, and by employing Marxist class analysis as the theoretical framework, I seek to accomplish three goals. First, on an empirical level, I aim to add to our understanding of the process through which the American working class was inculcated with modern industrial discipline. Second, there is a need for more theoretical work on the development of industrial capitalism in the United States and on the development of the capitalist state and its social control institutions. Third, I hope to answer important questions about the political, economic, and social forms that repression takes and about its impact on class society.

CHAPTER TWO

The Urban Police Institution in the Trans-Appalachian West, 1865–1890

THE PERIOD BETWEEN the Civil War and the First World War marks the midpoint of large-scale industrial development in the United States. Most of the significant characteristics of the factory system matured during this time, especially in cities west of the Appalachians. Prior to the Civil War the major industrial regions of America were concentrated in the East and Northeast. While these areas were undergoing industrial revolution, such cities as Chicago, Pittsburgh, Milwaukee, Buffalo, Detroit, and Cleveland remained small- to middle-sized commercial centers with very little industrial development.

Marxists consider the victory of the Northern industrialists over the Southern planters, which unleashed the industrial capabilities of the North, to be the turning point in the establishment of one mode of production over another. The railroad and western lands combined to shift American industrialization over the Appalachians, and the commercial Great Lakes ports and river junctions of the old Northwest Territory became America's largest and most important industrial centers in less than thirty years. This was an industrial revolution much more rapid and complete than that of England or of the eastern seaboard.[1]

Moreover, the growth of these cities occurred simultaneously with a high level of industrialization, making them the first true industrial cities in America, in contrast to the East, where industrial satellites grew up around commercial centers. Cities with populations in the tens of thousands after the Civil War embraced a half-million or more residents by 1915, most of them workers. The heavy industry that accounted for the most intensive expansion was concentrated in this region: iron and steel in Pittsburgh, Cleveland, Chicago, Buffalo, and Youngstown; rubber in Akron; machinery in Cincinnati, Milwaukee, Chicago, Toledo, and Detroit. By 1900, 8 of the country's 15 largest cities were in this region. Of the 13 cities with populations over 250,000 in 1910 and with more than 40 percent of their labor forces involved in mechanical and manufacturing work, 10 were in the Great Lakes/Ohio Valley region. (see table 1).[2]

Population growth illustrates only a small portion of the revolutionary changes wrought by industrialization. In North America this process was characterized by large-scale immigration, producing cities populated largely by foreign-born and semiskilled workers and their children. The proportion as well as the absolute numbers of both workers and immigrants skyrocketed after the Civil War: by 1900 the proportion of a city's workers employed in industrial and mechanical trades often exceeded 60 percent; the proportion of immigrants and their offspring was seldom less than 60 percent, often reaching 70 percent and even more than 80 percent in Milwaukee and New York City.[3]

The turmoil that this rapid development suggests was increased by the material conditions of working-class life. The volatile economy forced regular periods of unemployment; prevailing wages were generally low; and often whole families had to work to maintain a marginal standard of living. Housing conditions were equally depressing, with families often crowded into a few small, airless rooms with poor sanitation. Perhaps a third of all European immigrants found the reality of the American dream to be so unappealing that they returned home. Others kept moving west in search of improved opportunities, going "on the tramp" to look for laboring jobs in fields, railroads, lumber camps, and mines.[4]

Early efforts to organize workers to improve these conditions often went aground against strongly entrenched manufacturing

Table 1. 1860–1910 POPULATION OF GREAT LAKES/OHIO VALLEY CITIES WITH OVER 100,000 INHABITANTS IN 1910

City	1860	1870	1880	1890	1900	1910
Buffalo	81,129	117,714	155,134	255,664	352,387	423,715
Chicago	109,260	298,977	503,185	1,099,850	1,698,575	2,185,283
Cincinnati	161,044	216,239	255,139	296,908	325,902	363,951
Cleveland	43,417	92,829	160,146	261,353	381,768	560,663
Columbus	18,554	31,274	51,647	88,150	125,560	181,511
Dayton	20,081	30,473	38,678	61,220	85,333	116,577
Detroit	45,619	79,577	116,340	205,876	285,704	465,766
Grand Rapids	8,085	16,507	32,016	60,278	87,585	112,571
Indianapolis	18,611	48,244	75,056	105,436	169,164	233,650
Louisville	68,033	100,753	123,758	161,129	204,731	223,928
Milwaukee	45,246	71,440	115,587	204,468	285,315	373,857
Minneapolis	2,564	13,066	46,887	164,738	202,718	301,408
Pittsburgh	77,923	139,256	235,071	343,904	451,512	533,905
Rochester	48,204	62,386	89,366	133,896	162,608	218,149
St. Louis	100,773	310,864	350,518	451,770	575,238	687,029
St. Paul	10,401	20,030	41,473	133,156	163,065	214,744
Toledo	13,768	31,581	50,137	81,534	131,822	168,497

Source: U.S. Bureau of the Census, *Thirteenth Decennial Census of the U.S.*, 1910, Vol. 1, *Population 1910*, p. 80.

interests, usually backed by the immense legal authority of the state. Wholesale dismissals were threatened and carried out. Labor spies infiltrated even embryonic working-class organizations and virtual armies of strikebreakers were on call around the country. In spite of this opposition, workers formed a wide variety of fraternal associations, ethnic self-help groups, labor unions, and political action or discussion groups. Together, these provided the spark for political actions that by the 1880s and 1890s made local working classes important political forces to reckon with.[5]

The dominant role that the trans-Appalachian region assumed in many forms of industrial innovation was reflected in civic innovation as well. An openness to police innovation led to changes in the police institution in this region that were more rapid and more complete than those in the East. As a result, most of the important transformations in the police institution during this period began in the West. Within the region, striking similarities appear in the development and expansion of all local municipal institutions, including the police.

Although I collected data for all the cities of the region, my primary focus of analysis will be those cities with populations of 300,000 or more in 1900, for it was there that industrial development reached its highest level. Three of these cities were selected for detailed study on the basis of local political and economic factors. Buffalo in 1905 had a larger proportion of its workers—69 percent—in the mechanical and industrial labor force than any city in America. In addition, the city lay under the tight control of its businessmen and tolerated only a relatively weakly organized working class. Milwaukee supported the third-largest industrial and mechanical labor force in the country (56 percent of all workers) and also what was probably the strongest working-class political organization of any large city in the region, one that offered a strong challenge to local manufacturers and businessmen. Chicago, by virtue of its size (even then the second-largest city in America), its leadership position among cities in the region, and its high level of both manufacturing activity and working-class political resistance, presented a compelling case for further research. The process of industrialization in smaller cities of the region followed similar patterns, and a number of these cities—including Akron, Allegheny, Columbus, Duluth, Erie, Gary, Grand Rapids, Indianapolis, Minneapolis, Oshkosh, Rochester, St. Paul, Toledo—were of substantial industrial importance. To the extent that data are available, secondary examination of these cities will be undertaken as well in order to provide a complete regional analysis of the impact of class struggle on the development of the police.

DEVELOPMENT OF THE MUNICIPAL
POLICE INSTITUTION

The conventional image of a mid- to late-nineteenth-century policeman pictures a slow, fat, whiskey-swilling Irish cop, crooked, but still politically protected, obviously incapable of carrying out any policing function effectively or reliably. Such an image presents a gross distortion. Municipal policemen carried guns and clubs, which they used frequently, and they made at least as many arrests as do policemen today. Even acknowledging their inefficiency, a ten- or twelve-hour beat patrol allowed policemen considerable opportunity to structure urban social activity. Moreover, discipline and coordinated action gave the urban police a capacity for socialization far beyond what their numbers indicated. This paradox of rising levels of police capability juxtaposed against an image of ineffectiveness is not hard to understand, given the complexities and contradictions of the police role; in fact, it probably describes the police institution in the 1960s and 1970s as well.

Before analyzing the policing of the late-nineteenth-century class society, it is necessary first to describe the late-nineteenth- and early-twentieth-century police department. What kind of an institution was it? What kinds of capabilities did it have? Who controlled it? What kinds of social control activities did it engage in and why? From the outset it must be clear that I do not accept the prevailing interpretation, which views the late-nineteenth-century police as corrupt, inefficient, and incompetent "adjuncts of the machine." The corruption and political control that concern most historians are obviously important elements in understanding the police of the period, but they must be seen within the context of police activity as a whole. The evidence clearly shows that corrupt, machine-dominated police departments also engaged in a solid succession of anti-working-class activities, effectively representing the interests of the bourgeoisie in the class struggle. In contrast to historian Robert Fogelson, who argues that the policeman at turn of the century was little changed from his mid-nineteenth-century predecessor, I maintain that, beginning with the "Great Strike" of 1877 and accelerating with the "Great Upheaval" of the mid-1880s, the urban police institution was transformed into an efficient, well-organized, and disciplined system that was capable, for the first time, of asserting a powerful regulating effect on urban life—of *policing* urban society.[6]

It is perhaps ironic that although few present-day historians of the police agree with my position, the chiefs of police of the late nineteenth century clearly did. In speeches presented at the various annual meetings of their professional association, the International Association of Chiefs of Police, beginning in 1893, the chiefs affirmed that their departments had been completely transformed in the space of twenty to thirty years. Chief William J. McKelvey of Brooklyn noted improvements in almost every aspect of police work in 1896, and Chief Francis O'Neil of Chicago singled out the application of electric technology to police work for special praise in 1903.[7]

Capital's turn to the police to handle some aspects of the reproduction of the working class cannot be separated from a more general move by the bourgeoisie, beginning in the 1840s with the industrial revolution, to use public institutions in general for that purpose.[8] This socialization of expenditures necessary for the reproduction and expansion of capital encompasses public expenses for education, public health, welfare, police and fire protection, building inspection and housing, and public works. The post–Civil War period saw a rapid expansion of these early efforts, with local capitalists devoting substantial resources in order to control and direct the various components of the state apparatus to the ends of the capitalist class. The extent of municipal growth during this period is almost unfathomable by current standards: police departments numbering only a few dozen men grew to five hundred or one thousand or more by 1900. For example, in 1889 Captain William Reed of the Central Police Station in downtown Pittsburgh commanded in his single precinct more men than were on the entire police force when he joined the 31-man department in 1846. This example could easily be repeated for education, social work, and other social service areas. Something of the relative importance of these areas can be seen from the proportion of urban public expenditure each received in 1905: education led with 24 percent; police protection was second with 14.2 percent (excluding money for corrections); health, 9.5 percent; fire, 8.5 percent; charities and corrections, 6.6 percent.[9]

The origins of the various municipal police departments are far less relevant to this study than are the changes those departments went through under capitalist development in nineteenth-century America. Whatever the police institution was when initially created (often by simple merger of existing night watch forces, constabulary forces, or city marshal's officers), it had become something very different when it finished out the century as 1,000-man departments, spread over dozens of station houses, that patrolled many blocks of the city several times each day and possessed military capabilities to deal with strikes or other mass actions. Eric Monkkonnen's conclusion that city size correlates most closely with the date of creation of the first uniformed police forces is not surprising, but at the same time it fails to explain the relationship of the police to capitalist industrial development. We need to know more about the political process through which the police institution was created, enlarged, and changed and through which police orders and policies originated. Finally, although the municipal police were indeed a local institution, it is important not to deny their national character. Developments were repeated in city after city, and the telegraph facilitated both personal contact and quick communication among the police departments of different cities.[10]

Rather than seeing the development of the first modern police forces as a departure from existing institutional forms, it is possible to see a great deal of continuity between them. The police underwent steady change both before and after the creation of unified day-and-night forces staffed by full-time officers, the event that marks the creation of the police. These were not the first full-time forces; the day constables who worked on a fee basis had been full time. Nor were they necessarily larger than the watch forces they replaced; most often they were about the same size, and most men were kept on night duty, serving exactly as a watch. These early forces were often not uniformed, and although full-time commitment was required, no effort was made to train the men or pay high enough salaries to prevent frequent turnover, so that much of the ineptness that characterized watch forces carried over into local police forces.

In general, the period between the creation of a unified local force (most often between the 1840s and 1860s) and 1915 was characterized by frequent reorganization and innovation. As uniforms were added, more experience gained, forces enlarged, and organizational forms bureaucratized, local police forces became progressively less like the watch and constabulary forces they replaced. Hence, rather than dating a first police force, it is important to see the creation of these early police forces as being a 20-year or more process that varied from city to city but led to a common form. Moreover, the late-nineteenth-century force can still be recognized in our modern American police department: it was highly centralized and bureaucratized along quasi-military lines; men were recruited for a police career and given specialized training to accompany a quasi-professionalized job description; it often employed 1,000 or more officers; most police work consisted of patrolling the city for deviations from middle-class standards of public order and evidence of more serious crime; and the latest forms of technology allowed a tightly integrated force that could be ordered into action in any combination of units or in any part of town.[11]

This fully developed police force clearly is a long way from night watch forces and constables serving papers for a fee. It is also a long way from the first full-time police forces, with their leather badges and uniforms and their precinct captains who were local bosses only marginally subservient to the police chief. In terms of organization, the pre-1880s police departments resembled middle-sized family-owned industrial establishments, whereas the departments of twenty years later resembled middle-sized monopoly capitalist industrial establishments. Paternalistic domination by chiefs, minimal standards for admission and training, poorly defined bureaucratic structure, little specialization among the ranks, weak central structure, and strong precinct structure characterized the pre-1880s departments. The two decades between 1880 and 1900 saw a profound restructuring of departments organizationally: strong downtown chiefs were backed up by a strong centralized administrative bureaucracy; definite standards of recruitment and training were adopted; highly specialized units were established; standards of professionalism and discipline were enforced. In short, police departments assumed the outline of their current form. The industrial revolution transformed social institutions, leading to organizational forms particularly suited to the needs of expanding capital. It is in this context that we shall consider the establishment and transformation of policing in the central region of the United States, focusing on how the class struggle structured the first stages in the rapid expansion of the police.

ORIGINS OF POLICING

Major American cities established full-time police forces over a twenty-year period, beginning with New York City in 1845. New York's 800-man force organized under captains (one for each city ward) succeeded a watch force, headed by a watch commander in charge of each ward, and police officers who were attached to courts and acted on a fee for service. Under the new system, officers were political appointees serving first one-year, later two-year, terms. Although the force was nominally under the direction of a police chief, real power remained at the precinct level. The Democratic legislature that created the police delayed establishing the actual force until Democrats regained control of City Hall from the Whigs.[12]

The New York system was widely adopted across the United States: by Chicago in 1851, by New Orleans and Cincinnati in 1852, by Philadelphia in 1855, by St. Louis in 1856, by Newark and Baltimore in 1857, by Detroit in 1865, and by Buffalo in 1866. A closer look at a few of these cities will outline the political context of the creation of the police and underscore my point that it is not the creation date per se that is important but the process.

Prior to 1856, St. Louis had three police forces. The city marshal and his deputies were court officers who enforced city ordinances and kept criminal records. The city guard, the traditional night watch, consisted of a captain, six lieutenants, and 42 privates. The day police were composed of a lieutenant and 7 privates who arrested transgressors and reported offenses to the city marshal. St. Louis's first police act, in 1846, created a police department in name only; it codified the above system (plus the office of jailor) but left the several parts as separate units. An 1856 police ordinance changed the title of city marshal to chief of police, combined the three separate police forces into one 150-man department, and prescribed uniforms for the first time. The men were to be organized into three platoons serving eight hours each, but the number of platoons was reduced to two and the number of men to 120 before the system was even tried. The state legislature took control of the force in 1861 and returned the size of the department to 150.[13]

Similarly, Chicago's first police act, in 1851, declared the police force to be the sum total of all constables, policemen, and watchmen of the existing organizations in the city. One police constable was elected for each ward, and the city council appointed as many night watchmen as it deemed necessary. The city marshal, who was elected annually, held in addition the office of chief of police. In 1855 Know-Nothing Mayor Levi Boone and his city council passed a police reform bill that separated the chief of police from the city marshal's office, eliminated the night watch, and created an 80-man, three-shift police force. A new police bill in 1861 put the force under a three-man board of police commissioners, who were first appointed by the governor of Illinois and later (after 1863) elected from separate districts.[14]

Cincinnati also built its police force directly out of its watch force. In 1848 the night watch committee was given power to control the day watch. Two years later the city council created a chief of police and six lieutenants. Two of the lieutenants were assigned to the day watch, four to the night watch, with the chief of police controlling both. Watchmen were elected from their wards, with the chief assigning five from each ward to night duty, one to day duty. In 1859 the state legislature passed a police reform ordinance that created a board of police commissioners for Cincinnati, eliminated the office of city marshal, and transferred his functions to the chief of police.[15]

In Buffalo the constable and watch system lasted through the Civil War. Because the city council repeatedly turned down requests to establish a day-and-night police system, local Republican businessmen went to Albany in 1866 and persuaded the state legislature to create a Niagara Frontier Police Force for Buffalo and its neighboring townships. One hundred members of this 200-man force were assigned to Buffalo. In 1872 the Democratic legislature created a Buffalo municipal force under police commissioners appointed by the mayor.[16]

Even a small city like Dayton, Ohio, exhibits much the same pattern. A chief marshal and a deputy marshal had the power to appoint two night watchmen in each ward. In 1868 the metropolitan police force was organized with the marshal as police chief, the deputy as second lieutenant, and 20 regulars. This arrangement lasted nine months before it was abandoned in favor of a return to the old system. A new metropolitan police system, established by the state legislature in 1873, consisted of six elected commissioners who appointed a "captain and acting superintendant" to administer the 40-man force.[17]

From these examples we can identify several themes in the

creation of the urban police at the beginning of the industrial revolution. First, it is clear that these police forces were constructed piecemeal from earlier forces and often preserved most of the original watch system. This process took several years, with major changes following along a variety of patterns. Each city was acutely conscious of developments in other cities; Dayton actually based the size of its police force on computations of the relative sizes of other city departments. New York City was always held up as an example, but local variations were many. There was by no means a common local agreement as to the form the police should take. Dayton tried, then abandoned, the metropolitan system; Buffalo's Democratic city council refused to create a metropolitan police institution. Chicago, St. Louis, and Cincinnati enlarged and reformed their police forces in conjunction with political maneuvers by Know-Nothings in a charged atmosphere of class struggle between native-born Americans and Irish and German immigrants. In these cities the police emerged as a partisan arm of the Know-Nothings.

The waves of riots—by immigrants against Know-Nothings and by Know-Nothings against immigrants, by immigrants against symbols of oppression, and by whites against blacks— that swept American cities during the 1840s and 1850s are well known. According to John Schneider, at least 70 percent of America's cities with a population of 20,000 or more in 1850 saw major disorders between 1830 and 1865, totaling 80 major riots. The complex reasons for these riots are rooted in changing class relations of the period. Chicago's "lager beer riot" occurred when German workingmen marched on the downtown district to protest tax regulations passed by the Know-Nothings that were aimed at closing working-class saloons while preserving downtown taverns used by the wealthier class. In Cincinnati's Bedini riots of 1853 (often dismissed simply as anti-Catholic), German "forty-eighters," survivors of the abortive revolution, protested the visit of papal nuncio Father Bedini, who had betrayed the revolutionary cause. The police attacked protesters, and one police officer and one demonstrator were killed. Know-Nothing mobs in St. Louis set about wrecking Irish boardinghouses, and several rioters were killed in the ensuing battle. In St. Louis the police were withdrawn, but in other cities they actively participated on the Know-Nothing side.[18]

A direct link is evident between these struggles and the impetus to reorganize and expand local police forces, a link that must be understood in class terms. Often direct reference was made to the inability of the existing police force to handle riots. Local commercial elites, concerned about the threat to property and wary of the problem of controlling a growing working class, moved to brace up local police forces. In St. Louis, Cincinnati, Chicago, Philadelphia, Baltimore, New York, and Boston, the police were strengthened by one class as a response to the threat that another class posed against its dominance.[19]

POST–CIVIL-WAR REORGANIZATION

By 1905 most urban police departments were six, eight, or even ten times their 1865 size. Chicago's force, with 2,196 men in 1905, was over ten times its 1865 size; Buffalo's, with 774 men, had grown more than eightfold. Other metropolitan forces registered comparable increases. Moreover, this absolute growth was accompanied by an increased *relative* strength; many forces had nearly twice the men per capita (see table 2).

Such sharp expansion cannot be taken for granted as the inevitable product of rapidly growing cities. Rather, it was the result of hard-fought political struggles over a number of opposing considerations. First, police forces, like other urban service institutions, were expensive. Before the late 1870s it was not clear how important the police institution was for the maintenance of the capitalist industrial order. Moreover, municipal financing was somewhat precarious, and regular recessions caught city governments short, forcing unplanned layoffs of the police, often at inopportune times. In Pittsburgh, for example, public monies ran out in April 1877, forcing the city to halve its police force just before the Roundhouse riots. Similarly, Chicago's force was cut in the middle of the unrest of the depression of the 1890s.[20]

Table 2. GROWTH OF POLICE FORCES IN GREAT LAKES/OHIO VALLEY CITIES IN RELATION TO POPULATION, 1880–1915

City	1880 Department size	1880 Population per officer	1890 Department size	1890 Population per officer	1905 Department size	1905 Population per officer	1915 Department size	1915 Population per officer
Akron	11	1,510	18	1,533	47	1,189	68	2,040
Allegheny City	62	1,269	113	929	159	891	*	*
Buffalo	192	807	303	843	774	501	830	560
Chicago	487	1,033	1,870	549	2,196	884	4,626	528
Cincinnati	339	753	468	634	549	858	709	957
Cleveland	165	970	290	900	544	633	803	476
Columbus	41	1,259	116	784	167	919	234	894
Dayton	35	1,105	58	1,055	134	753	145	928
Detroit	145	802	385	554	621	605	1,163	627
Grand Rapids			60	1,004	116	863	157	796
Indianapolis	64	1,172	95	1,109	252	799	386	709
Milwaukee	87	1,328	199	1,025	379	869	581	715
Minneapolis	32	1,465	216	772	244	1,033	331	1,030
Pittsburgh	120	1,958	294	816	577	853	901	622
Rochester			125	1,106	218	873	409	628
St. Louis	489	716	671	686	1,451	435	1,945	376
St. Paul	36	1,152	178	747	217	870	306	734
Toledo	54	928	84	984	146	1,028	222	927

Source: Computed from U.S. Census data and from the police reports of the individual cities.
*Allegheny City was annexed to Pittsburgh in 1907.

A second factor influencing police department size was debate about the necessity of police increases. Such arguments were generally based on differing assessments of the functions of the police and the effectiveness of existing police services. Police strikebreaking activity occasionally resulted in working-class resistance to police appropriations, thereby restricting department growth in cities such as Milwaukee, where aldermen responsive to the working class maintained some measure of political power. An angry Chicago alderman responded to a call for more police to combat a crime wave by arguing that his ward had far too many policemen and needed more garbagemen instead.[21]

Finally, size was influenced by demands for increased police efficiency. Some police chiefs, most notably Milwaukee's James Janssen, prided themselves on maintaining good police service with small forces and avoided requests for more manpower. Technological innovations in the form of the patrol wagon and the signal system were also touted as substitutes for additional men and held down the size of some departments.

As a result, the ratio of police officers to population varied widely from city to city. Milwaukee, for example, had less than half the men per capita of Buffalo, a city of roughly comparable population and composition (see table 3). Since most arrests were for discretionary public order offenses, a higher police-citizen ratio often meant a lower arrest rate since fewer officers made fewer arrests.

The characteristics of nineteenth-century police forces that have attracted the most attention are their instability, corruption, and level of political control. But these features have been misunderstood. There was, for example, an unmistakable tendency toward increased stability of tenure among the rank and file. The advent of municipal civil service laws applying to the police, first introduced in Milwaukee and Brooklyn in 1884, strengthened this trend, but greater stability of tenure was evident even before these measures and continued in cities that had no civil service laws or had politically dominated or corrupt civil service boards. The upheavals in municipal politics of the 1850s

Table 3. RELATIVE STRENGTH OF POLICE FORCES IN GREAT LAKES/OHIO VALLEY CITIES, 1890

City	Population	Area in square miles	Size of police force	Average population per policeman	Police per square mile
Buffalo	255,664		303	843	11
Chicago	1,099,133	174	1,870	589	19
Cincinnati	296,951	24	468	634	19
Cleveland	261,426	28	290	900	10
Columbus	91,000	14	116	784	8
Detroit	205,669	23	385	554	17
Milwaukee	204,150	18	199	1,025	11
Minneapolis	165,438	63	216	772	3
Pittsburgh	240,000	28	294	816	11
Rochester	138,327	17	125	1,106	7
St. Louis	460,357	63	671	686	11
St. Paul	133,156	51	178	747	3
Toledo	82,650	21	84	984	4

Source: Department of Public Safety, *Third Annual Report*, (Pittsburgh, Feb. 1, 1891), p. 328. Numbers are rounded from fractional percentages. Eastern and western cities originally in the chart have been omitted. Buffalo was computed from 1890 census data.

that had occasionally led to complete turnovers in such police forces as those of New York and Chicago had been eliminated for the most part, although elections still brought many promotions and demotions, particularly in the higher ranks. However, as the departments grew, they also became more stable in membership. Buffalo's annual police turnover in the 1870s averaged 50 percent; by the 1890s it was only 10 percent. These statistics were repeated throughout the region. A reduction in purely political dismissals accounts for part of this difference; more important were improvements in the working conditions of rank-and-file police officers.[22]

There is no question that late-nineteenth- and early-twentieth-century urban police forces were "adjuncts of the machine," as Fogelson puts it, and that they were also corrupt and relatively inefficient. The argument is about the meaning of these facts and their relative importance in the context of daily police operations. Fogelson, Walker, and Richardson have interpreted the entire history of the police in terms of a drive for "reform" and "professionalization" in an epoch of corrupt and inefficient practices. This liberal conceptualization distorts the issue of the power that was at stake and takes the word of nineteenth-century reformers at face value.[23]

The term *reform*, as applied to the police institution, embraces two distinct phenomena that are often confused: the first was a crude struggle for political control of the police in which one side labeled itself "reformers"; the second refers to a series of technological innovations and structural changes that transformed the police institution by the end of the nineteenth century and laid the foundations of our modern "professional" police. To describe these phenomena with the value-laden, imprecise term *reform* obscures the diverse sources of change in the late-nineteenth-century police institution and distorts the class politics of the period into a simplistic reformer-machine dichotomy that does not adequately explain political differences. In fact, many "professional" police innovations were introduced by political machines, not by self-styled reformers.[24]

The class character of the struggle for political control of the police is also oversimplified when the conflict is viewed as one involving petty-bourgeois and bourgeois reformers versus working-class machines. Although it is clear that the working class was an important political force in American cities in the late nineteenth and early twentieth centuries, it is also evident that they exercised much less political power than their numbers should indicate. Montgomery points to the lack of a working-class political program before the successes of the Social Democratic party, which we shall examine more closely in Chapter 5. The key to understanding the urban political machines of the period is to regard them as a temporary form that incorporated some working-class participation into bourgeois and petty-bourgeois political circles and thereby perpetuated a reasonably effective urban government, promoted political stability, and maintained conditions favorable to the orderly expansion of capital. Workers had some influence over the actions of such machines, but they would never have thought that they controlled them. Indeed, the involvement of those machines in strikebreaking activities and in the mass arrests of public order offenders and tramps thoroughly disproves this argument. When Mayor Carter Harrison of Chicago withheld police strikebreaking services from Cyrus McCormick in 1885, for example, McCormick himself went to see the mayor. When the strike was resumed the next year, police were barracked inside the McCormick reaper works.[25]

Working-class protests against oppressive police behavior provided an immediate incentive for building a police system insulated from working-class political power, but it was more a matter of preventive action than it was a problem of wresting control of the police from the working class. Even when workers electorally won control of police departments, they did not have an affirmative model of a "workers' police." Their actions were usually limited to punitive measures following particularly repressive strikebreaking work by the police, and new chiefs usually did no more than promise not to repeat such behavior. Milwaukee's socialists came up with some proposals for transforming the class basis of the police, including renaming policemen "safetymen" and merging the police and fire departments. But these early socialists lacked enough political power to bring about fundamental alterations in policing practices.

The police policy innovation that probably brought the most important short-term relief for the working class came from a petty-bourgeois Christian progressive tradition. Mayor Samuel "Golden Rule" Jones of Toledo and Mayor Tom Johnson of Cleveland instituted a policy of releasing petty offenders from the police station under their own recognizance after entering their names in a "Golden Rule" book, a policy that cut arrests by as much as 75 percent. These experiments were tried in dozens of cities between 1907 and 1914 and were hotly debated at annual meetings of the International Association of Chiefs of Police.[26] Yet even the Golden Rule policy can be said to have served bourgeois interests. Although it was promoted as a pro-working-class measure, it also increased police efficiency by avoiding "wasteful" arrests and allowing patrolmen to concentrate on social control.

The issue of police corruption is closely related to the question of police work and police discipline. Paradoxically, as police departments became larger, more professional, and more efficiently organized, they also became more corrupt. It becomes apparent that although corruption is in the long run incompatible with Weberian conceptions of rationalization, bureaucratization, and professionalization, it is not necessarily incompatible with the achievement of short-term objectives. There is no inherent reason why a highly corrupt police department cannot effectively serve the bourgeoisie in the class struggle.

At the same time, it is possible for a police force to become so corrupt that it cannot perform routine functions, a level that a number of American municipal police forces approached in the late nineteenth century, most notably Chicago's. In such a situation, routine police functions are no longer carried out: calls for police assistance go unanswered, spectacular crimes go unsolved, and strike or crowd control work is handled badly. Moreover, corruption automatically encourages highly individualistic and entrepreneurial police activity, which conflicts with disciplined and organized police action.

No accurate reconstruction of the level of police corruption in the nineteenth century is possible. Accusations of corruption were numerous and indicted behavior ranging from simple bribe-taking to protection of vice and after-hour or Sunday saloon hours, which were integrally tied to fairly large-scale vice operations. Criminal activity of various sorts appears to have been protected in some cities. Officers on occasion were themselves accused of committing major crimes and of taking advantage of their position to cover crimes.

RANK-AND-FILE WORKING CONDITIONS

The class basis of the police institution must be understood in terms of day-to-day police practices and the political struggle over these practices. It is easy to overestimate the impact of political control and inefficiency on the police. But as Mark Haller correctly points out, even during the years of extensive political control of the Chicago police department, the rank and file enjoyed substantial job security. It was simply impossible to turn over an entire police department with every election, and major upheavals occurred only a few times before the end of the century.

In his well-known 1904 investigation of the Chicago police, August Piper described the department as hopelessly corrupt and inefficient, "there being practically no discipline." Many of Piper's contemporaries came to the same conclusion about the police departments in their own cities. Yet one might have asked Piper how the Chicago police managed to make over 30,000 arrests, answer hundreds of thousands of requests for police assistance, and regularly break strikes. Obviously, in spite of the chicanery Piper observed (and he saw a great deal), the Chicago police force was very much in business and had a substantial impact on the life of the city. Indeed, Piper may have missed the most important point: the officers he observed "cooping up" in saloons "conversing with citizens" were exercising a nominal amount of control over their work process, thus enabling them to put up with grueling 12-hour shifts in all kinds of weather.

Hence, such activity may well have increased the department's overall efficiency.[27]

From the standpoint of rank-and-file officers, better working conditions and more job security must have been the most important changes in their daily routine. There was an unmistakable trend toward increased stability of tenure and decreased day-to-day political control after the 1880s. The application of civil service laws to police departments had some effect on this trend, but the impact of these laws has been exaggerated. As has been pointed out, stability at the lower ranks was already increasing because machine patronage considerations had to be balanced against the need for minimal standards of police efficiency, which required the maintenance of large numbers of reasonably experienced police officers. The working conditions and pay scales of rank-and-file police officers were substantially improved to reduce voluntary resignations, and police work became a very attractive occupation. By the 1890s wages exceeded $800 a year for patrolmen in most major cities (see table 4), compared with perhaps $400 to $500 for unskilled or semiskilled workers. Even skilled workers with higher wages lacked the job stability and opportunities for advancement available to police officers. Police work offered year-round employment in an age when many workers faced seasonal layoffs.

Long hours were a principal disadvantage of police work in the late nineteenth century. Twelve-hour shifts and seven-day work weeks were common, and a portion of an officer's time off was spent on reserve sleeping in the station house, often in filthy rooms over the cells. By the 1890s, however, police work featured shorter days, regular days off each month, and attractive pension and benefit systems. This process took many years because it represented a heavy strain on city budgets. In an attempt to keep down costs but maintain efficiency, Buffalo in 1894 replaced its two platoons, each of which worked 12 hours, with three: a day platoon on a 10-hour shift and two 7-hour platoons that worked afternoon and night shifts and spent some extra time sleeping at stations on reserve. The new system automatically reduced the size of the patrol force on any given shift

Table 4. POLICE CHIEFS' AND PATROLMEN'S SALARIES IN MAJOR AMERICAN CITIES, 1899

City	Population	Total on payroll	Salary of chief	Salary of patrolmen
1. Greater New York	3,480,000	7,151	$6,000	$800 to $1,400
2. Chicago	1,875,000	3,294	$6,000	$1,000
3. Philadelphia	1,250,000	2,614	$4,500	$2.25 to $2.75 per day
4. St. Louis	651,821	1,039	$4,500	$1,000
5. Baltimore	540,000	850	$2,500	$18 per week
6. Boston	500,000	1,121	$3,500	$1,000 to $1,200
7. Buffalo	400,000	745	$3,500	$720 to $900
8. Cleveland	400,000	372	$3,500	$780 to $1,000
9. San Francisco	350,000	562	$5,000	$1,224
10. Cincinnati	350,000	531	$5,000	$780 to $1,020
11. Detroit	340,000	562	$4,000	$700 to $900
12. New Orleans	300,000	375	$3,000	$600
13. Washington	300,000	614	$3,300	$900 to $1,080
14. Pittsburgh	300,000	436	$3,000	$2.50 per day
15. Milwaukee	270,000	310	$3,600	$960
16. Newark	250,000	326	$2,500	$3.00 per day
17. Louisville	225,000	287	$2,500	$2.25 per day
18. Jersey City	210,000	382	$3,000	$1,000
19. Kansas City	200,000	204	$3,000	$840
20. Indianapolis	200,000	170	$2,000	$825

Source: International Association of Chiefs of Police, *Proceedings of the Annual Meeting* (1899), p. 14.

by one-third, but it substantially strengthened the reserve potential of the force. Some cities that converted to the three-platoon system found it too expensive, however, and reverted to the old system.

The 1880s also witnessed nationwide efforts to "professionalize" the police and to emphasize "neutral" legal principles to govern the actions of a trained police department. The extent to which these innovations benefited rank-and-file police officers is unclear, but they did contribute to separating the police from the day-to-day political control of industrialists and machine politicians. Nevertheless, a professional police department committed to enforcing the law by keeping the streets open during a strike served the same function as one that was simply a tool of the industrialists, though it did so with greater legitimacy. And these same principles tended to insulate political machines from working-class backlashes aimed at the police.[28]

The rise of a professional police ideology was coupled with efforts to instill discipline within police forces. Departments scheduled regular drills, training the entire force in paramilitary companies that could be readily mobilized for strike work or other anticrowd actions. Police training programs emerged during the 1890s as well. Although these were not the schools that developed later in the twentieth century, a new officer was required to attend classes at headquarters for a few hours each week during his first months on the force. This removal of recruit training from the purview of precinct captains tended to encourage the emergence of a strong centralized police force. Moreover, these training programs could be prescribed for veterans as well when in the judgment of the chief these officers needed additional training.

As part of the drive for discipline, police administrators instituted formalized departmental hearing procedures. Drinking on duty, failing to be on post, insubordination, and violation of various departmental rules incurred such penalties as fines, demotions, suspensions, transfers, reprimands, and dismissals. These disciplinary measures greatly strengthened departmental discipline but also created great resistance among the rank and file and became, along with wage demands, a major impetus to the earliest police union organizations, which were referred to as fraternal organizations because of the fierce antiunion sentiments among police administrators and among many of the rank and file.

What, then, was the nature of rank-and-file police work? By and large, it consisted of 12-hour shifts spent walking long beat patrols. Usually more than 80 percent of a municipal department was assigned to such work. While on their beats the officers were to look for suspicious behavior, watch property, and answer citizens' queries—general activities not very different from those of patrolmen today.

This heavy emphasis on the patrol function—that is, the regularized police presence and potential to intervene in and control any social situation—is the key to understanding the evolution of the police function and the nature of the police work process. It was dull and routine work, physically and emotionally taxing. Police administrators not infrequently ignored their officers' "normal" socialization in saloons and barbershops; they expected some rest periods and felt them to be necessary to enable officers to last out their beats. But police reformers, drawing on industrial models, demanded more efficient patrolling from the rank and file, which translated into miles patrolled and less time in saloons. This idea of the highly visible patrolman on his beat as a symbol of state power was very important in the early conceptualization of the police role. Enormous resources went into this police patrol function, but with unclear results.[29]

The tendency of some historians of the police to see patrolmen as irrelevant and inefficient in the shaping of the class struggle turns on the impossibility of assessing the effectiveness of the patrol function. We know very little about what Robert Percival and Lawrence Friedman have characterized as a vast "trawling operation."[30] We do know, however, that we cannot use arrest data as an index of police patrol activity. Most police intervention in working-class community life stopped short of arrest, even during the most serious strikes. Rather, the arrest power was reserved as a coercive measure to ensure compliance with police orders. The average patrolman in 1890 made well under one arrest each week, a record roughly comparable to the current level. In Chicago, each officer made 44 arrests a year on the average; in Buffalo, 41; Cincinnati, 36; Milwaukee, 30; Cleveland, 33; Detroit, 29. Thirty-five percent of all arrests made in cities over 30,000 were for drunkenness. Other status and public order offenses—disturbing the peace, vagrancy and tramping, and violations of city ordinances—accounted for a roughly equal number of arrests. Thus, 70 to 80 percent of all arrests were for these public order offenses, and virtually all of those arrested were workers.[31]

Arrests for other common offenses reflect the same class enforcement patterns. Assault and battery represented the most common serious crime, but more than 90 percent of the arrests on this charge were for misdemeanor offenses, logically simple extensions of drunkenness and disorderly conduct arrests. Prostitution and gambling together accounted for about 5 percent of all arrests, roughly equal to assault and battery, and prostitution netted the greater proportion of these arrests. These were anti-working-class arrests, representing police efforts to regulate the vice industry; they were never intended to eliminate the exploitation of prostitution. Often police used arrests as a means of taxing prostitutes or as a means of reducing competition for houses that paid bribes for the privilege of doing business. Similarly, the large gambling interests were seldom bothered. But the numerous working-class forms of gambling and individual entrepreneurs, especially travelers, were more vulnerable to arrest. Thus, although gambling and prostitution are offenses that exploit the working class, enforcement of them took on anti-working-class forms.

Amazingly, little serious crime needed police attention. Of 1,212,574 arrests in 1905 in the United States, 2,239 were for murder, 14,305 for robbery, and 81,509 for housebreaking. Rates of serious crime remained remarkably stable during the industrial revolution in the United States, although there were extraordinary fluctuations between years and between cities (a result, at least in part, of poor reporting).[32]

Overall, the post–Civil War pattern of arrests roughly resembles the current pattern, in which felonies are about 10 percent of all arrests. The vast bulk of all police work entailed the maintenance of certain prescribed standards of public order, and the method of doing this was primarily not by arrest but by the threat of arrest—embodied in the person of a police officer. The development of the modern urban police institution turned on the assumption that police presence alone could structure urban behavior patterns, at least in some segments of the population, independently of the arrest power. Police regulation of working-class behavior succeeded largely through the mere possession, rather than the exercise, of the portion of state coercive power that they commanded.

CONCLUSION

The police institution became increasingly capable of repressive activity as it was reorganized and strengthened throughout the late nineteenth century. As part of this specialization in repression, many of the functions traditionally held by the police were removed to newly created municipal institutions, beginning in the 1870s. These services included health inspection, building inspection, street and lamp inspection, welfare investigations, census-related work, messenger relays for city hall, and such direct charity functions as running lodging houses or offering free lodging to indigents in rooms at the police station. In the central regions of the nation the development of the police and other public institutions was directly coextensive with industrialization. In addition, it is clear that the Great Lakes/Ohio Valley region was the center of far more than its share of police innovation in the late nineteenth century: civil service laws were first extended to police in Milwaukee in 1884 (an honor shared with Brooklyn), the telephone was applied to police work in Cincinnati in 1878, the patrol wagon and signal system was developed in Chicago in 1881, a school of instruction was established in Buffalo in 1893, and the Golden Rule policy was inaugurated in Cleveland and Toledo in 1907. Moreover, these innovations usually extended to other cities in the region, before they were adopted in the East, West, and South. Thus the central region exercised the kind of influence over police innovation in the nineteenth and early twentieth centuries that the unification of the New York City force had exercised in the pre–Civil War period.

CHAPTER THREE

The Patrol Wagon and Signal System, 1880–1900

RISING LEVELS OF CLASS CONFLICT in the 1880s and 1890s over-reached the physical ability of the police institution to contain them. Existing police forces proved inadequate to deal with more frequent and violent strikes, to supervise the working class on a daily basis, and, particularly, to monitor immigrant neighborhoods and recreational activities. In general, as in the rebellions of the 1960s, the police response was widely criticized as clumsy, inefficient, and often either an over- or underreaction. The rapid adoption of the patrol wagon and signal system, the single most important technological innovation in policing prior to the radio-equipped patrol car, was one clear result of this struggle. It represented a key element in the general reorganization and expansion of local police forces in the 1890s and early 1900s.

Police technology at the time of the Civil War consisted of telegraph lines connecting station houses. The cop on the beat was not linked to headquarters, nor was the citizen needing police services. If an emergency developed, messengers had to be sent out to bring in enough officers to handle the problem, or a bell or other warning could be sounded to assemble the entire force. A citizen who needed police help had to go out and find an officer, which often necessitated a trip to the precinct station. Sergeants or "roundsmen," who were charged with supervising the conduct of beat patrolmen, had no effective means of doing so. Precinct captains were isolated from headquarters and became powerful figures controlling police policy in their precincts. This kind of organization characterized the first 30 years of police services in every large city in the country, even though the technological means for tightening discipline and control existed after the development of the telegraph in the 1850s.

The story of the development of the signal system and patrol wagon is best told by John Wilkie, a Chicago police reporter who himself made a contribution by designing the light wagon that was a central feature.

> One day in the summer of 1880, while attending a society picnic, Mr. Harrison, at that time Mayor, and Austin J. Doyle, then Secretary of the Police Department, dropped into a chat, in the course of which it was suggested that it would be a great thing for the department if there could be some means devised whereby the men on the beat could communicate with the station at any time they desired to do so. It struck both parties to the conversation that this should be a simple matter, at least in the hands of an electrician.
>
> Upon returning to the city that evening Secretary Doyle saw Prof. Barrett, superintendent of the Fire Alarm Telegraph, and detailed to him the talk he had had with the Mayor. It was then suggested that a system somewhat similar to the Fire Alarm Telegraph might work in the police department, wagons could be located at central points in the various districts, and that they could respond as the steamers did to an alarm. The Professor thought it over during the night, and the next morning presented for the inspection of the Mayor and Secretary Doyle, a plan which provided for the system as it exists to-day, with the exception of a few minor changes in the electrical features. The plan was approved and the electrical department was set at work on the manufacture of the necessary instruments.[1]

The basic system that Barrett designed and manufactured connected the best available communications with the fastest possible transportation equipment. Scattered through each police precinct were to be a number of call boxes, locked and secure from the weather, and each containing three pieces of equipment: a "calling mechanism" that could be set to send a small number of signals—including "riot," "robbery," and "send help"—automatically with the simple pull of a lever; a telephone to permit two-way conversation between officer and switchboard; and an alarm bell that could be rung in each box from headquarters to signal men on the beat to run to the box and call in for a message. The alarm bell was dropped immediately, but the remaining features became the basis of the systems adopted across the country.[2]

Although the telephone, contained in an inner box, was reserved for the use of police officers, any "reputable" citizen could apply for a key to the outer box, which gave access to the calling lever that would summon police. Moreover, for a fee of $25 in 1881 (about two weeks' pay for a laborer) a call box could be installed in any residence or store, and about 400 boxes were initially purchased in this way in Chicago. This service, rendered to the wealthy and to businessmen, clearly shows the class basis of this innovation: the public police apparatus was merged with a private system of mobilizing officers. As a prevention against false alarms, later systems contained a device that retained the key until an officer showed up and released it.[3]

Both the transportation necessary to respond to calls from the boxes and the administrative structure of the system were equally simple. The patrol wagons devised by John Wilkie were patterned after existing ambulance and fire wagons. Constructed of the finest and lightest materials, they provided seating for three in the front, auxiliary seating along the sides, and room for prisoners or stretchers in the center. First-aid and fire equipment, as well as police equipment, completed the fittings. Horses were initially kept in harness at all times, and wagons could leave the station within a minute of receiving the call. Later systems featured harnesses that dropped over the horses and automatic door-opening devices to speed departure further.[4]

Lieutenant John Bonfield, who later distinguished himself in strikebreaking work, designed the administrative apparatus for the system. Again, the innovations were simple but served as the basis of the system for years. Bonfield recommended hourly reports from men on the beat, with at least two boxes on a beat so that the men would have to keep moving between them. The patrol service itself was an elite unit; the men assigned to it were much more active than beat officers and involved in many more police actions.

EXPANSION OF THE SYSTEM

By 1902, according to the U.S. Census, there were 148 police patrol systems in every part of the United States and in cities of every size: 34 systems were found in cities of over 100,000; 30 in cities of 50,000 to 100,000; 39 in cities of 25,000 to 50,000; 33 in cities of 10,000 to 25,000; and 12 in cities of under 10,000. These systems ranged from one or two boxes linking outlying or "trouble" sections of the city with the police station, as in Escanaba, Michigan (population about 8,000; system installed in 1892), to more than 1,000 boxes in Chicago.[5]

Cincinnati and Milwaukee developed systems at about the same time. Cincinnati's, which was begun in late 1881 and was fully operational by January 1884, followed immediately in the wake of another major communications innovation there: Cincinnati was the first police department to make full use of telephones for communication between station houses. Eight lines were working in police stations in 1879, less than one year after Bell's first patent on the telephone. The full implication of this development can be quickly seen by comparing the number of phone messages—363,080—sent during 1880, the second year of its use, with the 10,385 sent over the cumbersome telegraph dial system used ten years before. The use of the telephone in police communications made possible a fully coordinated, citywide policing apparatus. Telephones quickly replaced the clumsy coded signal devices in the patrol wagon and signal box system.[6]

Other cities adopted the signal system immediately following Milwaukee and Cincinnati. By 1886, the year Buffalo adopted it, at least 20 more cities had the system: Minneapolis and St. Paul;

Detroit and Grand Rapids; Dayton, Toledo, and Columbus; Joliet, Peoria, and Hyde Park, Illinois; Denver, Allegheny City and Philadelphia, Pennsylvania; St. Louis; Baltimore; Washington; Hartford and New Haven, Connecticut; New Orleans; Brooklyn; and Lynn, Massachusetts. By the time Buffalo and later cities came to consider the system, it was beginning to be mass produced and sold by traveling agents of the major companies, including the Gamewell Signal Company of New York and the Municipal Signal Company of Boston. Cities with existing systems were used as models to sell more systems, and police officials frequently traveled to other cities to inspect the competing systems in operation.[7]

Within five years of Chicago's invention of the system, at least 25 cities had adopted it. By 1892, 11 years after its first application, 56 systems had been installed nationwide. In 1904, 148 systems were reported in operation.[8] Use of the system was concentrated in Great Lakes/Ohio Valley industrial cities throughout the 1880s; by the 1890s it had spread to all regions of the country. The social context of this rapid diffusion of police technology will now be considered.

STRIKE AND CROWD CONTROL

The patrol wagon and signal system greatly improved the general efficiency of police work; with regard to controlling mass action, it was essential. Whereas earlier methods might require hours to round up enough police officers to march in force to the scene of a strike or other demonstration, the patrol wagon system could move 10 to 20 officers to the scene in 5 minutes, double or triple that number in 10 or 15 minutes.

City after city cited the system's reputation for crowd control as one of the primary reasons for adopting it. The Chicago police force's widely publicized use of the wagon against workers in the series of incidents in 1885 and 1886 that culminated with Haymarket stimulated other police departments' interest in the system and encouraged city councils to approve appropriations for it. Buffalo Police Superintendent Emmanuel Phillips's request for a city council appropriation for the system is typical:

> Experience during the labor troubles of the past summer convinces me that I cannot too strongly recommend to your honorable body the necessity of introducing the patrol wagon system as an auxiliary to our patrol force . . . as it enables us to concentrate a large force of officers at any threatened point a few minutes after an alarm was given; and as the aim of the department was to prevent a row from starting, the prompt appearance of a large force of officers had a desired effect.[9]

"The police say that the patrol wagon has a more soothing effect on the Poles than a dozen policemen," noted the Buffalo *Courier* after a food riot in the Polish district.[10]

Table 5. OPERATION OF BUFFALO'S PATROL WAGON AND SIGNAL SYSTEM, 1887–1896

Year	Total calls	Wagon responses	Patrol wagon arrests	Number of wagons
1887[a]	726	801	1,121	1
1888	128,513	4,438	5,306	4
1889	142,638	5,645	6,793	4
1890	144,787	6,171	7,169	5
1891	148,684	6,994	7,687	5
1892	143,540	6,953	8,370	5
1893	131,130	8,255	9,355	5
1894	159,884	10,524	15,222	6
1895	166,827	11,266	15,202	7
1896	843,300[b]	12,734	16,848	7

Source: Buffalo Police Department, *Annual Reports.*
[a]The system was installed during the year 1887, hence it was only in use for part of the year.
[b]Prior to 1896 each officer was to call in only in an emergency or to receive instructions. Beginning in 1896, each officer was to call in each hour routinely.

Officials in Pittsburgh agreed: the patrol wagon was "equal to a dozen policemen. No matter how great or turbulent a crowd may be the mob gives way at the approach of the wagon." Consistent with this view, police officials approvingly referred to Pittsburgh's 145 signal boxes as a "civilizing agent."[11]

The application of the patrol wagon system to strike and crowd control took several forms. Obviously, the ability to move large forces of reserves rapidly around a city was an important element of any strike control strategy. Similarly, the location of signal boxes every few blocks enabled headquarters to coordinate police efforts over a large area more efficiently. But there were additional applications as well. The patrol wagon itself served as a weapon: it could be driven zig-zag through crowds to break them up or several abreast down a street to clear it. Moreover, the patrol wagon made it possible to use mass arrests as a means of crowd control. Before, prisoners could not easily be taken because there was no means to hold them and remove them to the station without setting aside large numbers of officers, who usually could not be spared.

CRIME CONTROL

A second major selling point for the new system was its utility in controlling, and even reducing, the crime rate. Some idea of its application is found in Flinn's and Wilkie's analysis of the system's operation in Chicago:

> It would be the easiest thing in the world for three or four men to clean out any banking institution in the city in broad daylight. . . . Supposing someone carried information to the nearest station, say a quarter of a mile away? And supposing a number of officers started for the place on a keen run?
>
> Let us suppose that this were attempted today in any large city. At the first appearance of the desperadoes, someone about the place would jump to a small, dial-faced box against the wall, turn a pointer on the dial to a division marked "thieves," and pull a little lever on

the side of the box. Within a half a minute there would dash up to the door a wagon loaded with blue coats. . . .[12]

Moreover, it was argued that every reputable citizen provided with a signal box key thereby became a policeman. These private citizens could be expected to call the police through the signal box if they observed trouble, significantly reinforcing their local police. It was even argued that the patrol wagon would exercise a powerful deterrent effect by increasing the certainty of capture.[13]

Although the impact of the patrol wagon and signal system on crime control cannot readily be evaluated, arrest statistics show no decrease in crime after the adoption of the system. In fact, many cities registered a sharp *increase* after the adoption of the system, mostly in the form of public order arrests.[14]

POLICE EFFICIENCY

Police work has always been labor-intensive, requiring substantial annual outlays for large forces of men at good wages. Cautious city governments early began looking for cost-cutting methods, which generally took the form of manpower reductions. The patrol wagon system did not reduce the numbers of officers already on the force, but it precluded the necessity of further increases. Superintendent William McGarigle of Chicago raised this issue at the time of the creation of the system when he argued that a good system would do the job of 200 men at a fraction of their cost—that is, a one-time capital outlay of $100,000 for the system versus $180,000 annually for 200 patrolmen (at $900 per year, not including pensions, supervision, and other costs).[15]

McGarigle's argument was too attractive not to win approving notice around the country. Mayor Thomas Brown of Milwaukee recommended that the city council make a study of the use of the patrol wagon and signal system in other cities on the ground that "the efficiency of the force can be largely augmented without a numerical increase by the introduction of the Police Alarm Telegraph."[16]

Other cities focused on different types of efficiency, most specifically on speed and mobility or on ability to cover a wide territory. In Buffalo and Cincinnati the expanding physical size of the city was offered as a rationale for purchase of the system.[17] Saginaw, Michigan, with a 46-man department in 1891, followed the lead of other small- to middle-sized industrial cities and installed the patrol wagon system in 1895 after a four-year campaign.[18]

RANK-AND-FILE WORK DISCIPLINE

A final form of efficiency attributed to the system was its utility in controlling and disciplining rank-and-file officers. Police officers, like other workers, vigorously resisted management attempts to reorganize, discipline, and control their work process. Often it took a major series of police reforms to strengthen the organization of the department enough even to begin to require hourly reports from officers. Chief Janssen of Milwaukee instituted a system of regular one-hour call-ins in 1888—six years after the system had that capability. Superintendent William Bull took similar action in 1893, also six years after the establishment of the system. In Philadelphia the importance of call-ins was recognized from the outset: "Patrolmen as they go their rounds of street duty are required to report at the street stations on the various portions of the beats. . . . This requirement guarantees the faithfulness of the force and prevents any shirking of duty or continued absence from post."[19]

One of the clearest statements of the importance of this system for controlling and disciplining rank-and-file officers can be seen in a letter from Lewis Withey, one of Grand Rapids's four police commissioners, to the Saginaw chief of police:

> Prior to the adoption of the police signal system by our department in 1885, we were obliged to trust to each man to perform his duty

conscientiously, and we had no means of knowing whether he did so or not, except from the occasional visit of the roundsman. We were constantly annoyed by reports that when a policeman was wanted he could not be found. . . . An officer would often stop in an open stairway or vestibule in inclement weather for shelter, and keep on the watch of the roundsman. He could leave his beat and visit with his friends by the hour in some saloon, and unless caught in the act, we were not cognizant of it. We had more cases of drunkenness, sleeping on beats, complaints of absence when wanted, and disturbances where the officer appeared after the fracas was over in one week, than we have now in a year. . . .

In 1885 we put in the Police Signal System and located a sentry box at the end of each beat, giving the patrolman sufficient time while going over his beat, to answer questions, try doors, and whatever work was required, and we insist upon his sending in his report on schedule time, or giving his reasons for not doing so. The men at first did not approve of it and did all they could to make it unpopular, but the more they kicked against it the more we liked it, and a few fines and dismissals went far towards removing their objections, and we have no complaints now from any quarter. Now we know where our men are. Each one of them is heard from, anywhere from fifteen to twenty-five minutes, day or night. One officer cannot report for another, or play off on us any of those tricks which no one knows how to do better than a policeman. The number of cases of stomach ache, where whiskey is necessary to relieve the pain, has materially decreased, and sickness is not taken as an excuse for any shortcoming because the officer can telephone in his troubles and be relieved without delay. . . .[20]

The police rank and file immediately recognized that the system could be used to organize and control their labor as they walked their beats. In addition to much bitter grumbling against the system, methods of sabotage were devised. One officer could be given the responsibility of turning in signals on schedule for a number of officers. Because it was expensive to wire them individually, boxes were often wired in series. One officer taking his phone off the hook could obstruct an entire line, thus freeing other officers from the responsibility of calling in regularly.[21] A poem published anonymously in the *Chicago Tribune*

illustrates the resentment against the heightened level of supervision introduced by the signal system. That system, the author
complained, could "shmell iv'ry dhrap ye've been tastin' the
night."[22] Rank-and-file resistance was one reason many departments did not institute the call-in requirement until their systems
had been in operation for as long as ten years.[23]

Rank-and-file patrolmen had another reason for opposing the
system. From the outset it was presented in part as a labor-
saving device that would replace expensive patrolmen, who
were becoming even more expensive with the advent of pension
plans. Chicago Police Chief McGarigle's estimate of the new
system's cost efficiency was the major argument for spending so
much money so quickly on a system untried in any other American city. Hence this system represented the first technological
threat to the labor-intensive nature of police services.[24] Police
officers had class interests very different from those of management, particularly with regard to work-process issues. Although
these men could be mobilized into action against the working
class, this role was fraught with internal contradiction.

CONCLUSIONS

The patrol wagon and signal system, far from reducing the need
for additional manpower, as proponents had argued, actually facilitated department growth for several reasons. First, the system provided the technological infrastructure for managing
much larger police departments. Second, the system was *reac-
tive;* without large numbers of men on patrol, the system would
lay idle. Third, a department needed specially trained officers,
drivers, operators, electricians, linemen, and hostlers to operate
the system and to keep it functioning. Buffalo's Gamewell system, for example, a very standard and efficient one, required 70
men—nearly 10 percent of the force—to operate its five wagons
in 1894.[25]

Most significantly, the patrol service system laid the technological foundation for the integration of police forces into one

coordinated unit, a clear shift away from localized, precinct-based structures. With efficient transportation and communication mechanisms, command functions could be centralized downtown—a process that will be examined more closely in the next chapter.

By the end of the nineteenth century the urban police institution was much better equipped, more organized, larger in size, and more disciplined than it had been 20 years before. Many of these changes can be traced to the development and spread of the patrol wagon and signal system. The application of new forms of technology did not in itself cause these changes to occur but was in fact a product of the changing police institution. Forms of technology that had long been available were adapted to the police institution to permit increased communication, rapid expansion, and higher levels of discipline.

In order to present a more detailed analysis of the development of the police institution during the industrial revolution, the focus will now shift to a closer look at the patterns of bourgeois domination of the process of police expansion and reorganization in two industrial cities: Buffalo and Milwaukee. Though similar demographically, these two cities produced distinct police organizations out of their local political structures.

CHAPTER FOUR

The Buffalo Police, 1865–1900

BUFFALO PRESENTS A MODEL of police expansion under a well-organized local ruling class. Between 1865 and 1900 the emphasis on Lake Erie shipping and trade gave way to manufacturing, and Buffalo became the nation's second-largest rail center, processing grain and timber and supplying iron and steel products. By 1910 Buffalo had a larger proportion of its labor force in industrial work than any other city in America. The city's working class, however, was poorly organized and lacked the political power to alter local decision making.

Buffalo's police force was specifically constructed to intervene in the class struggle on the side of the bourgeoisie. Exactly what this meant can be seen quite clearly in a letter from F. Tuma, master mechanic of the Erie Railroad, to Buffalo's superintendent of police immediately following a 1906 strike. The letter was reprinted in the department's annual report, clearly as a kind of advertisement to prove the worth of police services and to support the department's claims for more appropriations.

> . . . on the morning following the strike of the machinists on the 24th at this shop, without any request the officers were sent from No. 11 Station early on the morning of the 25th informing me that they were sent to render any assistance they could to protect the company's

property, and would furnish as many officers as it was deemed necessary to protect the company's property and employees. . . .

Also thanks for letting me have just what men I thought was best to cope with this kind of work, and I trust they will be able to handle the situation in the future as they have in the past.[1]

Apparently the municipal police institution was so completely under the control of the local capitalist class that much of the actual direction of police antistrike work was delegated to the employers themselves, without even the pretense of neutrality. In fact, the Buffalo police force was always dominated by the major business interests in the city—first commercial interests, then industrial interests. The working class had no involvement in shaping or controlling the police force.

BEGINNINGS OF THE BUFFALO POLICE

Unlike Pittsburgh, Cincinnati, Chicago, and Detroit, Buffalo had not developed a modern police force by the end of the Civil War. Local political decision makers, primarily commercial businessmen, simply did not see the need for one. So long as the watch force succeeded in confining disorder to one district, and so long as no major riots disturbed Buffalo in the 1840s and 1850s, businessmen could not agree on spending the sums necessary to establish a large police force.

In 1866 three Republican businessmen attempted to persuade the city council to pass a police bill. Jonathan S. Buell, a commission and insurance agent and secretary of an oil company, O. J. Green, a downtown grocer, and James Adams, owner of a tanning company, were determined to impose a modern day-and-night police force on Buffalo in place of its watch force. When their efforts failed in the city council, they took a 10,000-word police bill, authored by Buell, to Albany, where it was lobbied through the Republican state legislature. The new act created a regional police force under the authority of the governor, who appointed Buell, Green, and Adams as the city's first police commissioners, with Buell as chairman of the Police Board. The three returned to Buffalo, had employment application forms printed, and began interviewing applicants for the new Niagara Frontier Police Force. Besides personally hiring candidates, the commissioners made rules and regulations and reduced or dismissed officers who did not meet their approval. This direct control of the Buffalo police by local businessmen continued through the next 40 years. In 1870 a Democratic victory in state-wide elections saw the removal of Buffalo's three Republican commissioners and their replacement by three Democrats. Democratic control of both city and state removed much of the original political impetus for state control of the Buffalo police, and in 1871 the state legislature passed control of the police back to the city through three police commissioners, the mayor, and two appointees, one from each party.[2]

The Niagara Frontier Police Force lasted just five years. Though patterned after the state-run metropolitan police forces then being tried in New York City, Illinois, and Missouri, Buffalo's was nevertheless a regional force and incorporated rural areas and small towns in Erie and Niagara counties. However, of the 200 men who patrolled Buffalo and adjacent rural townships, about 136 were on duty in Buffalo—eight times the manpower of the former watch force. The effect of this increase is easy to measure in terms of arrests. During its first six months the new force made 6,192 arrests in the enlarged area but mostly in Buffalo, as opposed to 1,859 during a similar period in 1865—a threefold increase. Fines collected registered an even greater increase: for the entire year of 1865 fines collected amounted to $5,965; for the first six months under the new system they reached $16,629. This figure is not linked to an increase in crime; rather, it represents increased regulation of existing behavior. Closer analysis of the pattern of arrests shows that this regulation was directed toward working-class recreational behavior, indicating the class basis of law enforcement under the new Buffalo police force. Of the 6,192 arrests in 1866, 3,827 (62 percent) were for the four most common public order offenses—drunkenness, drunk and disorderly conduct, disorderly conduct, and vagrancy—and an additional 1,071 (17 percent) were for misdemeanor assaults, probably mostly another public order offense stemming from general working-class rowdiness. Thus one measure of the impact of the new force in Buffalo was the threefold increase in arrests for public order offenses.

From police reports, which list suspects' occupations, it can be seen that virtually all of those arrested in 1866 were workers: laborers, 1,719 (28 percent); sailors, 810 (14 percent); boatmen, 445 (7 percent); no occupation, 327 (5 percent); servants, 243 (3 percent); and others from virtually every working-class occupation. The greatest proportion of those arrested were born in the United States (2,483, or 40 percent), but a disproportionate number (1,945, or 31 percent) were Irish. Seventy-eight of those arrested were males. More than half of the females arrested were recorded as "prostitutes," but there were no arrests for the offense category "prostitution;" rather, females were most commonly arrested for disorderly conduct, assault and battery, and larceny.[3]

The transformation of the Niagara Frontier Police Force into the Buffalo Police Department in late 1872 did not alter the trend of arrests. The first Buffalo police force had 204 men, substantially expanded from the 136 that the Niagara Frontier Force had stationed in Buffalo. Not unexpectedly, they made 2,001 more arrests in 1873 than the regional force had made in 1872 (12,535 versus 10,534). Again, all of the increase was in the categories of drunkenness, disorderly conduct, and vagrancy. More important, although arrests remained at about the 1866 level, the proportion of public order arrests had become a greater proportion of the total—66 percent—while an additional 14 percent more were for misdemeanor assault and battery. In addition, there were many new descriptions of offenses, spreading public order arrests over dozens of new offense categories, such as "misdemeanor," "disturbing religious meetings," "violating city ordinances," and "peace warrants."[4]

The 1873 force remained virtually unchanged for ten years and was typical of urban police forces of the period. About 200 men were organized into two 12-hour shifts and into eight precincts, where primary authority rested with precinct captains, whose appointments were largely political. After an election about half of the captains might be replaced. The annual turnover rate among the patrolmen, including both voluntary resignations and political removals, was about 50 percent. As in other cities in the United States, the force took on an increasingly Irish complexion.

Some efforts were made to maintain a disciplined force: a regular military drill was assembled twice a week; the most flagrant violators of discipline were dismissed; and captains were required to keep a written record of the personal qualities of individual officers. The force remained inefficient nonetheless, in part because of the continual need to train new officers and because of the relative inexperience of the force. In 1873 three-quarters of the patrolmen were recruits. The result can be seen in arrest figures: between 1874 and 1887 arrests dropped, usually to two-thirds or three-quarters of the 1873 figure—in 1879, to a low of about one-half that rate. Since the population was growing, the real decline in arrests was even greater. It was 1888 before even the absolute number of 1873 arrests was equaled, and by then Buffalo had doubled its 1870 population. It also had a completely reorganized police department.[5]

CAPITALIST CONTROL OF THE BUFFALO POLICE

The slow decline of the Buffalo police between 1873 and 1888 was more than made up for in two decades of rapid growth after 1888 in response to a sharp increase in the tempo of the class struggle in Buffalo. Class violence had occurred prior to 1888, but not with the frequency and on the massive scale that finally convinced local capitalists to invest in a stronger police force.

As in many other cities in the United States, behind Buffalo's class politics there kindled volatile party politics. Republicans and Democrats regularly fought election campaigns filled with graft and corruption. Marshaling the forces of both parties were not working-class political machines but the most successful businessmen in Buffalo, carrying their notion of laissez-faire competitive business practices into the political arena. Political power meant jobs for supporters, public contracts, streets paved and improved, and a hundred other valuable benefits associated with control of municipal government. Such possibilities were too valuable to turn over to a working-class machine, even one under strict supervision. As a result, Buffalo was the only eastern city with a sizable Irish population that never saw the Irish in major political positions.[6]

Working-class-based machines in Buffalo struggled over jobs, bribes from saloons, and labor contracts, but not over control of the development and expansion of capital in Buffalo. The machines existed alongside political parties dominated by the owners of all the major factories in Buffalo and by petty-bourgeois professionals and mid-level functionaries of all kinds. No machine boss ever served as mayor of Buffalo. Similarly, the two police commissioners were always businessmen or manufacturers. Political office was not a symbolic exercise of bourgeois power. The men who held public positions in Buffalo devoted most of their time to those efforts, often putting their business interests aside for a period. This personal involvement on the part of the bourgeoisie extended to all city services—education, welfare, public health, as well as the police—and was absolutely essential in the formative years of capitalist development. There existed no professional class of educators, police officials, or welfare workers who could be trusted to develop public institutions that would provide for the orderly reproduction of the working class. Not even the bourgeoisie were certain of exactly what the needs of expanding capital were, since the capitalist system was new and developing. Innovations in other cities were eagerly studied, debated, and, when appropriate, copied, but there was no system of urban development under capitalism that could be copied as a whole.

Local politics during the 1870s and 1880s kept Buffalo and its police force in turmoil. There were 12 mayors between 1870 and 1900, four Republicans and eight Democrats. Two Republicans who served terms in the 1870s were defeated by Democrats, then returned to defeat Democrats in the 1880s and serve again. The average term as mayor was only two and one-half years. Virtually all of Buffalo's major industries were represented in the mayor's chair at one point or another between 1870 and 1915.

The mayor appointed two police commissioners, one from each party to ensure its nonpartisan character. These men, too, represented Buffalo's major enterprises. For example, Commissioner Frank Sears (1878–1879) was a partner in a malting firm; Robert Mills (1880–1883) owned a shipyard and dry dock; Frank Illig (1889–1894) ran a downtown hardware business; William Churchyard (1890–1891) directed the Buffalo Planing Mill and Bellows Factory; and Charles Rupp (1895–1902) was a building contractor. Edgar Jewett (1894) of Jewett Refrigeration Company was the only man to be appointed a police commissioner and later to be elected mayor.[7]

Service as a police commissioner was not simply a civic duty or an honorary public office. In those years for which records are available (mostly during the 1890s), the board met between 100 and 150 times per year—that is, between two and three times per week. Commissioners, who were officially considered to be only part-time employees, received about three times the pay of a full-time patrolman—$2,500, as opposed to $900 for a first-grade patrolman and $1,000 for a sergeant in 1895. In 1885 and 1897 the police commissioners made extensive inspection trips to other cities at their own expense.[8]

The police commissioners exemplify the bourgeoisie's need to assume personal control of public institutions to ensure that those institutions developed in ways favorable to capital. The lack of models for the operation of urban institutions allowed capitalists to take direct control of those institutions. Even the idea that the police should stay neutral in strikes or in other situations where the community was divided did not have wide currency. Good business and law and order stood for virtually the same set of principles. This agreement did not prevent the major political parties from struggling bitterly over the police, however. What was at stake was the immediate benefits that control over the police could bring. In the long run, however, capitalist domination of the economic system went unchallenged, and the fundamental class basis of the police institution remained undisturbed.

For example, one universally noted function of the police in this partisan political warfare was to assist the party in power at election time. A major scandal erupted in Buffalo in 1892, when the police were accused of preventing some citizens from voting. No officers were punished, however, and the captain in charge, Michael Regan, was later promoted to police chief in 1906.[9] To the extent that police involvement in ward politics precluded a more efficient, more centrally administered police force, it also caused the department to neglect capital's need for strong regulation of both the day-to-day activity of the working class and the occasional, but serious, strikes and other forms of mass action.

In Buffalo, as in other cities, a major struggle developed over the power of partisan politicians to hire and fire police officers at will. Here the short-term interests of both parties demanded as much patronage as possible in order to pay off the soldiers who did the political foot work of the machine. Furthermore, the interests of the capitalist class as a whole required both patronage jobs for working-class individuals as a means of structuring working-class political activity and a city government sufficiently broad-based to serve the interests of expanding capital. Offering jobs and services to the working class served to legitimate the democratic political framework in which capitalist domination of public institutions occurred, and the police department, like other city service organizations, had to supply its share of patronage. At the same time, however, high police turnover prevented the development of expertise on the part of both patrolmen and administrators. Policemen on all levels were untrained and capable of only a few kinds of basic functions. And because they owed their jobs to one set of politicians and would soon lose them to another set, no matter how good their work, they had little incentive to do a competent job. Moreover, no matter how effective the department's work, its legitimacy was questionable, because any police action could be criticized as policy carried out for some political interest.

Brief biographies of Buffalo's twelve police captains, published in 1893, clearly show the chaos inherent in a police career in Buffalo in the 1870s and 1880s. Fully half of the twelve had experienced career irregularities. John Kraft of the Fourth Precinct had been appointed captain in 1880, was demoted to patrolman for political reasons in 1883, and was reappointed captain three years later. Captain John Martin of the Tenth Precinct had been a sergeant prior to 1887, when he resigned to serve at the New York Central Station as a patrolman for five years. Resignations were a common response to political changes in the department: Martin could have been dismissed if he had refused to yield his rank. He was promoted straight through all the ranks to captain in 1892. Captain Edward Forrestal enjoyed a meteoric rise: he was appointed captain in 1883 without even one day's experience on the police force. In 1887 he was demoted to patrolman, then in 1891 promoted again to captain.

Insecurity affected all levels of the force. During the 1870s about one-third of the force resigned or was dismissed annually on the average. During the 1880s this figure was reduced to a 13 percent resignation and dismissal rate. But even this rate meant about 40 jobs a year in a department of fewer than 300 men.[10]

This instability profoundly affected police work. Where promotions depended on political connections, there was no emphasis on developing police skills. Officers were reputed to make unnecessary arrests just to get off patrol work. Escorting a prisoner to the station, completing the necessary book work, and waiting for court was usually good for perhaps four hours out of Buffalo's infamous weather. Buffalo installed patrol boxes beginning in 1885 as one attempt at supervision, but men were required to call in only once per 12-hour shift, a situation that prevailed until 1894, when hourly call-ins were required. Arrest rates sagged seriously in the late 1870s and again in the 1880s. Patrolmen lacked the motivation to make arrests and spent as little time as they could walking their beats. In 1888 the chief of police proudly claimed that a 30 percent increase in arrests (almost 3,000) reflected the growing efficiency of the force, not rising levels of crime, violence, or disorder in the city.[11]

It is important to note, however, that despite Buffalo's recurrent political upheaval, dismissals and turnovers never reached such proportions that the force was completely disorganized. Officers on all levels, including captains and chiefs, made accommodations with both political parties that allowed them to keep their jobs after an election. Obviously, no party felt free to replace the entire force. Some level of stability was always maintained; some high-ranking officers always kept their jobs.

Expansion, technological innovation, and administrative centralization came into immediate conflict with the corruption and partisan politics of the Buffalo police. Buffalo, like virtually all other American cities, faced regular police scandals. Here it is important to differentiate between two distinct types of problems. First, the problem of police corruption—bribery, thefts, and protection of vice—was indeed serious, but not necessarily inimical to either day-to-day patrol of working-class communities or special crowd control or strike work, so long as the force was not so inept that no work could be done. The real problem was a tendency toward complete immobilization and breakdown of police services as officers devoted increasing proportions of their time to these activities. Moreover, corruption undermines the legitimacy of the police institution. Periodic anticorruption drives attempted to keep the level of corruption within acceptable bounds.

Similarly, the problem of partisan political control can be understood in Weberian terms: it undermines the continuity of the police bureaucracy when reorganization is continually undertaken for purely external considerations; hence, the bureaucracy loses its effectiveness. In Buffalo partisan political control was in fact bipartisan, but it had the same result: both Democratic and Republican officers were regularly reduced in rank or dismissed from the force. Such interruptions do not seriously impair the function of a watch force, but an aggressive force intending to police the social life of a city must have stability in its administrative ranks.

Contributing a measure of stability was the Board of Police

Commissioners, the dominant force in the Buffalo police until the late 1890s. The board was composed of representatives from both parties, which had the effect of reducing party influence. More important, these commissioners were all substantial businessmen, representing the largest industrial and mercantile interests in the city, and they tended to put class interests above partisan politics where they came in conflict.

The much-touted effort in 1894 to remove the Buffalo police from politics involved only the elimination of partisan political influence on the police, interference of the police in elections, and regular political firings in the police department. It did not extend to the elimination of bourgeois political control over the police and other municipal institutions. The foundations of this reorganization, moreover, had been laid by other capitalist reformers eight years earlier, in 1886, with the institution of civil service regulations, which were selectively and corruptly implemented. A reformer and dry goods merchant, Daniel J. Morganstern, was appointed police superintendent in 1891 to complete some of this separation of direct political interference from the police. He encountered strong resistance, however, and was removed in 1894. William S. Bull, a wholesale paper dealer, was appointed to finish the job.[12]

Though reduced, direct intervention by politicians in the police department did not end; it merely took on different forms. Police officials emerged as important political figures in their own right. The police department still depended on public institutions for appropriations, retirement benefits, and salary scales, and Buffalo's powerful police commissioners still hired and fired the superintendent of police. Nevertheless, direct control of the police during periods of intense class struggle is a distinct liability for a city government responsible within the electoral process. Hence, there are clear advantages in and for a tough, independent police chief who carries out policies that serve the requirements of an expanding capitalist economy. His independence, of course, is carefully structured within a legal framework so that simply carrying out legal rules serves the necessary purpose of reproducing the working class.[13]

In Buffalo the first steps toward this autonomy of the police occurred in the appointment of stronger chiefs who remained in office for longer periods of time. A 20-year run of weak police chiefs with two- or three-year terms ended abruptly with the appointment of William S. Bull in 1894. The candidate of young, chiefly Republican reformers, his first action was to announce that political recommendations would no longer have any effect on the appointment or retention of officers, a promise that was more or less kept. Bull also fully used the signal system to ensure that men were walking beats, and he reorganized crowd control strategy. During his tenure patrolmen's wages and hours greatly improved, particularly with the adoption of the three-platoon system and eight-hour shifts.[14]

Ironically, his successor as Buffalo's second reform superintendent was Mike Regan, who had been implicated in the vote fraud scandal of 1892. Like Bull, a strong commander, Regan was nevertheless Bull's opposite in that he was no businessman but a rough-and-tumble cop who had survived 20 years in the First Ward, Buffalo's toughest. Uncompromisingly anti-immigrant and anti-working-class, he believed that "the Italians are a dangerous class for they break the law," and he defended police beatings of Italians. Regan saw his job as maintaining order exactly as prescribed by the conventional bourgeois values of the time. Strikes were acceptable so long as they were orderly, which also made them ineffective. Immigrants were a special police problem because they lacked "American" values and needed constant watching. Saloons wasted workingmen's money and promoted laziness and recklessness. Alcohol was a problem because the working class misused it.[15]

The great changes in administration and technology brought about by businessmen-reformers transformed the police department after the mid-1880s, but they also had the effect of making the department too complex to be effectively administered by a nonprofessional. Gone were the days when J.S. Buell and two friends could author a bill providing for all aspects of the operation of a police department, interview and hire all the patrolmen, and personally supervise all details of the department's operation. In the shift from businessmen-superintendents to career police officers, however, the bourgeoisie did not lose control of the department, for the tough police chiefs who professionalized the department and inculcated value-neutral ideals of law and order accomplished class goals precisely.

EXPANSION AND RATIONALIZATION

Showing who controlled the Buffalo police is only one part of showing *how* the department, over a 20-year period, was restructured into a powerful strikebreaking force under the control of the manufacturers. Before the 1880s, Buffalo's businessmen could not agree that the city even needed a strong, well-organized, and disciplined police force. During the 1870s and early 1880s the city had allowed the force to decline in strength proportionate to the population. Thus, although the local bourgeoisie completely dominated the police force and all other public institutions, they had not yet decided on the extent to which they would actually use this power.

This indecisiveness was consistent with a national trend. The capitalist class was divided over the question of the use of public institutions and public expenditures to socialize some of the costs of capitalist expansion. Low taxes and laissez-faire economics had a strong traditional appeal to local capitalists, but by the 1880s and 1890s these ideals were being overwhelmed by the dimensions of the "urban problem"—slums, improper sanitation, unsocialized immigrants, unpaved streets, poor housing, and the growing class struggle. Many thought the Great Strike of 1877 to be an aberration. By the time of the eight-hour movement and the Haymarket violence of 1886, however, the class struggle had become a central force in urban life. In other words, as large-scale industrial development moved forward, existing social institutions for the reproduction of labor proved inadequate. This growing disparity can be seen in education, welfare, and recreational institutions as well as in the police institution. The police institution, moreover, had a unique function in addition to the reproduction of labor, namely, social control—the violent defeat of any working-class challenge to the existing order.

There was no cataclysmic shift in policy that brought about this transformation of urban life in Buffalo. Rather, it reflected evolutionary changes in the mode of production and the class structure. Buffalo not only grew larger; it also grew along sharply divided class lines. The bourgeoisie clearly recognized this division during the 1877 Great Strike in Buffalo, which assumed the proportions of a general strike. All manufacturing activity in the city ceased in support of striking railroad workers. Such dramatic events clearly alarmed the city's ruling class.

Though poorly trained, poorly disciplined, demoralized by a high turnover, and completely inexperienced in mass strike control tactics, the Buffalo police, augmented by a few civilian volunteers, succeeded where the militia had failed in breaking the strike, clearly establishing its capabilities locally (and nationally) in the eyes of the bourgeoisie.[16] From this point on, the strike control capabilities of the police were steadily augmented, but not without opposition from the working class.

At the same time that the number of officers available to handle the larger strikes increased, the strikes became better organized. Strikes of several hundred workers in the 1880s grew to strikes of several thousand workers in the 1890s. Railroad and dock strikes, common in Buffalo, were especially difficult to police. Factories had a limited number of gates and occupied a fixed area, but railroad and dock operations covered many miles inside Buffalo's city limits. Furthermore, though a "wildcat" strike might be broken by a club-swinging charge or by simply letting in enough scabs to take the workers' jobs, the organized strikes that were called more and more frequently by labor unions could not be so easily broken. Manpower increases in the police department made more men available for difficult sustained antistrike activity.

The police strategy that evolved during the longshoremen's strike of 1884 remained at the core of the Buffalo department's strike work through the First World War. The police detailed a large number of reserves in stations near the strike area, and patrolmen were assigned to keep the strike area under surveillance. Forty "specials" were appointed from the list of rejected applicants for police employment, replacing the citizen volunteers used in 1877. Those who served best were kept on as vacancies opened, thus completing the permanent separation of the police function from citizen participation in Buffalo.[17]

Eighteen-eighty-four also marked the Buffalo police department's recognition that good strike control work required more regular appropriations from the city council. From this point on, police requests for additional men were often based simply on the fact that strike work overextended the department's resources. Although that work accounted for only a small proportion of all police activity, preparation and readiness for strikes was a full-time job. Much of the overhead of the Buffalo police went to maintaining a large force of "reserves," full-time police officers who spent up to one-half of their work time on call at stations. This reserve was obviously intended for crowd control work.

The strain that strike work placed on the system was exactly communicated to the city council in a request for additional manpower in 1890:

> In this connection it may be well to call your attention to the large amount of extra duty which is always imposed upon the patrolmen whenever there is a strike. Owing to the comparatively small number of officers which are at my command for such occasions, it becomes necessary to utilize the officers of the platoons off duty for extra labor, thus compelling them to be on duty continuously both day and night, while the trouble lasts. During the strike in September last, the officers did about ten days of such extra duty. The duties of the officers are surely arduous enough on ordinary occasions, and to compel a man to be on duty day and night without sufficient sleep and rest, so long, is more than should be expected of any ordinary mortal.[18]

The greatest growth of Buffalo's department, in numerical terms, occurred between 1883 and 1905, the years of most intense industrialization. Until 1883 the size of the force remained at about 200, unchanged since the creation of the department in 1872. Between 1883 and 1903 the force grew from 229 to 783—nearly a fourfold increase—while the population roughly doubled. By 1915 the size of the department stood at 907, nearly its present size. Proportionally, the Buffalo force grew from 1.4 officers per 1,000 population in 1866 to 2.1, a level maintained from 1895 to 1905. In this respect, Buffalo's force was comparable to those of other cities of equal size.

A number of factors contributed to this growth. As already noted, however, the police administration put its argument for more men in terms of strike control needs. Accordingly, the greatest periods of increase were years following severe strikes—the mid-1880s, the mid-1890s, and 1900. Furthermore, the creation of more specialized police functions, such as those associated with the patrol wagon and signal system, required large numbers of men; the system, of course, was developed specifically with strike control in mind. The large increase in size brought with it a rapidly expanding bureaucratic apparatus, which in turn required even more men. This expansion was an indirect response to heightened class conflict and cannot be narrowly attributed to self-aggrandizing bureaucratization. Finally, the switch from a two-platoon to a three-platoon system required doubling the force in order to maintain the same number of men on each shift. This change, again, was due in large part to the increasing demands made on the department in its attempt to monitor the class struggle; men simply could not work 12-hour shifts, seven days a week, and still be expected to remain on reserve and stay at peak efficiency in case of mass actions.

When increases were granted, they were justified on the basis of Buffalo's expanding population and size—more miles to patrol, more people to control—or in the wake of specific strike control problems, such as those of 1890, 1892, 1894, and 1899.[19]

The explicit linking of an expanding property base to the need to increase the size of the police department clearly supports an interpretation that the protection of propertied interests underlay police expansion. Note how all these factors come together in the police chief's annual report for 1887:

The last increase to the Police force was made August 31, 1885, when 10 patrolmen were added. Since that date the population of the city has increased 30,284, and the value of property calling for police protection in proportion. The numerical strength of the force should increase proportionately with the population and the building up of the outlying districts of the city.[20]

Neither the police commissioners nor the Buffalo police chiefs ever argued that a rising crime rate per se required a strengthened police force.

POLICING CLASS STRUGGLE IN THE 1890s AND AFTER

On both an absolute and a proportional basis, the Buffalo police were more active in the 1890s than ever before. Their presence was felt in the repression of strikes and other mass actions and in the day-to-day monitoring of public order offenses, such as vagrancy and tramping. Paradoxically, this high level of police activity and the force's great effectiveness in the class struggle occurred precisely at the time when reformers were most critical of police corruption and inefficiency. Therefore it is important to look beyond the words to see the social impact of the rationalization of the police department.

First, with regard to the policing of mass action, Buffalo in the 1890s saw a full range of working-class resistance to the factory system and to the exploitation brought about by depression. Buffalo was hard hit by the depression of 1893-1897; more than 20 percent of all workers were unemployed, including perhaps 50 percent of the Poles. On either side of the depression, the 1890s also saw two of Buffalo's most serious strikes, both involving virtually the entire community and attracting national attention. National guard troops occupied the city during the railroad switchmen's strike of 1892, but the police were more important in containing the strike. The grain scoopers' strikes of 1898 and 1899 again involved the entire community and the entire police department, which patrolled along the docks. The strikes lasted so long that a special police station was established at the strike location. In addition, smaller, "routine" strikes occurred almost every year.[21]

Crowd control functions followed similar patterns but on a smaller scale. Spontaneous rebellions such as the Broadway Market food riot, the destruction of asphalt-laying machines by Polish road-building workers, religious riots caused by a rift in the Polish Catholic Church, and political resistance to police disruption of socialist meetings were handled on the precinct level, where the club-swinging charge was the basic police weapon. It was for these situations that the patrol wagon and signal system was ideal, bringing police officers quickly to the scene before a crowd coalesced.

As the level of violence in these situations increased, so too did police antipathy for the immigrants who were often involved. A disproportionate share of the routine crowd control work of the Buffalo police involved immigrant communities, particularly Polish and Italian ones. There appears to have been a deliberate policy of placing ethnic police units in neighborhoods containing ethnic groups to which they were traditionally hostile. In the 1890s, for example, Buffalo's force was largely Irish (perhaps 70 percent) and German. German captains commanded precincts on the East Side staffed by German patrolmen and populated by Germans and Poles. Irish patrolmen served under captains of Irish descent in precincts that included Irish, Wasp, and Italian neighborhoods (see table 6). There was considerable hostility between the Italians and the Irish and between the Germans and the Poles. The two groups in each case competed for jobs and residential space, with Italians moving into Irish neighborhoods and Poles moving into German neighborhoods. Police Captain Kohler of the Polish Eighth Precinct had nothing but contempt for the Poles. His denial of Polish misery in the depression is characteristic: "They are hungry but they have not yet reached the starvation level." As evidence of Polish wealth, he argued that the Poles he arrested always had enough money to pay their fines.

Table 6.   ETHNICITY OF BUFFALO PATROLMEN AND
CAPTAINS, BY PRECINCT, 1890

Precinct	Irish officers	German officers	Captain
1	49	6	Irish
2	26	1	Irish
3	25	4	Irish
4	4	14	German
5	12	5	Irish
6	22	4	Irish
7	22	3	Irish
8	6	20	German
9	10	3	Irish
10	13	2	Irish
Substation			
1	7	2	German
2	5	5	German

Source: *Annual Report of the Chief of Police of the City of Buffalo,* 1890.
Ethnicity of individual officers was determined by ethnic origin of surname.

The Poles acquired a reputation for turbulence after the
Broadway Market food riots in September 1893. Angry over
high food prices at a time of high unemployment, they attacked
some stalls in the Broadway Market. Police beat and dispersed
the crowd. A meeting was held the next night in a rented hall to
protest the police action, but the police stopped the meeting, and
a second riot broke out. Up to 500 Poles, led by socialist "agita-
tors," marched on City Hall to demand jobs. Again the police
stopped them, violently. Similar marches in 1894 met the same
response. Riots originating in a split among Polish Catholics
came the next year, and destruction of road equipment occurred
in 1897. Gangs of Polish laborers showed up at locations of city
jobs, demanding to be put to work. Often they brought shovels
and simply went to work, lining up for pay at the end of the day.
Instead, the police were called, and the workers were beaten
with clubs. All such conflicts were defined as simple police

problems. Arrests and beatings were frequent. The toughest police captains in Buffalo commanded the Polish precincts.[22]

If the Poles were regarded as turbulent, the Italians were seen as a "criminal" class. In fact, patterns of police control in Italian neighborhoods did not differ much from those in Polish ones. When an Italian Union parade was blocked in downtown Buffalo by irate nativists, a fight broke out, and the police entered to control the Italians. Police officers trying to arrest two Italians carrying home a beer pail were blocked by hundreds of neighbors. A patrol wagon rescued the officers and their prisoners. In another instance, a police officer carelessly discharged a gun on a street crowded with children in the Italian community, provoking women to march on City Hall. Blocked by the police, they turned to march on police headquarters, where several were arrested for disorderly conduct. Twenty years earlier, the Italian consulate had taken note of the Buffalo situation when it protested the police's handling of knifings in the Italian community. The police had arrested all the Italian males in Buffalo, searched them, given them a lecture on law, and released them. They found two knives.[23]

These kinds of class control problems, like strikes, were incorporated into the repertoire of police response patterns. Though paramilitary organization, large size, expansive bureaucratic organization, and specialized training were the keys to handling large strikes, the smaller, day-to-day riotous situations required a quicker response, which in turn depended on the patrol wagon and signal system and the presence of strong, well-trained men on the wagons.

CHAPTER FIVE

The Police as a Class Question in Milwaukee, 1865–1912

MILWAUKEE, LIKE BUFFALO, CHICAGO, and other cities in the region, grew rapidly to become a large manufacturing center by the late nineteenth century. The biggest industries were metal products, followed by clothing, leather, furniture and wood products, brewing, and printing. By 1910, when its population reached 373,857, Milwaukee was the twelfth-largest city in the United States. In terms of industrial activity proportionate to total economic activity, it was the third most industrialized large city in the country (after Buffalo and Detroit), with 56 percent of its work force engaged in "industrial and mechanical" occupations in 1910. Known as the most "foreign" city in America in the late nineteenth century, Milwaukee tied with New York City in having the highest proportion of foreign-born residents among its population (in 1910, 78 percent). Moreover, no city could boast that a larger share of its foreign stock came from one country: 68 percent of the foreign-born in Milwaukee were from Germany, giving the city its well-known flavor–the German "Athens."[1]

CLASS POLITICS IN MILWAUKEE

Milwaukee's heavy industrialization and large proportion of immigrants were closely linked with the phenomenon that distinguished Milwaukee from all other major industrial cities in America: its class-conscious and militant working-class politics, which after 1880 usually took the form of a working-class party that challenged both Democrats and Republicans for control of local governmental institutions. In 1882, 1888, 1910, and 1914 the workers' party won local mayoralty elections, and in most other elections some workers' party candidates won office. Win or lose, however, the threat of a politically organized and articulate working class could never be ignored by Milwaukee's ruling class. After the 1890s Milwaukee's Social Democratic party, working through the Central Labor Union, became the best-known and most successful of America's local working-class parties. But it is important to note that the success of the Social Democratic party followed the earlier struggles of Milwaukee's People's and Populist parties, which worked through the same trades-union base.[2]

This strong, well-organized working-class political movement articulated class issues in relation to all local governmental institutions, and it had a considerable impact on the police, which Milwaukee workers had long regarded as under the control of the local ruling class. As a result, the police became a political issue in Milwaukee. But the points of contention were not the police role in vote fraud or the partisan political control of the department. Rather, attention focused on the class nature of enforcement policies, as exemplified by the police role in strikes, police enforcement of vice laws (or lack of enforcement), police attacks on the saloons, and the day-to-day monitoring of working-class communities. Moreover, though working-class criticism of the police was common in all cities, in Milwaukee it was backed by political power. Politicians responsive to the working class resisted many police demands for increased resources, fought anti-working-class legislation, and struggled to assert some influence in the development of the Milwaukee police. This political articulation of the class struggle achieved its highest form through Milwaukee's Social Democratic party before the First World War, particularly during the one-term administration of Emil Seidel, Milwaukee's first socialist mayor (1910–1912).

The complex role that Milwaukee socialists played in the class struggle reflects the dialectics of local political developments. The Milwaukee Social Democratic party was thoroughly reformist. Communists criticized its members as "sewer socialists" at a later period because of their emphasis on civic betterment and their downplaying of the class struggle during the administration of Mayor Daniel Hoan (1916–1940). The emphasis of the socialists on electoral politics and on work in the trade unions was a conservatizing influence. Nevertheless, the prominence in municipal politics of socialists experienced in labor-union politics meant that Milwaukee witnessed a higher level of class consciousness and a more clearly articulated class struggle for control of municipal institutions than any other industrial city.

From 1882 on the Milwaukee Federated Trades Council, initially composed of sixty participating unions with a total of 13,000 members, was a powerful local political force. A People's party was followed by a Populist party, but once the Milwaukee Social Democratic party was founded in 1897, it was immediately an important force in the labor movement, largely through its recruitment of long-time union activists. By 1899 the Social Democrats had taken control of the FTC through an interlocking directorate of party officials who sat on the executive committee of the FTC. In turn, the FTC elected delegates to the Social Democratic city convention. Most Social Democratic candidates for public office were union members. The FTC, affiliated with the AFL, was the backbone of socialist electoral strength in Milwaukee.[3]

Milwaukee's working-class political forces were arrayed against a ruling class composed of the manufacturers and businessmen who controlled the economic life of the city. The strength of Milwaukee's bourgeoisie in strikes, political campaigns, and anti-working-class agitation clearly shows that a strong working class does not by any means indicate a weak ruling class. Most of the large businesses and manufacturing plants were owned and controlled by local families through the 1800s. These families were closely associated, belonging to a few clubs and social organizations, and they acknowledged one another as sharing social interests. The members of the Brewers Association, for example, had an agreement not to recognize their employees' unions and not to make agreements with their employees without first clearing them with the association. Antiunion sentiment ran high among Milwaukee employers.[4] The prolonged and violent strikes of 1886, 1896, 1901, and 1910 all had their origins in employer refusals to recognize unions or to grant minimal wage increases.

This ruling class held unquestioned control of the city and state Republican party and put up a solid series of businessman candidates for mayor. Moreover, the Republicans in Wisconsin generally controlled the state legislature. If they lost control of Milwaukee, they could push through state legislation to supersede city council law making. They made use of this power for regulation of the police at least three times: in 1885 they passed a police reform bill in Madison that they could not get through the Milwaukee City Council; in the early 1890s they secured life tenure for chiefs of police in order to insulate them permanently from local politics; in 1910 they deprived Social Democratic Mayor Seidel of the last of his powers over the police.[5] The mass working-class vote that the Republicans earned was most often that of the Germans, who were traditionally Republican from the time of the Civil War. The socialists constantly looked to the right and in a reformist direction for ways to win this vote.

The Democratic party in Milwaukee was more complex. On one level, Milwaukee, like all Great Lakes area industrial cities, had a strong "bourbon Democratic" tradition, represented by major businessmen and industrialists. Below them was a political machine based in the downtown and South Side Irish and Polish wards. Politicians in the machine were most often small businessmen who provided various services for their working-class constituents, such as finding jobs, helping to mediate between workers and governmental agencies, and directing petty welfare services. Although the Democrats were probably closer to the working class than were the Republicans, they clearly showed where their interests lay by several times forming fusion tickets with the Republicans in order to defeat working-class People's or Social Democratic party candidates. A listing of Milwaukee's mayors in the post–Civil War period clearly shows the domination of manufacturing and commercial interests in both parties.[6] Furthermore, aldermen, police, fire, and public works commissioners, and other major public officeholders also belonged to the ruling class, though many of them were small businessmen.

Both the Democrats and the Republicans (and later the Social Democrats) operated efficient political machines responsible for placing their own partisans in public offices. Of these, Mayor David Rose's Democratic machine, which governed from 1898 to 1906 and from 1908 to 1910, lasted the longest and was the most corrupt. The changing fortunes of Republicans and Democrats turned on the shifting loyalty of working-class constituents. Republicans enjoyed the allegiance of Wasps but vied with the Socialists for the German vote (Roman Catholic Germans more often voted Republican than did Protestant Germans). Democrats normally counted on the Irish and Polish votes, but by 1900 the Social Democrats had made strong inroads among the Poles, who came to hold the electoral balance of power.

Further complicating the electoral politics of Milwaukee was the three-party system after 1882, which made it possible to win control of city government with a plurality of votes rather than a majority, thus ensuring coalition politics in the city council. Generally, Republicans and Democrats formed fusion tickets to defeat the Social Democrats. The socialists remained outside of the system and did not engage in coalition building (although they were clearly not above considerable wheeling and dealing). This meant that the socialists were more likely than the other parties to go down to defeat on issues of principle, and on police issues the socialists were often defeated along straight party-line votes. Nevertheless, they registered a strong working-class protest against the police.[7] So long as funding for the police had to go through the city council, it was impossible to avoid at least some working-class resistance.

DEVELOPMENT OF MILWAUKEE'S POLICE DEPARTMENT: FORMATION AND CHANGE

The early Milwaukee police department bears a close resemblance to Buffalo's, but after the mid-1880s the class struggle gave Milwaukee's department a unique shape. In 1855 the Milwaukee police were established as a 12-man force consisting of five Germans, three Irishmen, and four native-born Americans. The force remained small and inefficient until the 1880s. Although the working class steadily opposed increases in the size of the force during the post–Civil War period, it was gradually enlarged. Salaries were doubled and men were added in 1866. There were 42 men by 1870, and 25 men were added in 1874. The 87 men on the force in 1883 were increased to 93 the following year.

This small force, with a pattern of slow, incremental growth, was forged into a large, disciplined, and efficient force over a 30-year period that also saw the city's most intense industrial development. By 1914 the department had grown sixfold. Its strength of 586 men meant roughly twice the number of officers per capita as in the 1880s. This growth pattern parallels that of comparable police departments of the period, although Milwaukee's force always remained considerably smaller in size and correspondingly more disciplined and efficient.

The force in its early years was nominally patterned after those in eastern cities, especially New York City. Chief William Beck, a Granville politician and farmer who had earlier served as a New York City patrolman, directed the department for almost all of its first twenty-seven years. If Beck's competency as chief was typical of the force, Milwaukee's police before 1880 were very inept. Twice ousted for political reasons, his erratic administration easily justified dismissal for incompetence, a charge never seriously levied against him. In 1861, the year of his first removal, he badly handled both a bank riot and a lynching, losing a prisoner in his custody to a mob. Back on the job in 1863, Beck emphasized tough, personalized dealings with offenders: "Never arrest a man until you have licked him in a fair fight first," he instructed his men. His force was not uniformed until 1878. Although salaries were increased after the Civil War, turnover remained high and political firings frequent. The force was unstable, inefficient, and not very reliable as a mechanism to maintain public order. Beck's incompetence was probably repeated down through the ranks.[8]

The ten years following Beck's administration witnessed the short, stormy careers of generally incompetent police chiefs, typical of the 1870s and 1880s in Buffalo and other cities as well. Daniel Kennedy served one year in 1879–1880 before being removed for mistreatment of prisoners. Robert Wasson served two years in 1883–1884 (after Beck had been brought back for one more chance) before being removed for corruption. He favored a wide-open town and failed to maintain discipline among his officers, who were repeatedly reported drunk and abusive. When he was asked about his policy on gambling, Wasson replied that he had "no particular policy," that "gambling was a thing belonging to our civilization." Lemuel Ellsworth was Milwaukee's first reform chief, appointed by Mayor Emil Walber, a Republican reformer who introduced civil service to city agencies. Ellsworth served only ten months before being removed after a hearing revealed both his inability to control the force and his participation in a scheme by which two of his detectives had illegally kept a reward for locating money that a disabled Civil War veteran had left for safekeeping with a saloon keeper. Ellsworth took his cut of the money (one-third of the $200 reward), returned it when he heard that an investigation was on, and lied to cover his actions. Florian Ries, a Republican politician who previously had headed the county workhouse, took over the department after Ellsworth but did scarcely better. He lasted almost three years before he was forced to resign amid a scandal involving the department's inability to solve robberies and rumors that police officers were paid off by the robbers—if they were not committing the robberies themselves. Like Ellsworth, Ries had been unable to control the force or maintain an effective level of discipline. Chief Ries had also been something of a liability, for he had directed the department's extensive strikebreaking actions during the Great Upheaval of 1886, which brought down a barrage of criticism both for his failure to put down the early demonstrations leading to the call for the state militia and for the anti-working-class strikebreaking actions of his force.[9]

This record of corruption and ineptness overshadows the fact that the 1880s saw substantial reform in the department. Mayor Emil Walber (1884–1888), elected as a reform Republican, was committed to police reform in particular. The impetus for this reform came from Republican manufacturing and commercial interests, who recognized the need to consolidate their control over the police following the Milwaukee working-class's first citywide electoral victory, largely over police issues.

During the cigar makers' strike of 1881–1882 a number of clashes between strikers and strikebreakers had resulted in arrests of strikers. Workers tried to swear out warrants for the "arrest of employers who committed gross outrages upon the laboring classes," but, of course, authorities refused to issue the warrants. The union charged that workers had been arrested and sentenced simply for having "the audacity to pass Asherman's Cigar Manufacturing Company," and the Trades Assembly resolved to pursue justice at the ballot box and to run a full slate of candidates against the Republicans.

Their nominee for mayor was John M. Stowell, a Democratic manufacturer known for his favorable treatment of workers. For comptroller, they nominated Henry Smith, a socialist, Greenbacker, and Democrat who had led the fight in the state legislature against a tramp law that would have defined as a vagrant any worker who refused to accept the prevailing wages in a particular area. The Republicans nominated Harrison Ludington, former mayor and governor and a wealthy banker. Democrats then met and opportunistically nominated the Trades Assembly candidates. Workers appointed a campaign committee and poll watchers for every precinct, and their ticket won by a substantial margin: Stowell, 9,635; Ludington, 7,321. In the fall election workers' candidates won seats in the state assembly and the offices of county sheriff and treasurer.[10]

This vigorous working-class political effort fell apart by 1884. The beginning of the depression that year finished off the effort, but ethnic rivalries, an embezzlement, and political disagreement also contributed. As their mayoral candidate, the Republicans carefully selected Emil Walber, a German lawyer, to make inroads into the German vote, a strategy that succeeded. By 1885 a rising level of strike activity made it clear that Republicans needed to consolidate their control over the police and strengthen the institution. The state legislature passed a reform bill that increased the size of Milwaukee's police force by nearly half (131, up from 93) but also carefully specified the size, function, and organization of the department and laid out most of its operating regulations. On Walber's initiative this expanded and reorganized department was also the first police force in the United States under civil service protection. When the Great Upheaval of 1886 tested the limits of this new force, it held up remarkably well.[11]

CHIEF JANSSEN AND THE POLITICS OF
PROFESSIONALISM

John T. Janssen, a former lieutenant who had worked as head of security for the Milwaukee and St. Paul Railroad, was appointed Milwaukee's third police chief in 1888. He lasted for 33 years and was renowned as one of the country's foremost police chiefs. The strong discipline that Janssen imposed on his men forced them to perform their duties rigorously, and the department became tightly organized and efficient. He worked long hours, attending to the smallest details. But although Janssen is often lauded as the creator of the country's best police force, his record is by no means entirely commendable. He was a vicious autocrat who tolerated no opposition within the department, and he was reputed to keep a black box containing incriminating data on Milwaukee's politicians in order to prevent them from interfering in his domain. He was strongly antiunion and antisocialist, and he actively used the police to break strikes. Corruption and vice flourished in Janssen's department, making somewhat irrelevant the question of whether Janssen himself was "on the take." Janssen vigorously believed in a policy of "containment" for the city's vice district, which amounted to regulating and protecting it. At the same time, Janssen took a highly moralistic attitude toward working-class saloons and dance halls, urging stricter regulations and ordering his force to maintain tighter controls over them.[12]

Republican measures in the state legislature made Janssen the first large-city police chief to gain life tenure, an obvious source of extreme personal power. Milwaukee's four-man (later five-man) Fire and Police Commission acted as little more than an advisory body, with the chief in strong control of the department. In many cities the convenience of a strong police chief effectively beyond the reach of any elected officials was a common adjustment to the growing political power of the organized working class: in the event of a working-class political victory, the police could remain an effective anti-working-class force. But Milwaukee went further than most other cities of the time toward putting power in the hands of one strong chief.[13]

Although this extraordinary degree of autonomy removed the police from partisan politics, it by no means removed the department from the bourgeois political system that it served. It was not necessary for Milwaukee's bourgeoisie to maintain direct day-to-day control of the police in order to have their class interests served.[14] Milwaukee's chief could be removed only for misconduct in office after trial by the police board, a weak body with few powers other than setting departmental recruitment standards—and with no resources to conduct an investigation of the police. The autonomy of Chief Janssen enabled him to tell socialist Mayor Seidel to "go to hell" when Seidel demanded the chief's resignation for brutality against women picketers during a garment strike.[15]

Milwaukee's police chief was appointed by the mayor and confirmed by the Fire and Police Commission. The four members of the commission were also appointed by the mayor, one each year for a four-year term. In 1911 the Social Democrats expanded the membership to five men serving five-year terms in order to gain control of the commission. Initially, no more than two of the men could be from any one party, but this restriction broke down when two-party control of Milwaukee ended. Prior to the rise of the socialists, manufacturers and businessmen dominated the board.

Twenty-eight men served on the Fire and Police Commission between 1886 and 1914. Most served one four-year term, several served two terms, and resignations before the expiration of a term were frequent. Twelve commissioners (42 percent) were manufacturers, either owners or high-level managers of enterprises including brewing, shipbuilding, furniture making, clothing, and cigar manufacturing—some of the major employers in Milwaukee. Ten others (36 percent) were involved in commercial enterprises, evenly divided between large-scale enterprises, such as the Plankinton Bank, a large clothing store, and a large hotelkeeper, and small businessmen, including two saloonkeepers. The remaining six were professionals: five lawyers and a newspaper reporter. (The socialists appointed a lawyer and a saloonkeeper.) With the exception of Seidel's appointees, the commissioners generally supported Chief Janssen's policies and worked for increases in both men and appropriations for the police department. Size increases were resisted by aldermen responsive to working-class interests. One request for 25 additional men was turned back with the comment that if the chief needed more men he could "withdraw men from city hall. On council days especially there are many bluecoats about the building." A measure to add 100 men led to a 3–3 tie in the council's police committee.[16]

When they could not stretch public means to provide the level of police service they required, private businessmen materially supported the police. In 1893, after working-class aldermen defeated a measure to establish a mounted patrol because such patrols were frequently used in strike control work, business-men made private donations to put a mounted patrol on Grand Avenue. During strike periods businessmen formed "law and or-der" leagues, which often donated their services as "specials" to support the police.[17]

Significantly, one of Janssen's first measures upon taking of-fice was to tighten departmental discipline. Most important, each officer on patrol was required to report in hourly on the call boxes, an order similar to the one Superintendant Bull gave in Buffalo in 1894. By maintaining a careful record of these calls, it was possible to make sure that each officer was actually patrol-ling his beat.[18]

Charges were brought against individual officers who failed to carry out their duties, and the charges and their disposition were published in the department's annual report. At times during Janssen's first years, charges were brought annually against 20 percent of the force, and never less than 10 percent. Most of these charges dealt with indiscipline on duty, and many involved drinking offenses: drinking on duty, entering a saloon, neglect of duty, insubordination, and conduct unbecoming an officer. Pen-alties were assessed in the form of suspensions (usually for 10 to 20 days) and fines of 10 to 20 days' pay. By the second decade of Janssen's administration the rate of charges was less than half that of the first decade. The right to appeal to the Fire and Police Commission afforded individual officers some protection from Janssen if they were suspended or dismissed. Although all sources agree that Janssen was a tough disciplinarian, it is also clear that he was selective. High-ranking officers with citywide reputations for graft were protected. Disciplinary measures were aimed at rank-and-file patrolmen who failed to meet de-partmental standards of efficiency.[19]

In addition to attending to tighter discipline and to the im-proved use of available technology, such as the patrol wagon and signal system, Janssen well understood the value of public im-age. He began the tradition of an annual police parade so that the condition of "Milwaukee's finest" could be publicly inspected. Such displays became important civic events in dozens of American cities. Officers on the beat were expected to maintain high standards of appearance—a small but significant part of the legitimation of the state's police power.[20]

Janssen also brought the 1885 civil service regulations into regular use. Recruits were selected on the basis of written tests, character tests, and physicals. Usually one-half to two-thirds of the applicants failed the written test. This policy of selectivity, coupled with the pay of $700 per year (lower than comparable cities, but still higher than most workingmen could expect), greatly reduced turnover in the department. Janssen failed to secure higher pay for his men because of the resistance of politicians responsive to working-class constituents, who disapproved of police conduct. Ironically, his opposition to a work week shorter than seven days brought him into bitter conflict with socialist Mayor Seidel, who granted police officers two days off a month as part of a general improvement of working hours for all city workers.[21]

It is no accident that Janssen's autocratic power and his use of the police on the side of the bourgeoisie in the class struggle introduced the innovations—civil service tenure, freedom from direct political control, regular standards of recruitment and training, discipline and competent service—that laid the foundation for the professionalization of the Milwaukee police. Janssen was instrumental in the early years of two professional police organizations. From 1897 to 1899 he was president of the National Police Chief's Association. In 1902 he formed the Wisconsin Association of Police Chiefs and headed the organization for many years.[22]

POLICING STRIKES IN MILWAUKEE

I have already argued that working-class political resistance to police expansion was the major reason for Milwaukee's comparatively small police department. This resistance was born in strikes, where the class interests of the police were clear. Milwaukee workers remembered police repression in strikes for many years, and working-class representatives in the city council used police strike behavior to justify voting against increases in the police force. Thus, although the police actually spent little time proportionately on strikebreaking work, each strike event was highly symbolic of the prevailing class relations. Employers spared no expense or effort to defeat workers. In turn, Milwaukee workers fought hard to win strikes. As already mentioned, police strikebreaking efforts during the cigar makers' strike of 1881 provoked formation of a workingmen's ticket that captured the mayoralty in 1882. When the Republicans regained the mayoralty in 1884, they took steps to establish a police force that would protect their class interests in the face of substantial working-class electoral strength.

Milwaukee had more than its share of strike activity: the thirteenth-largest city in the country in 1900, it ranked tenth in number of strikes, eleventh in total workers out, and eighth in number of establishments struck. Between 1881 and 1900, Milwaukee witnessed 187 strikes, which affected 1,722 establishments and directly involved 38,977 workers as strike participants. Thousands of equally militant workers joined in as supporters. Two of the largest strikes shaped the strike response of the Milwaukee police: Milwaukee's contribution to the Great Upheaval of 1886, the most extensive nationwide strike activity of the time, and the streetcar strike of 1896. We have seen that although the police represented a continual challenge to working-class recreational activities in Milwaukee, workers there achieved more latitude in their personal affairs and freedom from arrest in their use of liquor and saloons than workers did elsewhere. With regard to strikes, however, it was a completely different matter, for reasons that will be discussed shortly.[23]

The Great Upheaval of 1885–1886 sorely tested police resources. Mayor Walber, in recapturing the mayoralty from the workingmen's coalition in 1884, acted immediately to strengthen the police department. The coalition, though it had not reduced the size of the department, had not maintained it in efficient condition. In his inaugural address Walber emphasized this issue:

"complaints of police inefficiency had reached" him, and he promised to give the matter his full attention in the form of civil service protection and increased manpower. The result was an entire reorganization of the police: the state legislature passed a police act; civil service regulations were applied to the police department; and 28 officers were added, bringing the total to 131. These measures had just been completed when the general strike of 1886 strenuously taxed the police and intensified the demand for the department's reconstruction.

This urgency was doubly felt because of the nationwide character of the strikes. The Great Upheaval, like the 1877 railroad strikes, greatly worried capitalists because it revealed a united working class with unexpected strength in dozens of cities simultaneously. Moreover, unlike the strikes of 1877, those of 1886 were planned as part of the nationwide eight-hour campaign, a workingmen's movement that proclaimed the dignity of labor and the rights of labor to decent hours and working conditions. German socialists figured prominently in the movement, which had its antecedents in the period of the Civil War. But the notion of a workingman's right to more time for family, education, and recreational activities sharply contradicted capitalist views of labor.

The conflict in Milwaukee approached the level of a general strike and effectively closed down the city.[24] The brutal repression of the movement, which included the shooting of workers in a suburb of Milwaukee led labor leaders in Milwaukee, St. Louis, Chicago, and other cities to launch a new labor party. The Wisconsin People's party, formed at a statewide convention in June 1886, achieved more electoral success than any of the others. Campaigns in the fall of 1886 featured People's party candidates for governor, for representative to Congress, and for other offices. Henry Smith, the People's party candidate for Congress, was sent to Washington.

The next electoral test came in the spring 1887 aldermanic and judicial elections. The Democrats and Republicans, alarmed at the People's party showing in the previous November, nominated a fusion ticket for the open judgeships. This fusion ticket lost by more than 1,000 votes in Milwaukee but was saved by the vote in outlying communities. Five People's party aldermen were elected. The critical test, the mayoral election of 1888, saw Democrats and Republicans running another fusion ticket against the People's party candidate. This time, however, the socialists withdrew support from the People's ticket, which then lost by about 900 votes. Although People's candidates contested the mayoralty after 1888, they never again came close to winning.[25]

SOCIALISTS AND THE POLICE

The Milwaukee Social Democratic party, founded in 1897, became the chief political antagonist of the Milwaukee police. By 1899 the socialists had formed an interlocking directorate with the Milwaukee Federated Trades Council. This meant that trade-union politics in Milwaukee became predominantly socialist, both in terms of union leadership and in terms of the rank and file. Socialists undertook much educational work among union members and held many well-attended political meetings.

In the 1910s the reformist emphasis of the Social Democrats made them practically indistinguishable from liberal Democrats and Progressives. Although these reformist forces had been present in the earlier years as well, the party had then consciously aimed its program at the class interests of workingmen. One aspect of this program was resistance to the police. On a political level the socialists knew who the Milwaukee police worked for and understood the repressive functions of the capitalist state. As examples, they cited police harassment and arrests of socialist demonstrators and campaign workers and police interference with union activity. Moreover, Police Chief Janssen harbored a personal hatred for the socialists and used the full extent of his considerable powers to repress them. Socialists in turn marked Janssen as a class enemy and used every opportunity to expose him and the police. Tactically, it was important for the socialists at least to neutralize, if not remove, Janssen from his control of the police force in order to stop the police from interfering with their work. By constantly keeping pressure on the police, the socialists served notice that they were not to be meddled with. Socialist proposals relating to the police ran the gamut from far-reaching and brilliant reforms consistent with the class vision of socialism to equally brilliant instances of petty harassment that made the police look foolish or exposed them as agents of capitalist domination. What is important is that the socialists articulated a working-class view of the police and raised coherent, careful criticisms of the police that rarely appeared in other cities.

At the outset, socialists preferred to focus on the public service aspects of police work rather than on repression. Mayor Seidel wanted to use the police to stop factory smoke, inspect garbage, and stop truancy. He thought that officers should regularly visit every house on their beats to ask whether "all was well." Chester M. Wright, a member of the socialist Fire and Police Commission, proposed renaming the police "safetymen."[26]

This attitude was consistent with the socialists' support of police as city workers. Though police wages were adequate, working conditions were poor; hours were long, and there were no days off. One of the first clashes between Seidel and Janssen occurred when the Democratic Socialist city council granted police officers two days off a month without pay deduction. Janssen argued that this would "cripple the force" and cost the city $27,000 a year.[27] Janssen tested the council by canceling all days off for September 1910. The city council responded by censuring the chief:

> Resolved that the said chief is hereby informed that the council will insist on his showing a decent respect for the laws it passes and that a further unnecessary interference with the workings of the law giving day-offs to the policemen on his part will subject him not only to the censure of this body but that such further steps will be taken as may be necessary to make the law effective.[28]

Janssen generally had no choice but to allow the men their days off, though he did it grudgingly.

Other socialist measures called attention to the class basis of justice in Milwaukee. Councilman Edmund T. Melms introduced a resolution making it unlawful to transport prisoners through the streets in an uncovered patrol wagon. "No one is deemed guilty until convicted, yet they were driven through the streets and exposed to view as criminals. The rich are not treated that way." Socialist aldermen demanded a full investigation of the Hattie Zynda murder case, focusing on the failure of the police to provide services to the Polish community. Further, they demanded an investigation of police clubbings of Polish workers.[29]

The high point of socialist harassment of the police was a measure to cloth the police in khaki uniforms, an obvious reference to their repressive military character. "Czar" was a common nickname applied to Janssen (as well as to Chief Michael Regan of Buffalo), and the socialists freely played on the political meaning of the term. The council also proposed to reduce Janssen's salary from $4,000 a year to $3,500. Mayor Seidel suggested that the police deliver water bills and save the city postage costs.[30]

Janssen was a powerful political figure and resisted the socialists with force. He refused to use a $4,200 ambulance that the socialist-dominated city council had purchased for the police department on the grounds that it was unsafe, a position he supported with medical testimony. He called a socialist plan to combine the police and fire departments "tomfoolery." Most directly, he told Seidel to "go to hell" for criticizing him for his handling of a garment workers' strike.[31]

The socialists' electoral victory carried with it real political power that allowed them to accomplish some objectives in the class interest. For example, the socialist council consolidated the police and fire alarm systems and removed the power to appoint the system's superintendent from Janssen and gave it to the mayor. Furthermore, in 1911 a new Fire and Police Commission Bill added a fifth commissioner, giving the socialists effective control (the commission was composed of two Social Democrats, two Republicans, and one Democrat who voted with the Social Democrats). But at the same time the state legislature took care to protect Janssen. He was given the right of appeal to the circuit court in the case of suspension or dismissal. Nor did the socialists have much effect on police strike activities until after Janssen's retirement in 1921.[32]

CONCLUSION

The class struggle in Milwaukee shaped the police department in a number of ways but failed to structure most police activities. Where police policies could be indirectly controlled by the city council, results favorable to workers were sometimes achieved. Among the victories obtained by councilmen responsive to working-class demands were the small size of the department (kept small through law appropriations), the low public order arrest rate, and the relative lack of interference in the working-class social institution, the saloon. Where police policies turned on administrative matters, such as police conduct during strikes, working-class politics had much less effect. The police remained a powerful bourgeois weapon in the class struggle, conducting vicious antistrike work in the major strikes of 1886 and 1896 and in dozens of smaller strikes, including those that occurred during Mayor Seidel's term.

Working-class political activists managed to slow down the direction of police development in Milwaukee, but they could not stop it or change its function. The socialists, playing the game of urban politics, made many compromises with more powerful political forces. This is the major failure of working-class electoral politics in a political system dominated by the bourgeoisie. Moreover, the legal order, with its professionalism, autonomy, and value-neutral ideology, effectively insulated the police department from public supervision under the guise of protecting it from political control. The police were responsible only to an autonomous chief who ran the department like a czar and served the interests of the manufacturers and businessmen who put him in office. A system of neutral laws required the police to smash strikes and to control working-class recreational behavior. The socialists did not seriously threaten the status quo because the multilevel political system, operating under bourgeois rules, was always one step ahead of them, even though they clearly had some local impact. Within the framework of the capitalist legal system, the socialists had few options open to them. More important, the Milwaukee Social Democrats accepted the legitimacy of the existing capitalist legal order, even though they maintained a critical attitude toward its class system.

This analysis suggests a modification of the commonly accepted notion that working-class-controlled police forces were ineffective and unreliable for strike control purposes. In Milwaukee it is clear that working-class political representation—as powerful as in any city in America—was not enough to obtain even the neutrality of the police, much less a pro-working-class force. Milwaukee's working-class parties were hamstrung by bourgeois conceptions of the police function. It takes more than an electoral majority in one city to reverse years of capitalist hegemony. Moreover, the socialists themselves lacked a coherent vision of what they should do with their power. Instead of furthering the class struggle, they turned reformist, incorporating much of the middle-class reform effort. This reformism limited them to a holding action that could restrain development of the police institution but not fundamentally alter its direction.

The brief surveys of changes in the Buffalo and Milwaukee police departments during the late nineteenth century could be repeated for other cities as well. Police developments in dozens of local contexts occurred as part of an essentially national system. Accordingly, the next four chapters will focus on patterns of policing the class conflict in the Great Lakes/Ohio Valley region. Four distinct arenas of class struggle will be analyzed: control of strikes and other overt forms of working-class political action; control of working-class recreational activities, chiefly saloons and liquor-related activity; regulation of vagrancy and tramping; and policing of common felony crimes.

CHAPTER SIX

Cops as Strikebreakers

SURELY THERE IS no more outstanding symbol of the class struggle of the late-nineteenth- and early-twentieth-century United States than the great strikes that rocked the very core of the country during that period. The stories of a few of these are commonly found in American history textbooks: the Great Strike (1877), Haymarket (1886), Homestead (1892), Pullman (1894), Lawrence (1912), and Paterson (1913). Equally important, however, were the frequent smaller strikes that occurred in virtually every industrial city, large and small, during this period. Larger industrial cities saw hundreds of strikes—Chicago had 92 on at one time in 1904 (see table 7). Collectively, these strikes were characterized by a high level of violence, leading to well over 300 deaths, plus uncounted injuries, and lending credence to arguments that the United States had the most violent industrial revolution of any Western nation.[1]

Ironically, histories of the police are written as if this industrial violence never happened or as if the police institution had little to do with it. The common euphemism is that police departments were occasionally called upon to control "social disorder." On the contrary, as I shall argue, industrial violence was not "social disorder" but class violence—essentially state-created as well as state-suppressed—and the municipal police were inextricably involved in both the creation and the suppression of

Table 7. STRIKES IN MAJOR GREAT LAKES/OHIO VALLEY
CITIES, JANUARY 1, 1881–DECEMBER 31, 1900

City	Total strikes	Number of establishments struck	Number of employees out	Loss to employers
Allegheny and Pittsburgh	500	5,432	175,795	$3,099,815
Buffalo	164	1,210	40,627	1,291,215
Chicago	1,737	17,176	593,000	22,123,344
Cincinnati	250	1,236	57,098	1,273,476
Cleveland	207	879	45,569	1,106,194
Detroit	116	483	22,193	567,367
Milwaukee	187	1,722	38,977	1,133,810
Minneapolis	114	696	16,996	331,795
New York City[a]	5,090	33,161	962,470	11,813,291
St. Louis	256	2,511	71,889	5,369,326

Source: *16th Annual Report of the Commissioner of Labor,* 1901, *Strikes and Lockouts,* p. 29.
[a]Included for comparative purposes.

that violence. Furthermore, the need to control and suppress this class violence motivated much of the effort to expand and reorganize the police institution.[2]

Social historians and labor historians studying the late nineteenth and early twentieth centuries have not made the same error as the historians of the police. The police institution is accorded an important place in local politics, just as workers' organizations and the labor strikes are accorded important places in the study of social history. David Montgomery has properly identified the strike as one important (but not the only) index of class conflict and of class consciousness among workers. He might also have added that strikes did much to strengthen the class consciousness of the bourgeoisie and the middle class, clearly drawing class lines in community life and politics. Herbert Gutman, in detailing the class dynamics of a number of small communities, has emphasized the importance of the local police in class politics, although in the small, often isolated mining communities he studies the police generally played a sharply different role than in larger cities.[3]

We might also note that whereas late-twentieth-century historians of the police may prefer to bury this class violence—for whatever reasons—the late-nineteenth- and early-twentieth-century local historians who wrote the official or semiofficial "house" histories of local police forces commonly celebrated the police antistrike and antilabor function. Although these studies are often flawed as history, they provide solid contemporary evidence of what local elites and police departments thought was important about their own history.

Strike violence had essentially one cause: workers and employers nourished incompatible notions about power and property. Striking workers believed that a property right in their work justified them in shutting down the workplace. Employers took the position that they had an absolute right to use their property as they saw fit and under any conditions they desired. They routinely met strikes with tactics designed to divide their workers by trying to induce some to continue work or, failing that, with nonunion strikebreakers, either professional scabs or simply new immigrant workers off the street. The confrontation between striking workers and police-protected scabs was at the root of virtually all strike violence of this period.

In this context the police had at least two choices. They could side with the workers and use their coercive power to force the manufacturers to remain closed until the strike was settled. If the manufacturers resisted, the police could have attacked their factories. The other choice was to detail numerous police units around the workplace and along the routes leading to it and to use police violence against the workers as they tried to protect their jobs against scabs.

Obviously, the police considered only the latter option, which in fact was the only legal one available. But as the "neutral" enforcers of class-biased law, the police institution becomes class-biased as well. Moreover, the police institution often went far beyond the law in the protection of manufacturers' interests—workers were attacked in their homes, political freedom was suppressed, and countless beatings and killings took place. The bourgeoisie and the petty bourgeoisie dominated the legislative process and accordingly created a legal framework that elevated their property rights over human life. Not until Franklin Roosevelt's New Deal did workers even begin to acquire a substantial property right in their jobs, though even then the rights invested in a worker's job were less substantial than the rights of the owners of the means of production.

I shall argue in this chapter that the evidence clearly demonstrates that the police engaged in strongly anti-working-class strikebreaking activity in the major cities of the Great Lakes/ Ohio Valley region during the period 1885–1915 whenever the occasion arose. I shall also show how police strikebreaking capabilities were developed over time and how individual police officers who may have had some sympathy toward striking workers were controlled in this anti-working-class activity. First, however, it is important to show why it is incorrect to cite Herbert Gutman's work as evidence that the police institution favored workers in nineteenth-century industrial disputes.

There is no general agreement on the extent to which municipal police served as effective agents of the industrialists in combatting workers' strikes. Bruce Johnson, Sam Walker, and others, in attempts to extend Gutman's work on the policing of strikes in small cities in the early 1870s, argue that the public police were sympathetic to the workers and hence an ineffective weapon in the class struggle. This important question of the class loyalty of the police institution has many implications. If the main coercive arm of state power was in the hands of the working class, then the state itself cannot be seen as an instrument of bourgeois domination.[4]

Gutman's work focuses on small industrial or mining towns (Newport, Kentucky; Braidwood, Illinois; Buena Vista and Johnstown, Pennsylvania) in the 1873–1874 period. At this early stage of industrialization capitalists and their allies had not yet fully consolidated their power. Most smaller towns never developed large enough police forces to suppress even a moderate-sized strike. Industrialists turned to other policing forms, especially private and state police, particularly in Pennsylvania. Moreover, Gutman himself offers examples of the police being used to beat down workers: the police in Newport, Kentucky, at first refused to protect strikebreakers but did so after being threatened by the mayor; the Paterson police, who in 1877 refused to help break a strike, viciously beat female silk workers in a 1913 strike, indicating quite clearly that power relations had changed in Paterson during the intervening 40 years.[5]

The common thread here is not city size; rather, it is the organization of work. The transformation of the organization of work during the late nineteenth and early twentieth centuries involved the continual undermining of the craft system, which had allowed skilled workers some degree of control over their conditions of work as they more or less carried out the entire production process. This system was replaced with a work process controlled by the capitalist—one in which each separate function was broken down to its simplest elements and carried out repetitively by unskilled workers, a process called Taylorization.[6]

This change in the labor process profoundly affected the form of class conflict. Skilled workers were in a much stronger position in a labor dispute than unskilled workers. Generally, in order to shut down the factory to await a favorable settlement, they had only to withdraw their labor, pick up their tools and go home. However, when the capitalists controlled the labor process, it was no problem to replace even thousands of unskilled workers. The strikes of the late nineteenth century involved thousands of workers defending their jobs violently against armies of strikebreakers recruited wholesale. Success required mass action once workers no longer controlled the organization of their work. It is this shift in the control of the labor process that chiefly distinguishes the violent strikes of the 1880s and later from the conditions Gutman describes for the 1870s. Nevertheless, his work clearly shows that strikes are not isolated events in community life but important arenas in which to study community power dynamics.

The organization of American workers to gain control of their work and their work product predates the late nineteenth century, but organization efforts greatly accelerated after the Civil War. Permanent local central labor unions, organized to make labor's power felt in local politics, date only from the 1880s in most cities west of the Appalachians. The political and economic importance of workers' organizations and of the strikes that those organizations led cannot be underestimated: nothing less than the control of the labor process was at stake and, through that, control of the entire national economy. The employers *had* to defeat the strikes to protect their livelihoods. The fundamental importance of this struggle for survival and dominance is demonstrated by the role that strikes played in working-class communities: whole communities turned out to aid the strikers, strike rallies drew thousands, and thousands of others joined workers to block factory gates and streetcar lines. The power of the organized working class could be felt by each worker as all marched together through the streets carrying banners, singing, and shouting slogans and threats.

THE GREAT STRIKE OF 1877

The same weaknesses in local structures of class domination described by Gutman for small cities in the 1873–1874 period became very obvious in large cities during the 1877 strike. Small, poorly disciplined police departments that up to this time had often been disregarded by the local bourgeoisie clearly established their importance with effective antistrike work. Given their limited resources and training, their achievements were nothing short of incredible. Particularly on the eastern seaboard, the local bourgeoisie had long recognized the importance of the police in strike work.[7] But national awareness of the need for effective police antistrike capabilities emerged only out of the 1877 strikes. The events of 1877 caught local forces off-guard, and in many cities they proved unable to protect corporate property from mobs of rebellious workers. Moreover, 1877 also revealed the power of the unified working class, and it terrified the bourgeoisie and the middle class. They called striking workers "communards," "revolutionaries," and "anarchists"; the *Chicago Tribune*'s demand that they be massacred was moderate for the time. Only during the Civil War had so many Americans fought one another at the same time. Pittsburgh, Buffalo, St. Louis, and Chicago were virtually shut down by actions that approached the proportions of a general strike. Philadelphia, Baltimore, Scranton, Terre Haute, Louisville, Cincinnati, and many smaller railroad towns also experienced large-scale strike activity. Some measure of the bourgeoisie's fear is suggested by the strike preparations taken in New York City, which saw no strike action: two gatling guns were placed at the heads of Wall and Pine streets to protect the financial district; 75 volunteers assembled to protect the Subtreasury building; 200 police were assigned to a workers' meeting, with 600 on reserve nearby; Tomkins Square, where the workers met, was connected with the armory and police station by a newly strung telegraph wire; and 1,000 sailors and marines were held in reserve, as were 8,000 rifles and 1,200 clubs.[8]

The 1877 strikes can only be understood as an expression of strong working-class solidarity and class rage at new forms of capitalist exploitation. Particularly west of Pittsburgh, the railroad issues that originated the strikes were subordinate to class issues. Socialists took leadership in many cities, including Chicago and St. Louis, and a high level of class consciousness prevailed. When asked by a reporter to explain the reasons for the strike, a Chicago worker replied: "We are fighting the goddamned capitalists."[9]

The expansion of police departments in the 1880s, the adoption of the patrol wagon and signal system, and the institution of organizational innovations occurred, if not as a direct result of 1877, then with the specter of 1877 never entirely out of consciousness. In city after city the municipal police proved the best of the various strikebreaking forces. Accordingly, in cities where the bourgeoisie and middle classes had paid only marginal attention to the police institution—often accepting it only reluctantly as a necessary evil and as a haven of louts to be tolerated but kept in check—a new effort had to be made to remake the police for a more central role in establishing a stable urban social order. Prior to the 1877 strikes, urban police institutions were not fully accepted as an important part of municipal government; after 1877, with rare exceptions, this went unquestioned.

The riot control situation in the Chicago strikes of 1877 was typical. Running battles were fought throughout the city by workers against police, militia, and citizen volunteers, but ultimately it was the police force that proved most effective in combatting the strike. Higher levels of training, more experience in city neighborhoods, and greater skill in using force won the battle for the Chicago police. By the last day the police were firing into crowds, resulting in a death toll perhaps as high as 35.[10]

Such actions legitimated the police in the eyes of the bourgeoisie and the petty bourgeoisie as the most reliable social control apparatus in the city, and the department was rewarded accordingly. A contemporary history of the Chicago police affirms that the riot of 1877 won respect for the police and ended political resistance to the police institution among the aldermen:

> Some good results followed the riot of '77. As already stated the military organizations of the city received more attention than ever before, and more liberal contributions. But of more interest to us is the fact that the Chicago policeman ceased to be looked upon as a mere uniformed idler from that time on. The policemen did not stand high in popular esteem previous to this time. . . . He was only tolerated because there still remained a doubt as to the wisdom of trying to get on without him. Nothing could be more indicative of this sentiment than the frequency with which propositions to lower the salaries of police officers came up in the city council, and the language used by the aldermen in reference to the force when these propositions were debated. Looking over the printed reports of these meetings now, we find some rather bitter criticisms that came from the mouths of city fathers who have since patted the force on the head, so to speak, and pronounced it the finest in the world.[11]

In one day of killing in 1877 the Chicago police secured for themselves the respect of the ruling class and their allies and secured for the police institution a place in the complex arena of community power as a well-trusted, coercive weapon of the bourgeoisie. Although this newly won legitimacy did not end occasional attempts to criticize the police or reduce their power, it solidly diminished such efforts and at the same time provided a strong impetus to growth in succeeding years. Police growth through the middle of the 1880s was in response to the events of 1877.

Nowhere is this point better demonstrated than in Pittsburgh, where as many as 100 people were killed by police and militia in the most serious rioting in 1877. Scarcely two months before the strikes the Pittsburgh force was reduced from 236 to 120 men as an economy measure. Nevertheless, at the outset of the strike the police went hard to work. Thomas McCall, a brakeman, punched and blackened the eye of Assistant Superintendent Watt of the Pennsylvania Railroad and was arrested by four policemen, who had to fight their way through railroad workers trying to protect McCall. He was held at the Central Police Station and kept secure in spite of the efforts of a mob of several hundred to rescue him. Unsatisfied with this demonstration of police competence, the Pennsylvania Railroad used its statewide political power to have the militia called up.[12]

The feeling of the local bourgeoisie appears to have been that the militia intensified the crisis. When the militia fired without orders into a crowd that included many women and children, an enraged crowd attacked the soldiers, forcing them back into a roundhouse. Two days of uncontrolled rioting followed, accompanied by the destruction of almost all Pennsylvania Railroad property in Pittsburgh—dozens of engines, hundreds of cars, and warehouses and other buildings. The local bourgeoisie thereupon decided to reassume control of the antistrike effort themselves, organizing around their local police force. The soldiers were removed to nearby East Liberty, specials were recruited to augment the police, the police department was restored to its regular strength, with the local bourgeoisie guaranteeing salaries, and saloons were ordered closed. The police cracked down so hard that the stations were often filled with masses of arrested, anonymous workers.[13]

Pittsburgh civic and political leaders were quick to blame the riots on the militia. More important, though, is the bourgeoisie's preference for a local police force. As in Chicago, the 1880s witnessed a very different Pittsburgh police department, the result at least in part of the Roundhouse riot. Some changes, such as greater stability of membership and increased organizational discipline, began early in the decade. A major police reorganization starting in 1887, together with the adoption of the patrol wagon and signal system, finished the task.[14]

The failure of the militia as an effective urban crowd control institution was noted in city after city during the intense conflicts of 1887. In the simplest terms, the 1877 strikes showed property owners that a good police force was better able than an army to protect their class position. The weaknesses of the militia were correspondingly the strengths of the local police. Whereas the militia was under state control, the police department was under local control. Whereas the militia was inexperienced at confrontations and moved in military formation, the local police already had practical experience in crowd control. Whereas the militia was unfamiliar with local situations, the policemen were residents. Militiamen worked part-time and were drawn too often directly out of the working class. Police officers, though also normally recruited from the working class, were disciplined into a full-time organization that emphasized obedience to orders. Moreover, the local police were under tighter, more direct political control, which meant better control over state violence.

This lesson was not lost in Buffalo. City authorities, embarrassed by the clumsy violence of the militia during the Great Strike of 1877, did not call on the militia again until 1913. Their reasoning was stated clearly by the Board of Police, which refused to call out the militia for the longshoremen's strike of 1884: "During that existing week there was considerable pressure made upon this board to call out the militia, but the Board firmly insisted that police could preserve the peace of the city and protect the property of citizens, and by its firmness the city was saved from the disgrace and danger of this extreme measure."[15]

STRIKEBREAKING AS A REGULAR POLICE SERVICE

Strike control was assigned to the municipal police institution beginning in 1877, but it was the mid-1880s or later before antistrike work was fully incorporated into the urban police function. Small departments, poorly disciplined and untrained for strike work, gave way to expanding departments, that although still unsure of the scope of their power, steadily increased both their capacity and willingness to break strikes. Strikes were anticipated and planned for. Specially selected forces were deployed, often to be barracked on the premises of the employers. Strikers were attacked with clubs and scattered wherever they congregated. Police patrolled strikers' communities, stepped up arrests for disorderly conduct and related offenses, and closed saloons and meeting halls. Police departments were often drilled in military formations, and many cities organized special companies that transcended local precinct organization. In effect, the department operated on a military model during strike activity. How the police reorganized to accommodate the new strike control function can be seen in some important strikes of the 1880s.

A longshoremen's strike in Buffalo in 1884 gave the local police department its first major opportunity to use a full-scale antistrike plan. The response was a primitive version of the pattern that would be employed for the next 30 years: a massive call-up of reserves as soon as the strike began, maintenance of a large force very near the strike area, and tight surveillance of the strikers. According to the annual police report for 1884, "All the members of the force who could be spared from precincts away from the river were massed at Station Number 1, where two large band wagons, with horses in harness day and night, were held in readiness to convey squads of men with the greatest possible speed to any point where their services might be needed."[16] The force was augmented by the appointment of 40 specials, at regular pay, from the list of rejected applicants who had taken the last patrolman's examination. This was not the citizens' patrol of the 1877 strike but a reinforcement of the regular force.

Police efforts during the strike were definitely one-sided. When a group of strikebreakers fired pistols at a menacing group of strikers gathered in the streets, the arriving police vigorously attacked the strikers:

> Word was sent to headquarters and Superintendent Phillips [then As-sistant Superintendent under Superintendent Thomas Curtin] placed himself at the head of all the reserve held in readiness at No. 1 sta-tion and was quickly upon the scene of action. An impetuous charge and a free use of the locust [club] soon cleared the street, numerous arrests were made, every saloon and place of resort in the "infected district" was closed and the backbone of the strike was broken.[17]

This small strike well illustrates police strike control methods during the 1880s. Whereas the 1877 strikes did not see the use of scab labor because they were so short and violent, this strike centered on scab labor. Employers could easily hire new work-ers to unload their ships and thus defeat the demands of strikers. The strikers had only two choices: to admit defeat or to prevent the scabs from working. Although it is clear that the police stood on solid legal ground in protecting scabs, the issue involved more than legal rights.

This issue became very confused in the heat of battle. The police and employers argued that they were protecting the lives of scabs rather than merely the property rights of employers; yet it is obvious that the scabs were not threatened apart from the struggle over the property rights of both workers and employers: had the docks been closed, there would have been no scabs. Furthermore, each side justified violence against the other by depicting the other's actions as illegal. Employers, echoed by police, argued that the real workers were peaceful but that "troublemakers," "vagrants," and "criminals" stirred up antag-onisms and threatened the peace. Workers in turn argued that the scabs were not workers but "criminals" or "bums." This tension was often fed by ethnic differences, since the newest and poorest ethnic groups were used as strikebreakers, often recruit-ed off the docks without being told that a strike was in pro-gress.[18]

Protection of the scabs was a difficult job. Police had to se-cure not only the grounds and adjacent areas involved in the strike but also those portions of the city where identifiable groups of scabs traveled. Security had two dimensions. First, the scabs had to be protected physically from blocked streets, beatings, and thrown objects. Second, they had to be shielded from the appeals and threats of striking workers. Verbal pressure, ranging from simple appeals to scabs as "fellow workers" not to take their jobs, to accusations of being traitors to their class, often succeeded in inducing scabs to quit. Employers eventually found it necessary to obtain court injunctions against the use of such words as "scab," "black sheep," and "baaa." The police often used considerable force to prevent workers from communicating with scabs.

The simplest way that the police might have assisted strikers was deliberate laxness in protecting scabs. The best way to support the employers was continuously to beat down entire workers' communities so that scabs could walk safely through them. The shift to more vigorous efforts on behalf of the employers can be seen in the Chicago police department's handling of strikes at the McCormick reaper works in 1885 and 1886. Cyrus McCormick, a capitalist in the most traditional sense, firmly believed in his right to do whatever he wished with his business, and he tried to run his plants during the strikes with scab labor recruited from several states.

In 1885 striking iron molders managed to keep out almost all strikebreakers, mostly through verbal threats and persuasion, but also by blocking roads and gates. McCormick nonetheless managed to get 25 scabs inside on a company tugboat. Other scabs arriving for work on trolleys and on company omnibuses were beaten, as was a busload of Pinkertons. McCormick called on Mayor Carter Harrison for more adequate police protection, but the mayor told McCormick to settle with the union—quite possibly in retaliation because McCormick had let his men out of work on election day to vote against Harrison. The situation grew worse, and McCormick was forced to settle.[19]

Harrison's refusal to allow the police to assist McCormick was more than one episode in a continuing political and personal feud. Rather, the whole question of the appropriate police role in strikes was still open. Within a few years, however, police protection of strikebreakers would be the normal expectation in every city in the country.

Less than a year later, McCormick refused to discharge non-union molders and locked out his men. Within two weeks he reopened the plant with scab labor, determined to smash the union. This time Mayor Harrison came to some accommodation with McCormick, for the reaper works was protected by 400 Chicago policemen. Hot meals were served to the police on company premises, with Cyrus McCormick himself pouring coffee. On reopening day, Inspector Bonfield, who had distinguished himself as an enemy of workers in a streetcar strike a year before, beat down union picket lines and opened a wide path for the strikebreakers. The strike dragged on for months, with the plant operating on scab labor protected by the police. On May 3 several hundred McCormick strikers left a mass meeting of the lumber shovers' union and attacked scabs leaving work, driving them back into the plant and breaking some plant windows. A special detail of 200 Chicago police arrived and attacked the workers with clubs and revolvers, killing two, wounding a few others, and clubbing an unknown number.

This bloody event, known as the Black Road riot, is little known in labor history, being overshadowed by the events that followed. Anarchist August Spies hurriedly left the meeting and in his anger wrote the famous "revenge" circular that called a meeting in Haymarket Square the next day, which ended with a bombing. This landmark event in labor history, in which seven police officers were killed in the act of brutally breaking up a workers' meeting, led in turn to a police massacre of a still uncounted number of persons who had been peaceably listening to the speeches. It also led to a much less well-known "radical hunt": police beat and locked up militant labor leaders all over Chicago for weeks, and broke up labor organization offices and newspaper presses.[20]

The change in police policy between the two McCormick strikes is also evident in the response to other strikes in Chicago during this period. Carter Harrison, elected mayor of Chicago in

1885 as a sort of Populist friendly to labor, moved steadily closer to the bourgeoisie during his first year in office. Like other members of his class, he was alarmed by the increasing proportion of foreign-speaking, "radical" workers and the rising levels of class conflict.[21] Three months after he had dispatched only a weak force to McCormick's 1885 strike, he ordered a streetcar strike brutally suppressed along all the major streets of downtown Chicago. Hundreds, if not thousands, of Chicago workers, mostly supporters of the strikers, were beaten down by the police. Streetcar strikes were among the most difficult to police because the strikers enjoyed great support among the riding public, who felt exploited by the car companies, and because the lines covered so many miles. The company was promised as many police officers as necessary to move its cars and on the first morning three cars were taken out, containing 8, 7, and 15 policemen, respectively. Additional police squads were placed along the streets, and two patrol wagons rode ahead, clearing out the crowds.[22]

Workers turned out all along the route to prevent the movement of the cars. Heaviest resistance was met during the noon hour, when workers from factories along the tracks threw stones, dirt, and other missiles. Mayor Harrison himself arrested a man tearing up the tracks along Halsted Street with a pickax. At least once, the police shot at missile throwers. While Harrison was stating that nine out of ten citizens of Chicago sided with the strikers and telling the company to negotiate a settlement, he also ensured that they had no need to do so by promising them all the police protection they needed to run their cars. After high-ranking police officials held a "council of war," Superintendent Doyle informed the press that, although the police could not provide labor to run the cars, they would do all they could to protect the company's property and preserve the peace. Captain Bonfield, head of the strike force, put it more bluntly: "If the railway company wants to run its cars it is entitled to protection and should have it. The cars shall be run if the company desire it, and people who do not wish to get hurt had better keep out of the way."[23]

The next day 400 officers turned out at the Des Plaines Street Station. Superintendant Doyle addressed them from the steps of the station: "Whatever your private views or mine may be, property must be defended, and the law must be upheld, and you are its defenders." Two hundred patrolmen were sent out in 17 patrol wagons to take up positions along the route; 200 more patrolmen marched down the street taking up positions as well. Bonfield then arranged the streetcars into a unit of three, with policemen in the front and rear cars; the middle (closed) car held 20 more men and served as a prison van and ambulance. A double advance platoon, led by Captain Bonfield, covered the width of the street. Bonfield addressed the crowd: "You must not molest us. You have all been warned, and now I repeat that unless you disperse you will get hurt. . . . Shoot the first man that throws a stone. March!" Bonfield's men then pushed back the crowd, clubbing people down as they went. At least 25 were seriously injured, scores more were hurt—and complaints rolled in to the mayor's office. Harrison defended Bonfield, however, and the inspector himself was proud of his actions: "Mr. Mayor, I am doing this in mercy to the people. A club today, to make them scatter, may save the use of a pistol tomorrow."[24]

Although the bourgeoisie in Chicago and other cities continued to criticize the police for failure to prevent strikers from closing their factories, it is clear that the police most often employed vigorous measures in defense of employers' property. This does not mean that the police encountered few problems in strike work: manpower shortages, poor training and discipline, and poor leadership took a toll. Even more important, the bourgeoisie underestimated the strength of an organized working class; large numbers of strikers and sympathizers spread over a wide area were difficult to control, even with determined police efforts. Many industrialists believed that a good police force should control all strike activity and that the existence of any strike violence at all was proof of police ineptness or sympathy with strikers.[25]

The Great Upheaval of 1886 had as much impact on the development of urban policing as did the strikes of 1877. The new patrol wagon and signal system proved a great success in the strikes of the 1880s, and cities rushed to adopt them. Similarly, the high turnover of both rank-and-file patrolmen and police administrators diminished greatly after the mid-1880s. Discipline and military drill generally improved as well. Obviously, other considerations motivated these innovations as well, but continual trial in open class warfare added an urgency to the development of new equipment and strategies.

STRIKE-CONTROL EFFORTS FULLY UNLEASHED

The full integration of strikebreaking into the police function paralleled other changes in the municipal police institution during the 1890s. Effective antistrike work required a level of discipline and training very rare in the 1870s and 1880s but increasingly common by the 1890s. Police units directed from a central location were often able to cover large sections of cities in a well-controlled and efficient manner. Developments in police tactics in the 1890s can be seen in the strategies employed to break three railroad strikes that tested police capabilities to their limits.

The Buffalo switchmen's strike, called on August 13, 1892, spread over miles of track both inside and outside the city limits. On the volatile Polish East Side, with the longest length of track, Captain Kilroy, the police department's expert in military discipline, deployed 60 policemen along six miles of track. Eighty-five officers were assigned duty at the city limits, sleeping in three cars loaned by the railroad. Brief skirmishes fought with crowds of strikers and neighborhood supporters generally ended in club-swinging charges by the police. In one such incident Philip Day, a coal and wood dealer, was severely beaten on his own doorstep while watching the police beat Jack Dennison, an engineer returning from the store with groceries.[26]

Crowds of strikers and supporters tried to stop the movement of trains in every way possible. A few scab trains were stopped, but others were able to get through. The union charged that police officers were acting as switchmen and assisting in the movement of trains, and officers were taunted for scabbing. A delegation went to see Mayor Charles Bishop, but their protest was ignored. One crowd of boys, seeing police officers riding on top of boxcars (where brakemen normally ride), called derisively: "Get onto de gay brakemen. Dey's too fat to stand up and dey's so weak dey have to carry brake sticks. I wonder who put up for dey suits."[27]

Suppressing the strike was clearly beyond the capabilities of the Buffalo police. On August 17 the police were augmented by 5,000 state militia under the command of New York Central Railroad Superintendent Doyle, also conveniently a general in the militia, and the police and sheriff hastily recruited 200 reserves. "They are there for blood if the lawless element makes a move looking for resistance," warned the reform Republican *Express*. In addition to direct combat against strikers and supporters in the railroad yards, the Buffalo police were mobilized across town and engaged in a series of actions against workers' communities in order to hasten the end of the strike. A mayoral proclamation forbade congregating in the streets in working-class neighborhoods, and the police enforced the rule. Taverns were ordered closed in working-class districts. Leaflets defending the strikers were seized, and the distributors arrested. Individual strikers and strike leaders were arrested, often on fabricated charges in order to get "troublemakers" off the streets. Chief of Police Daniel Morganstern ordered that the city be cleared of tramps.[28]

After a few more days of street fighting, the strikers capitulated. There were more complaints of militia members throwing switches and helping to run trains. Yet some militiamen and police reserves defected while facing striking workers, giving rise to the charge that there was substantial working-class sympathy among the police. The actions of the regular Buffalo police, however, contradict this interpretation: virtually the entire force worked unceasingly—and with a high degree of effectiveness, given the number of trains run against strikers' resistance. Their shortcomings appear to have been due to overextension along miles of track and to fatigue. If some officers harbored working-class loyalties, they were held in check through military discipline.[29]

The Pullman strike in Chicago in July 1894 interrupted every phase of city life. Unlike the Buffalo department, the Chicago police had not been upgraded much since 1886. The force was inefficient, undisciplined, and politically corrupt. Nevertheless, even though large forces of Pinkertons, state militia, and federal troops supplemented them, the local police were easily the most effective of all the agencies involved and were the sole source of public order during the first critical days of the strike. The entire regular force of more than 3,000 men, plus 512 specials (most of whom had served as regular or special patrolmen), worked twenty-hour days for the length of the strike.[30] As in Buffalo, the intervention of outside troops was owing not so much to the weakness of the Chicago police as to their exhaustion after days of continuous duty and to the railroads' demands for a massive show of force.

Depression-era struggles in Milwaukee came to a head in the streetcar strike of 1896, which produced the most intensive conflict throughout the city since 1886. Milwaukeans had voted overwhelmingly in favor of a municipal takeover of the streetcar franchise because of poor service and high fares under the privately held streetcar monopoly, but a conservative city government did not heed the popular will and signed a franchise awarding the company very favorable terms. When carmen struck the railway for higher wages on May 3, 1896, they enjoyed widespread popular support. The company's determination to break the strike, backed by extraordinary police support, ensured a high level of class violence.[31]

Police Chief Janssen promised complete police protection for cars run with scab labor, and he swore in 100 specials. Following a meeting with his lieutenants and then with the mayor, Janssen announced that he could put 275 men against the strikers but that he needed 400 more to cover the city adequately. Cards were sent out to carefully selected men all over the city asking them to be sworn in as specials. One-half of the night force was held off patrol on reserve, and men were assigned to every car barn. All these actions were taken before the workers even went out.[32]

Workingmen from all over the city turned out in support of the strikers. Every car barn was surrounded and stoned by crowds. Large reserves at each police station augmented the forces at each of the car barns, and squads of police were sent out to disperse crowds of up to 4,000 reported around the city. The chief had repeated conferences to plan strategy with the mayor, aldermen, company officials, and his staff officers.

Like the Buffalo police in the switchmen's strike of 1892, the Milwaukee police were accused of scabbing—of actually doing the work of union men to run the cars. Moreover, 12 streetcar inspectors (lower-level management in the streetcar company) were sworn in as deputies, two patrolmen were assigned to each car, and the mayor supported the professional scabs brought in from St. Paul, Minneapolis, and Chicago—an action that always escalated strike violence. Car service was temporarily suspended because the effort to run the system could not be maintained at such a high cost in property destruction and physical injuries. The strikers' victory was short-lived, however.

When the company renewed attempts to run all its cars, the police redoubled arrests, making 26 early in one day. For all this effort, 127 cars were run, nearly the normal number. The strike had been broken, largely because of powerful police repression of workers. "If the time comes when we cannot handle the hoodlums we will call on the militia," announced Janssen. "All circumstances considered I think everything has passed off well. We have not been as aggressive with the disorderly element as we might have been."[33]

The papers published partial listings of those arrested, along with their occupations, so we may see who these "hoodlums" and "disorderly elements" were. Of the persons arrested during the last two days of the strike, occupational data are available for 43, all workingmen, representing a wide variety of occupations: twelve laborers, five machinists, five schoolboys, three coopers, three teamsters, plus one each cigar maker, housewife, expressman, ice peddler, engineer, tailor, painter, newsdealer, patternmaker, conductor, baker, butcher, turner, shoemaker. These represent perhaps one-third to one-fourth of the total arrests, but the occupational breakdown is probably typical. Thousands of Milwaukee workers had turned out in support of the carmen, but they were beaten by the determined efforts of the police force, augmented by 150 specials.[34] Samuel Gompers called this strike "without parallel in the labor world." Violence was common in streetcar strikes everywhere, but the level of class solidarity found in Milwaukee was unusually high. The Milwaukee police emerged from this strike as a much more clearly defined enemy of workers and the workers' movement. Police appropriations were blocked, and council resolutions to increase the size of the police met with more resistance. It was eight years before the city council voted money for an increase in the size of the police force.

This type of violence characterized streetcar strikes in general. There were dozens during the period 1886–1915, with widespread community support for the strikers and correspondingly high levels of force used by the police to suppress them. Police departments regularly employed quasi-military organization and tactics during strikes, often sweeping large areas of the city clear of strikers, strike sympathizers, and working-class citizens generally. Fully electrical communication systems and full utilization of the patrol wagon and signal system supported these massive police actions. Police violence in the form of clubbings and club-swinging charges increased as well. "Specials" chosen from the ranks of the petty bourgeoisie or often from the private police forces maintained by employers regularly augmented police forces during strikes. More and more often, police officials took this anti-working-class violence for granted and ceased to be as defensive about their strike work as they had been in the 1880s.

SUSTAINED ANTISTRIKE ACTIVITY IN ONE CITY

After the turn of the century, employers began a concerted effort to break organized labor, and a major tool was the municipal police, this time augmented by professional strikebreakers who were hired more for combat than for work as scabs. By the turn of the century the municipal police had almost 30 years of experience in anti-working-class activity, and there was much less concern among employers about police laxness. A strong strike response had been inculcated into the routine urban police function, and police strategy seems to have shifted to violent offense. To some extent, the increased emphasis on violence resulted from heightened class tensions, from the isolation of predominantly Irish, German, and Anglo-American police forces from Polish, Bohemian, Jewish, and Hungarian workers, and from the high proportion of foreign-born unskilled workers dominating the work force in cities. The bourgeoisie saw these workers as much less predictable than even the anarchists of the 1880s. Hence, there was a much greater need for supervision and police repression. Typically, police presence was much stronger during strikes of this period than earlier, both in terms of numbers of men and in terms of tactics.[35]

Chicago witnessed a series of major strikes between 1904 and 1906. The stockyards strike of 1904 and the teamsters' strike of 1905 illustrate the scope of the full-scale antistrike efforts of the Chicago police, as well as the heightened militancy and organizational skills of the working class. For the stockyards strike, a police detail under the leadership of Inspector Hunt was dispatched to the yards even before the strike began. It was increased to 200 men on the first day of the strike, and to 375 on the second day, with 75 additional patrolmen assigned to the working-class residential and railroad district north of the yards. As strike activity died down, this force was reduced to 100 men, but it was increased to 400 men when activity again resumed. In addition, 70 plainclothes patrolmen and 90 detectives were assigned duty in the strike area. This special force was divided into companies under lieutenants, who further divided them into 2-man patrols. Five-man "flying squadrons" were later sent on patrol in major streets in the strike area to prevent the formation of crowds. Plainclothes men gathered information, watched the streets near the yards for vandalism, and searched suspicious characters for arms. Saloonkeepers were ordered not to sell "take out" beer or liquor to intoxicated people, and those who violated this edict were arrested.[36]

Clubbing became a major police tactic to keep streets clear. One typical incident became well-known because the police clubbed a female University of Chicago social worker half a block away from a disturbance.[37] Nevertheless, this strike was one of Chicago's more peaceful ones for its size, largely because the stockyards could easily be sealed off. Still, five strikers were killed—shot by scabs, none of whom was arrested by the police. At the same time as the stockyard strike, July and August 1904, there were 92 other strikes in progress in Chicago, with 800 patrolmen detailed to full-time strike duty out of only 1,800 patrolmen suitable for patrol duty (500 more patrolmen were infirm).[38]

The teamsters' strike of April 1905 involved all parts of the city and was far bloodier. Twenty-one persons were killed and 415 injured seriously. The strike broke out at Montgomery Ward & Company on April 8 and became a general strike of teamsters on April 27. From the first day, the company tried to operate caravans of nonunion wagons. Police were not able to protect all the drivers, but over the next days the incidence of blockading was reduced through vigorous police action.[39]

Hundreds of small encounters occurred throughout the city for weeks. Police officers were assigned to routine delivery wagons, and columns of policemen walked on both sides of wagon caravans. During the 105-day strike the police arrested over 1,100 protesters—five-sixths of them unionists—but much of the violence far exceeded police capabilities to repress it. The employers therefore hired Frank Curry, a professional strikebreaker who armed his men with leaded clubs and set out to open up the streets. This force was met by a crowd of workers and was defeated in a brief battle.[40]

The unionists' defeat of the scab army illustrates a unique feature of this strike: the willingness of the union to use organized force against scabs, but not against the police. The union employed as many as 200 "sluggers" in 10-man gangs assigned to stop scabs. The union clearly summed up its policy:

The only weapon the strikers had was violence, for under present conditions a peaceful and successful strike is an impossibility. . . . While there are in all our cities so many non-heroic, non-professional strikebreakers lounging on every street corner ready to die for unlimited beer, the striker, whether his cause is just or unjust, must be prepared to say to them, "See here! If you try to take our jobs while we're looking for a square deal we'll break your heads." Intimidation is the only argument that appeals to a certain class of minds.[41]

The bourgeois press condemned the union's action as evidence that all unions were "criminal." At the same time, employers paid 7,000 to 8,000 strikebreakers, many of them professionals brought in from outside of the city. Some were drivers, but most were guards, and the jobs were virtually interchangeable. As many as 1,200 blackjacks were distributed to about half of the black strikebreakers, and leaded hickory clubs went to others. Distribution of Winchester rifles was stopped at the plea of the city council.[42]

Typically, a wagon would be sent out as a decoy watched by a 10-man slugging squad. When the wagon stopped and a crowd gathered, the slugging team would attack the crowd from the rear, blackjacking as many people as possible. One professional strikebreaker and crew leader from St. Louis held the unofficial record of eight men knocked out in a single attack. Union leaders were also hunted down and beaten by these men. One of the employers' sluggers later informed the police that he had been ordered to "kill a nigger" in order to start a riot and force the governor to call for militia. A race riot almost did occur, and it may well be that other employers' sluggers carried out that order.[43]

To be fair, the Chicago police did not approve of the hired scabs—but neither did they often arrest them. The goons occasionally beat up police officers, and in any case they did not have much respect for the police. It was also patently obvious to the police who was responsible for the violence on the streets on a day-to-day basis, even if the bourgeoisie were willing to blame it on the strikers on the theory that "no strike, no need for strikebreaker violence."[44]

Whatever their shortcomings, however, it was the Chicago police who broke the backbone of the strike. The original strike force of 200 was quickly increased to 500. By May 2, 75 percent of the police force was detailed to strike duty, and the department issued a call for a thousand volunteers. One hundred men were drafted from the city water department, but only 38 qualified as policemen, and they were unwilling to fight. The department, stretched to its limits, clearly showed signs of wear after weeks of heavy work, but it was kept in the field. Regular escort service of wagon convoys, guards assigned to wagons, and immediate dispersal of any crowds collecting in the streets broke down the resistance of the strikers and got the wagons moving again.[45]

The employers had turned to private strikebreaking forces, not because the municipal police had failed, but because the strike was beyond the immediate capabilities of the city police. It was all the police could do to keep the streets open. The employers wanted much more extensive police work than that and, given the magnitude of the strike, needed more support to win it. Private goons extended the capabilities of the police, but they nonetheless relied on the police for arrests of strikers and strike leaders, for protection of wagon convoys, and for legitimacy— thousands of strikebreakers were sworn in as special police or deputy sheriffs. The ties between the police and the strikebreakers are obvious when one considers arrest patterns: the strikebreakers were clearly the major violent force in the city, yet almost all arrests involved disorderly conduct charges against citizens congregating in the streets and union members throwing rocks and blocking wagons.

The two great garment workers' strikes of 1910 and 1915 demonstrated that the Chicago police department had degenerated into little more than the hired sluggers of the manufacturers. Police strike activity in 1915 was similar in form to that of previous strikes. A 200-man strike force was initially called into service (including 100 mounted officers); 100 more were added the next day, and this force was eventually increased to 500. Officers were assigned beats around the clothing factories or to the streets to break up crowds. More officers were stationed at bridges leading into the Loop in order to keep strikers out of the downtown area.[46]

More than in any previous strikes the police acted as the agents of the manufacturers. Their major antistrike tactic was wholesale clubbing of strikers, carried out on such an extensive scale and in so cold-blooded a manner that the strikers won considerable support from "reform" women's groups and anti-machine aldermen.[47] The pattern of clubbing in both strikes was similar: clubbings were wholesale and indiscriminate, directed against both strikers and any member of the public at large who looked out of place in the strike district. Large numbers of women were clubbed by the police, with no attempt to hide their actions. A reporter for the *Chicago Daily Socialist* engaged in a dangerous experiment designed to show the one-sidedness and brutality of the police. He persuaded a few young girls to march past a tailoring shop and blow a small whistle. The police rushed out and arrested the girl with the whistle with considerable roughness and scattered the others.[48]

The arrests that often followed the clubbings were equally indiscriminate. One intoxicated officer simply blocked off his street and asked each person passing if he were a striker. Those determined to be strikers were beaten and arrested. Although this excess was stopped by headquarters, no effort was made to stop equally repressive behavior. Such arrests depleted scarce union funds, intimidated strikers, and proved an effective police weapon.[49]

Perhaps more serious is the complicity of the police in sluggings by the manufacturers' professional strikebreakers. In a few cases pickets were held by policemen until employers' goons could arrive and beat them severely in the presence of the police. One officer refused to consent to slugging by private guards on his beat, but the guards had him transferred out of the strike district within an hour. In more extreme cases the police officers assigned to a factory worked under the direction of the sluggers' boss, making arrests as ordered.[50]

Police control of street activity included both official mass picketing and crowds gathered around minor disturbances, often deliberately started by employers' guards as a pretext for a police attack on the strikers. Here mounted police proved an effective innovation. The horsemen simply rode over the crowds, trampling people as they scattered in all directions and earning the epithet "Cossack" from the entire labor movement. Clubbings from the horsemen and the ground patrolmen bringing up the rear finished these assaults.

The scale of police antistrike activity in Chicago during the early twentieth century is probably without parallel in American labor history, but the duration and intensity of strikes such as those of the teamsters and the stockyard workers were regular features in America through the late 1930s. The proliferation of heavily armed private police forces led to a great increase in violence, especially involving firearms. The municipal police were accessories to this increasingly lethal tactic, since they were notoriously soft on the employers' private armies, often deputizing or making specials of them, and ignored their gunplay. The police also became more willing to use firearms, not just as a reaction to forces beyond their control, but as part of escalating class violence that they had helped to foster.

STRIKE CONTROL IN SMALLER INDUSTRIAL CITIES

By definition, the municipal police had little to do with rural strikes and strikes in company towns. The primary business of the professional guard and strikebreaking forces originated and remained in these areas. The development of these private forces and such public forces as the Pennsylvania State Police followed that of the municipal police but stemmed from different political and economic bases.

The policing of strikes in smaller industrial cities closely followed the model of the larger cities. There is no evidence that the smaller size of these cities lessened the class conflict inherent in the relations of production, and serious strikes occurred. To the extent that there was a difference in police response, it can only be attributed to the fact that police effectiveness depends not simply on number of patrolmen per capita but on organizational efficiency. A police force of 500 men enjoys options in strike control work that a 100-man force simply does not have. Small forces were especially vulnerable to overextension and exhaustion after a few days of 24-hour strike work. The communitywide protection of scabs therefore became problematic after a few days. In other respects, however, small departments imitated the organizational changes of large city departments, including early adoption of the patrol wagon and signal system, tightening of administration and efficiency, and stability of membership. Parallel political struggles over the control of the police used the same "police reform" terminology.

The Oshkosh woodworkers' strike of 1898 offers a clear example of the difference between the small American industrial city of the late nineteenth century and Gutman's industrial city of the mid-1870s. Oshkosh, with a population of about 30,000, was Wisconsin's second-largest industrial city and was dependent primarily on a wood products industry. In 1905 its police department numbered only 21 men, including 16 patrolmen. When 2,800 workers belonging to the Amalgamated Woodworkers Union struck Oshkosh sash and door makers in May 1898, they enjoyed massive community support, but the employers refused to bargain with the union.[51] The police and specials exercised a supervisory function over crowds, even if they were unable to protect the scabs still working in the mills. Their passive role may possibly be attributed to sympathy with the strikers—and probably to respect for the strikers' overwhelming numbers.

Employers prevailed upon the government to call out 400 national guard troops, which were put under the command of General Boardman, head of an Oshkosh life insurance company. The strike dragged on for months with little violence because the workers refused to confront the militia, who had been ordered to "shoot to kill." As one striker sensibly put it: "Our object was to catch and beat the workmen. We did not intend to do any one any serious injury. I am sure they will not try to fight the soldiers, as it would be sure death to many." Soldiers meant stability, but not the end of the strike. That work fell to the local police.[52]

The large millworks of Paine and Morgan reopened on August 3 with crowds of strikers blocking the streets around the plants waiting for scabs—and the police ready to intervene to protect the strikebreakers. Police Chief Weisbrod and 20 men escorted Morgan scabs through a crowd as they emerged from work, meeting only verbal harassment. The next day the police took the initiative. Four officers under Albert Morgan led a flying wedge of 50 strikebreakers across the bridge toward the yards, but they were driven back. Chief Weisbrod, meanwhile, gathered all his men from the mills and marched them in formation across the bridge. The police attacked the pickets with clubs, "flailing away under a fusillade of stones, clubs, eggs and bags of salt." Strike leaders were singled out, "cut and severely pounded and the blood flowed freely from their wounds." Several women fighting alongside the men were arrested as a diversion and taken to jail. That night the scabs departed work without incident. Scabs at most of the mills were now deputized with police power and given clubs and badges.[53] Facing mills full of scabs with weapons and arrest powers, aggressive city cops guarding plant gates, police spies at union meetings, a manufacturer's "law and order league" backing the police, and arrests of union leaders—worker resistance faltered. Many laborers returned to their jobs, and although a rally bolstered their spirits, it could not turn the tide. On August 20 the strike was called off.[54]

The Oshkosh strike demonstrates that even a small police department could have a major impact in a large strike. Here 21 police officers, augmented by a few specials, were pitted against 2,000 strikers who had substantial support from their families and the rest of the community. The Oshkosh police maintained a low profile in the early days of the strike, gauging the temper of the situation and then acting swiftly to break the strike. Although the workers had substantial support among middle-class shopkeepers, the "neutral" ideology of law and order and the domination of industrial capital won in the end.

Another example of effective strike work by police in a small industrial city is the IWW rubber strike in Akron in 1913. At that time Akron boasted a population of 69,069 (1910 census) and a 62-man police force. On February 10, 20,000 workers walked out of the rubber plants. City officials subservient to the rubber barons determined to break the strike. A Citizens Welfare League raised vigilante troops from among the ranks of the bourgeoisie and petty bourgeoisie, and 700 presented themselves at police headquarters to be sworn in, provided with badges and clubs, and dispatched to the strike district under police direction. The peaceful progress of the strike ended suddenly on March 7. Five hundred strikers were listening to speeches by Wobblies and socialists and had formed a human chain in front of the Goodrich plant when Sheriff Fergusson asked the pickets to move across the street. As the crowd began to move, it was charged by 20 Akron police officers, reinforced by 30 special deputies. The Akron *Beacon Journal* describes the scene:

> The vigorous wielding of clubs soon had a telling effect. Steadily the clubs of the officers rose and fell as the excited mob was slowly battered back. As the strikers were unarmed, they could not long endure the severe punishment. Some of them seized bricks and stones and threw them. Mostly they fought with their fists.

The battle lasted 30 minutes. Sixty strikers and one police officer were injured. The only person arrested was an IWW organizer, who was charged with inciting a riot.[55]

This first battle of the strike shows the power of coordinated police antistrike work, even by the smallest of departments against a very large strike. The organized beating had a devastating effect on the strikers. This scene was repeated throughout the next two days, with squads of police and specials attacking workers' assemblies. The indiscriminate nature of the police clubbing can be seen in the fact that Sheriff Fergusson was accidently struck in the face by a special deputy.[56]

Following still more battles and riots, the mayor proclaimed martial law. Strikers were officially forbidden to demonstrate, picket, hold parades, or even unnecessarily use the streets. Vigilantes patrolled the streets in private cars, wore Akron police department badges, and carried clubs. At this point the strikers asked Governor Cox for national guard troops to protect them from the city police and their vigilante allies, but no help was forthcoming from the governor.[57] Under this high level of repression, the strike could not continue. IWW organizers were arrested and run out of town, severely weakening strike leadership. With use of the streets curtailed, it was impossible to rally strikers' spirits or to persuade nonstriking workers peacefully to stay out. Left to their own devices, the strikers drifted back to work.

Although Akron's small police department was not strong enough to control the strike alone, it nevertheless constituted a critical disciplined core around which a well-organized vigilante police action could be organized, and it sustained vigorous repression of a major strike for several weeks. Unlike the moblike vigilante actions of many cities in the nineteenth century, the vigilantes in Akron had police discipline at their core and operated as a well-organized and trained force.

A number of streetcar strikes rocked the Great Lakes/Ohio Valley area: Buffalo in 1915; Chicago in 1885, 1903, and 1915; Cleveland in 1899 and 1908; Columbus in 1890 and 1910; Detroit in 1891; Duluth-Superior in 1912; Evansville in 1907; Grand Rapids in 1891; Indianapolis in 1892 and 1913; Milwaukee in 1896; Muncie in 1908; Rochester in 1889; Saginaw and Bay City in 1895; St. Louis in 1899 and 1903; Terre Haute in 1902; Toledo in 1894.[58] Streetcar strikes were unique in that they fully involved the entire community. The streetcar was the only form of mass public transportation, and the physical growth of late-nineteenth-century cities depended on them.[59] Streetcar franchises — that is, the monopoly right to build car lines—were enormously profitable because, in addition to their regular high income from fares, the lines created great opportunities for wealth through land speculation. Not surprisingly, syndicates of investors bought up streetcar lines across the country, leading to the monopolization of the industry. A company therefore had much more at stake in a strike than a local union. Any settlement weakened the company with unions everywhere it operated. By the same token, profits from all lines could be used to absorb huge local strike losses. Although vigorous police action won many of the strikes for the employers, this power was of limited value in the long run.

When the operators of both the cable and the horse cars in Grand Rapids struck for higher wages and union contracts on May 10, 1891, the company announced that it would hire new men and run the cars as usual. Within a few hours a bottle of nitroglycerin turned up on the tracks. As the week progressed, workers tried to keep the cars from running, first by inducing others not to take their jobs, but later also by blocking the cars. In a typical incident a crowd of about 100 blocked the tracks, placing a bar of iron across them. When a car came along, the crowd turned a hose on the driver and conductor, dousing them with water. Two police officers on horseback responded to a call, and the crowd greeted them with shouts of "Pull them off, pull them off." The officers drew their pistols and rode through the crowd, creating an opening for the car. Two detectives in the crowd then made two arrests of the crowd's leaders (neither of them union men). A patrol wagon with 20 officers arrived, and the crowd was dispersed. One other arrest was made: J. S. Nelson was charged with using "ungentlemanly language toward an officer."[60]

As more cars appeared on the streets, violence escalated proportionately, stretching police capabilities beyond their limits—the officers simply could not cover all of the tracks or all of the crowds. Two officers rode each car while others lined the routes. There was considerable debate over the appropriateness of police arrests of persons who called out the word "scab." The police justice took the view that this was not an offense and dismissed charges against those brought in for it, but the police kept on making such arrests anyway.[61]

The community split along sharp class lines. The Central Labor Union took the position that the violence against the streetcar strikers was an attack on all the workingmen in the city. The union urged a boycott as the major tactic and claimed that it could control the violence better than the police; it even had 10 union men symbolically sworn in as specials. Opposing the CLU was a "citizens committee" organized by the secretary of the Board of Trade, who disclaimed any interest in which side won the strike; rather, the committee urged rigid enforcement of law and order. The mayor, police, and judges were soundly criticized for failing to maintain order. Citizen after citizen bemoaned that this was the first major disorder in the memory of even the oldest citizens in the city of 80,000. Major Edwin F. Uhl and two police commissioners reminded the committee that the city's 55-man police force was severely overextended by the strike and had done everything it could to contain the crowds and violence. Grand Rapids's bourgeoisie refused to acknowledge that disorder is inherent in the class dynamics of the city, and they couched their anti-working-class bias in the language of law and order.[62]

Perhaps symbolic of this conflict was a series of trials of strikers and strike supporters charged with using the epithet "scab" during the strike. A. W. Lyons was fined $8 upon conviction, while James Brittain, who elaborated the word with several obscenities, was fined $10 and costs but given 60 days in jail when he failed to come up with money for the fine. Burt Wilson put the matter to a jury trial. Wilson acknowledged that he had used the word but argued that it was not "immoral, indecent, or insulting, especially in the manner it was used in this case." John Coleman, a coachman called as a witness, put the matter more succinctly: "A scab is a scab, that's all." Wilson was convicted of disorderly conduct after the jury had been out 15 minutes.[63]

Streetcar workers in Duluth struck on September 9, 1910 to protest the dismissal of 9 men for union activity. The company immediately replaced them with 75 scabs from the Twin Cities. More strikers went out the next day, and 30 additional scabs arrived from Chicago. The entire police force was called to duty, joined by reinforcements from the sheriff's office.[64]

In the following days the violence escalated. According to one estimate, 5,000 strikers and sympathizers gathered at the car barns one night to throw rocks. The company did not even try to run its cars initially because of the strong crowd action. Thirty-

six special officers were sworn into the police force and detailed
to replace regular officers on beat patrols. The situation became
more complex on September 12, when the carmen in Superior,
Wisconsin (just across the bay), walked out in support of the
Duluth strikers; their strike, however, never reached the size of
Duluth's. A few cars were run with police protection, but the
overworked Duluth department could not protect all of them.
The county sheriff took over police duties from the local police
chief at the request of the mayor, but the original 30 police officers, plus 100 deputies (regulars and specials), remained on duty. More cars were run, and rioting subsided.[65] However, the
crowds adopted new tactics, hitting the running cars with stones
thrown by small groups that quickly dispersed and then re-
grouped at another location. The company responded by cover-
ing the cars with heavy wire for protection, and patrolmen stationed at the car barns both protected the barns from crowds and
rode the cars to keep the lines open.

The real break in the strike came on the political front. The
members of the Retail Merchants Association were as outraged
by the callous attitude of the Minneapolis company that owned
the street railroad as they were by the strike violence. Clearly,
local mercantile interests had nothing to gain from violent antiunion activity and much to lose. Citing the "Des Moines solution" to a strike the year before, whereby a court had ordered
arbitration because of the compelling public interest, Duluth city
councilmen sued the street railroad company for a similar resolution. Others proposed public ownership.[66]

By then, police activity was so efficient that at times all cars
were running. More than once, the *Duluth News Tribune* reported the strike all but ended, but each time the violence resumed.
Although effective police action could control most of the
streets by day, it could not end the strike violence. During the
second week strikers and their supporters fought pitched battles
against the scabs, while the police continued their role of protecting scabs and trying to keep the car lines open. After three
weeks, the company settled.[67]

In Duluth, as in Grand Rapids and other cities large and small
that faced disruption of commerce owing to strikes, the "neu-

tral" police function transcended local politics. The law-and-order ideology was essential to the interests of all capitalists, but there were limits to a coercively enforced law and order. Community-supported strikes often outstripped police efforts to control them, forcing searches for solutions that would reduce the level of overt class violence. This process, begun during the Progressive era, became one of the hallmarks of the liberal democratic captialist state in the 1930s.

The policing of strikes in small industrial cities did not reflect any less of an anti-working-class bias than that in major industrial cities. No sense of community transcended class in the policing of strikes in the early 1900s, as Herbert Gutman has argued for the 1870s. Whatever differences might have existed between the policing of strikes in small cities and large cities is better understood as a function of scale. Policing is more than a function of police per capita; cities with forces of 30, 40, or 75 men could not deliver the antistrike work of those with police forces of 300, 500, or 1,000. The organizational capacity of the police for antistrike work grew proportionately with departmental size.

THE RANK-AND-FILE POLICE AS STRIKEBREAKERS

It is both in the essence of capitalism and in the nature of highly disciplined bureaucratic organizations that individual members of the working class will routinely act against their class interests for short- or long-term individual gain. Hence, the czar's police were drawn from the working and peasant classes, as were the soldiers who made the Chilean coup. The police in America are largely drawn from the very cities they patrol and are called upon to beat and arrest friends, neighbors, and individuals with whom they may personally sympathize. How can this behavior be explained?

Employers almost routinely accused the police of "laxness," "favoritism," or "incompetence" in their antistrike work. Judging from police performance in nearly 100 strikes, however, the charges are not upheld by the facts and cannot be used themselves as evidence of police action or lack of action in favor of strikers. Rather, they mean that the police could not keep all scabs from being harassed, could not keep all gates unobstructed all of the time, could not prevent mass meetings and rallies under all circumstances. The employers desired a far higher standard of control in their communities than could reasonably be provided, given the violence of the class struggle.

From another point of view, the employers' criticism can be seen to have two functions. First, it prodded the police to ever higher levels of antistrike action—a steady reminder that a better job could always be done. Second, it served as a politically necessary counter-charge to the workers' repeated accusations that the police were acting on behalf of the employers. The police could point out that criticism from both sides indicated that they were acting "neutrally."

The few occasions where the evidence is clear that the police *were* lax in antistrike measures never turned on police rank-and-file sympathies for the workers' side but were always related to citywide political questions. For example, as part of their Golden Rule policies, Mayors Samuel "Golden Rule" Jones and Brand Whitlock of Toledo refused to permit the police to be used to protect scabs. In addition, where city policy permitted peaceful mass picketing, police work in strikes was much simpler and much less violent. When the Pope-Toledo Motor Car Company sought to operate "as usual" in spite of a strike in 1906, the presence of large numbers of pickets forced it to maintain its labor force in a virtual slave camp inside the bounds of the factory. Under such conditions it could not effectively operate, and the company was forced to arbitrate a settlement that was unusually favorable to labor. These policies, though, did not extend beyond the personal political strength of Jones and Whitlock. In the Cleveland garment strike of 1911, a scant three years after the adoption of the Golden Rule policy, the same police department was viciously beating strikers and protecting professional strikebreakers.[68]

Given the workers' inability to control the police institution through normal political channels, one remaining means of limiting police antistrike measures was to appeal to individual officers to resist orders and not to enforce antistrike measures. Clearly, in most such instances the officer simply looked the other way. Although police administrations encountered difficulties in socializing the rank and file to ignore thier class loyalties during strikes, there is little reason to doubt that, for the most part, these measures succeeded. Still, ensuring these loyalties was an important factor in structuring the police response to strikes.

The possibility of rank-and-file resistance required frequent measures to reinforce the department's legitimacy in the eyes of its officers. Resistance by an individual officer was severely punished and the officer made an example of. Police officers in Chicago's Pullman strike of 1894 and in Buffalo's switchmen's strike of 1892 were suspended for even a hint of sympathy for the workers. In both strikes the workers' cause had exceptional local popularity, and the departments took the most severe line possible to head off police resistance. In Cleveland, officers were suspended and fined for refusing a direct order to arrest bystanders during the Brown Hoisting strike of 1896.[69] The specter of a full-scale police mutiny was raised only twice. During a streetcar strike in Columbus in 1910, 32 patrolmen refused to obey orders to ride on scab-operated streetcars to protect the drivers. Three years later, in Indianapolis, 29 police officers refused a similar order. The significance of these police mutinies is not that they occurred but that there were only two of them in 40 years of strikebreaking activity.

The Columbus police had been working far beyond capacity for three weeks during that city's vicious streetcar strike when 32 officers refused to ride the cars any longer. Twenty-three special officers joined in the mutiny, bringing the total to 55, about 25 percent of the department's strength. The strike, though not the largest in the streetcar industry, had been characterized by high levels of violence, and it was the second such strike that year. The employers imported armies of heavily armed strikebreakers to operate the cars, and the workers resorted to dynamiting cars by placing explosives under the tracks. The police responded with tactics typical of the period: vigorous patrol and surveillance work, dispersal of crowds by flying squadrons, and arrests of identifiable workers' leaders (30 days for loitering was a typical sentence). On the day of the police mutiny one car had been blown up, two dynamiting attempts had been discovered, 14 persons had been injured, and 26 arrests had been made.[70]

Given such vigorous police antistrike enforcement for almost three weeks, why a mutiny? It is clear that the action was spontaneous, but its origins probably had much to do with city politics. While condemning the company's hired scabs, the city nevertheless supported them by releasing armed scabs who had been arrested on gun charges. Moreover, Mayor Marshall had just vetoed a bill providing an eight-hour day for police officers on the grounds of "economy" while forgetting to veto his own salary increase. Thirty-two men immediately refused the mayor's order to ride the cars, citing both personal danger and support for the strikers as their reasons.

Recognizing that they faced a unique situation in the history of police control of strikes, officials pleaded with the men to change their minds. "Try it for just one night," implored Police Chief Carter. "It would not be too late tomorrow for you to make up your minds definitely." The chief called a meeting of the patrolmen for the next morning's roll call, saying confidently to a reporter, "I don't believe that they will refuse to obey orders." The mayor, the chief, and the director of public safety each gave a speech, reminding the men of their duties and threatening dismissal for all who refused.[71]

The men remained unmoved, and several made speeches. One affirmed that "I would rather lose my job and take another which would make me work 24 hours a day than to be called a scab and lose the respect of the workingmen." The chief then announced that ranks were being formed to ride on the cars and asked those who would ride to form a separate line. Thirty-seven men stepped out of line and filed out of the station, the rebellious officers having gained 5 new supporters during the dramatic encounter with Chief Carter. Their ranks were later reduced to the original 32 as 5 officers, their futures clearly on the line, reconsidered and returned to work on the cars. Chief

Carter suspended the resisting officers the next morning. But this action did not stop the defections; one regular officer joined the mutiny over the following weekend. Furthermore, the mutiny spread to the 137 specials who had been sworn in and used on regular patrol duty, freeing regular officers for strike work. Twenty-three of these specials joined the mutiny as well, again catching the city by surprise. "I was never so stunned in my life," said Mayor Marshall upon leaving the police station. "I had heard rumors during the afternoon that the men would disobey orders, but I did not believe they would."[72]

The violence increased, fed in part by the police department's decision to permit the arming of the scabs. Mayor Marshall announced that he needed 2,000 "volunteers," but only 12 appeared. Half-service was maintained on the lines, but at high cost. Dynamiters attacked the car barns, blowing part of the roof off, and for the first time the police had to cope with daylight mobs. The next day the governor called out the national guard, citing the outstripping of local police resources as his reason. The strike remained extremely violent for most of the next week, but ended three weeks later. The remainder of the police force had been relieved of riding the cars as soon as the guard arrived. Thus, for all practical purposes, the mutiny had the effect of so undermining the department's strength that it remained a viable antistrike force for only four more days.[73]

The mutiny in Indianapolis on November 4, 1913, though similar in form and effect, occurred in a different political context. The company imported the usual armed gangs of scabs, and the local police were active in trying to keep the cars running and in protecting the scabs from violence. In order to reduce violence, the company withheld service, a routine move preparatory to building up strength to break the strike. It announced that it would run the cars, but that these would need police protection.[74]

Police Captain Kruger called out 10 men from the reserve detail housed at police headquarters and ordered them to board the streetcars. All 10 turned in their badges. Kruger called out 10 more, who did likewise. Kruger sent for Superintendent of Police Martin Hyland, and, after the superintendent's arrival, called up the last 11 men from reserve; only 2 agreed to ride on the cars. Twenty-nine badges lay piled on Kruger's desk. When Hyland informed the men that they were required to obey all orders, they responded that they would "fight in the streets, use their clubs and guns at risk to themselves, and face the missiles of the rioters, but they would not board the cars." Anxious to compromise, Hyland took the names of the 29 and announced that he would prefer charges against them. He then had their badges returned to them and sent them out with orders to march beside the cars. The men complied, but the company refused to run the cars without police officers on board.[75]

Without police officers on the cars, crowds of angry people effectively kept the lines stopped. In view of the Indianapolis force's inability to maintain control of the streets, the governor threatened to declare martial law, and he actually called up a reserve of national guard troops; but these were never put on the streets. Instead, the governor used his office to force a settlement that ended the strike, pending further negotiations, after only one week.[76]

At the subsequent trial of the 29 patrolmen before the Board of Public Safety, the men took the position that they believed that Mayor Samuel Shrank had countermanded Chief Hyland's order and that they had not knowingly disobeyed. Sympathetic to the strikers, Mayor Shrank had publicly taken the position that the men should not ride the cars. Patrolman Hanford Burk, the first of the suspended men called as a witness, was asked by the prosecutor to explain why he had had no objection to riding the cars on the Saturday previous to his Tuesday morning refusal to do so. For Burk it was a simple distinction: "Because the conditions were different Saturday than on Tuesday. There were citizens riding Saturday, and Tuesday there was no one riding but strikebreakers."[77] Officer Burk's distinction between protecting the lives of Indianapolis citizens and protecting those of scabs was not regarded as an adequate defense.

At least two of the commissioners had already made up their minds about the officers' disobedience. Commissioner William

Davis, committed to law and order at all costs, strongly favored conviction and dismissal. Commissioner Sisloff had been on record, with Mayor Shrank, as opposing the order to put men on the cars, and he had described the action as "criminal." Commissioner William L. Resoner, the swing vote, made it two to one for acquittal when he stated that it was not clear to him that the men had actually refused a direct order. Thus the men remained on the force. Chief Hyland, however, felt compelled to resign after 29 years on the force, claiming that he could not "remain at the head of a police force composed in part of men who have refused to obey my orders." Commissioner Davis resigned on the spot as well.[78]

These two mutinies are unparalleled in police history. Both were precipitated not by the issue of protecting company property but by one tactic in the arsenal of police work that was particularly effective and also particularly resented by workers: patrolmen riding on the cars with armed professional scabs. Such action demonstrated that the police department was not a neutral protector of all people's rights. Some of the men at least—a minority in both departments—were sensitive enough toward this issue to risk their jobs over it. The significant question is not so much how these police mutinies occurred but rather, given the origins of so many police officers in the working class, why there were not more mutinies. This question is especially important since many police historians insist on the working-class bias of the rank-and-file patrolman.

A basic factor in moving police against strikers was class divisions within the working class. Strikers were mostly unskilled laborers or relatively low-paid operatives, whereas patrolmen were disproportionately drawn from the skilled sectors of the working class. Moreover, even those police officers not drawn from the skilled sector were paid according to the living standard of the most skilled workers—$900 a year in Buffalo, compared with $400 to $500 for dock workers—and police officers often lived in the more middle-class sections of town. Moreover, policing in this period can be characterized as partially entrepreneurial in character. Various kinds of small enterprises, illegal and legal, brought in additional income: extra money for providing extra protection for businesses; a share of bribes for acting as a go-between for a higher-ranking officer; a cut of vice activity; and rewards for recovering lost property. In an extreme example, nearly 50 percent of the Chicago force in 1910 was detailed off patrol duty on various kinds of "special duty," often a synonym for some kind of paying slot in the machine. In this case a patrolman's pay was little more than a base salary to ensure loyalty in other kinds of activities. The remaining officers could aspire to such affluence even if they were not immediately gaining from this activity. These characteristics locate the police in the petty bourgeoisie or in a position of accessibility to the petty bourgeoisie.[79]

Second, exploitation of intraclass ethnic divisions between police and workers impeded class solidarity. Irish and Germans dominated most large-city police departments in the region, whereas the working class by 1900 had become predominantly Polish, Italian, Bohemian, and Jewish, a large percentage of whom could not speak English. There was considerable ethnic animosity toward these groups by older immigrants and native-born Americans. The new immigrants competed for jobs and scarce living space and threatened the existing social order for the older working class as well as for the petty bourgeoisie. Buffalo organized its entire police department along ethnic lines: Irish officers serving under Irish captains and sergeants generally patrolled Irish, Italian, and American districts; Germans served under German captains and sergeants and patrolled the German and Polish districts. This scheme, among other things, maximized ethnic antagonisms between Italians and the Irish and between Poles and Germans.[80]

The organization and discipline of police strike control work minimized the impact of an individual officer's reluctance to repress workers. Officers were removed from their everyday precincts and colleagues and placed in special strike forces. Strike patrolling was always done in teams. Serious strike work, such as breaking up pickets or dispersing crowds, required patrols of 10 or more under a sergeant or lieutenant. These units were part of larger 100- or 200-man units under specially assigned captains or inspectors and were much more tightly coordinated than regular police patrol work. Patrolmen were frequently drilled in military tactics in these special units. An officer's possible sympathies for strikers could be minimized if he were part of a vigorous clubbing unit. Moreover, transfers and suspensions were readily used to punish suspected infractions. In Chicago in 1894 an entire unit, inspector and all, was transferred off strike work and suspended to set an example for the force. The one officer who refused to cooperate with employer sluggers in Chicago's 1910 garment strike was similarly transferred within the hour. Several officers were suspended for laxness during the 1892 switchmen's strike in Buffalo, and the superintendent used the occasion as a warning to other officers and as a demonstration for employers of the seriousness and reliability of the police.[81]

Police officers were not well-trained and knew even less of the law, but it would be an error to assume that police work was completely unresponsive to legal norms. A further factor inducing the police rank and file to do strikebreaking work was the familiar law-and-order argument. Police administrators regularly aimed florid defenses of the rights of employers, workers, and the public at the conservative working-class and middle-class communities where most police officers lived, and the same language predominated in the speeches that captains and superintendents gave their men to raise morale for a police charge. When Superintendent Doyle of Chicago addressed his police "troops" from the steps of the police station and reminded them that "property must be defended, and law must be upheld, and you are its defenders," he offered them a rationale for the clubbing they did that day in the 1885 streetcar strike.[82]

To further legitimate police strikebreaking, city officials denounced strikers as "criminals" or suggested that real workers would not engage in mass strike action and violence. Strikers were viewed as part of the criminal classes, the same people the police combatted by all means, fair and foul, during the rest of the year. Such characterizations justified far greater force than either the rank-and-file or the public might have accepted against striking workers.[83] In summary, then, the major factors that ensured that working-class police officers would become effective strikebreakers were class stratifications both within the working class and between the working class and the petty bourgeoisie, ethnic differences exploited into animosities in the period of capitalist industrial development, police organization, military discipline, punishment for infractions during strikes, and legitimation of strikebreaking efforts by means of the law-and-order rationale.

One final factor might be introduced at this point, one that shifts emphasis from the police system to individual police officers. There is evidence that in the garment strikes of 1910 and 1915 individual Chicago police officers assigned to various factories were paid as much as $5 a day or more by employers—the same rate as for sluggers. Hence, police officers sold themselves as sluggers. Though, of course, it is impossible to say how widespread this practice was, employers almost routinely provided meals and often cigars and liquor to officers billeted on their property during strikes, and they commonly made substantial donations to the police pension fund after strikes. McCormick, for example, gave $5,000 after the 1886 strike. Given the prevalence of corruption in police departments of the period, there can be no doubt that bribery occurred in the strike control context.[84] Nevertheless, if the police in the Chicago garment strike had not been full of hatred for "Hunkies, Pollacks, and Wops," they could not so easily have been bribed.

POLICE REPRESSION OF WORKING-CLASS POLITICS

The strikebreaking function of the police was integrally linked to police repression of working-class political aspirations, which took the form of widespread use of public order offenses to harass, obstruct, and prevent working-class political activity. In city after city socialists, communists, anarchists, and Wobblies faced regular arrests for street corner speeches, raids on meeting halls, invasions of newspaper offices and campaign headquarters, denials of permits to hold meetings, and countless threats of violence. The political leadership of the 1885–1886 eight-hour movement was subject to continual police arrest and harassment. Chicago police vigorously attacked suspected anarchists after the Haymarket incident, engaging in a wave of wholesale raids, beatings, arrests, and destruction of newspapers and offices.[85]

At the turn of the century, socialists were subjected to the same harassment. Daniel J. Hoan, socialist candidate for Milwaukee city attorney in 1909, was ordered to "move on" by police when he attempted to address workers at a plant gate, a privilege routinely accorded other political candidates. Socialist orator Boris Reinstein was arrested in Buffalo in 1906 for "corner-lounging" after making a speech on a downtown street. After serving five days in jail he made a similar speech and was again arrested, this time for "obstructing a sidewalk." Two hundred Buffalo residents who turned out for a speech by Mrs. Louisa Parsons, widow of a Haymarket martyr, were barred by the police from entering a hall they had rented for the occasion. Later, Emma Goldman was prevented from speaking by the same method.[86]

The police would not have denied their harassment of radicals, for they saw it as a proper exercise of their law enforcement function. At the 1902 annual meeting of the International Association of Chiefs of Police, Chicago's Chief O'Neill summarized the effect of his department's "constant surveillance" of anarchists:

> There are still in Chicago a large number of anarchists, but they are no longer defiant. They have been made to feel the effectiveness of the law when the community is aroused, and by all outward appearances, fear the law, if they do not respect it. They no longer indulge in incendiary talk calculated to incite acts of violence. Close surveillance is kept on the leaders by the police in Chicago, and they cannot make a move of any importance that is not known to the authorities in a short time.[87]

IWW activities were singled out for special repressive measures. Milwaukee socialists were vehemently anti-Wobbly, leaving "Czar Janssen" free rein with arrests and harassment. Pittsburgh police arrests of Wobbly speakers led to one of the famous IWW "free speech fights" in August 1912: 45 members were arrested in one day as each in turn tried to speak. They were locked overnight in cells that each held 11 to 15 men, and in the morning each was fined $25—an amount that none of them had.[88]

Such repression was not limited to the various socialist groups. The term "anarchist" in its nineteenth-century context referred to the left as a whole. Thus the Populist "Industrial Army" movement met considerable police repression, especially of their right to free speech. As they traveled across America trying to hold mass meetings in public squares, the leaders of the various armies found their rights denied in city after city, including Toledo, Cleveland, Allegheny City, Pittsburgh, Buffalo, and Washington, D.C. When the industrials attempted to rent private halls for their speeches, the police often simply extended their prohibition on meetings to those forums as well.[89]

Although the full extent and ultimate impact of this police action is not known, we can reasonably assume that it restricted the political activity not only of anarchist but also of trade unionists and workers of milder persuasions. Clearly, political harassment by police was part of the repression of all anticapitalist activity, and in this regard the populists represented more of a threat than did the socialists. Working-class political activity was intimately related to strike activity, since both focused on control of worker's productive energies, and it was well into the twentieth century before these competing ideologies were reconciled by liberal democrats.[90]

CONCLUSION

It is estimated that as many as 57,000 strikes occurred between 1889 and 1915, with perhaps 10,000,000 workers involved by

1905.[91] Most strikes were small and of little concern to the police, but virtually every industrial city saw regular strikes that threatened existing class relations. Working-class victories, moreover, encouraged additional strikes. As a result, police action in serious strikes had a critical impact in the class struggle beyond the actual scope of a particular strike, and the need to counter police strikebreaking tactics influenced workers' planning of strikes.

Although the municipal police were not the sole strikebreaking force, their role was central. The militia and national guard were inefficient, wasteful, and poorly disciplined. They could occupy a whole section of a city, beat back a major crowd, or stand stationary guard duty, but citywide strikes called for more complex forms of policing. The part-time, poorly paid national guard was responsible for some of the major examples of weak antistrike work; it was used only in the largest strikes, and especially as a backup to local police in rural areas.[92] Much attention has been paid to Pinkerton's and other private guard or strikebreaking forces. Their involvement in strike activity increased greatly after the turn of the century—enough to be the subject of a Senate investigation in 1915 after armies of professional strikebreakers murdered dozens of workers. But the largest private guard actions were in mining strikes, not in cities, because the late-nineteenth- and early-twentieth-century city was too intricate a political arena to be freely roamed by gangs of hired goons. Moreover, the employers often got both more and less than they paid for when they hired private guards. Companies often hired expensive but lazy lumpen elements who did little work or did it incompetently. Guard companies also engaged in senseless brutality that won enemies for the employers without achieving strategic victories against the strike. The garment strikes in Chicago are a case in point. Finally, private guards needed police powers or police protection to operate freely on the streets. More often private guard forces provided services that did not compete with the police: they guarded factories, performed various duties inside them, and spied inside and outside.[93]

The municipal police, all in all, had a much better record. First, they were publicly financed and hence much cheaper to use—a classic example of the socialization of the means of reproducing capital. Second, they could be well trained and disciplined and more or less maintained in that state, even under conditions of corrupt political domination. Third, they had practical experience in day-to-day monitoring of working-class communities that both the militia and the private police lacked. Fourth, despite occasional lapses, the police were clearly more disciplined than any other social control force, including bourgeois and petty-bourgeois vigilantes. Fifth, and most important, the police were cloaked in the legitimacy of law and order. Over the 30-year period after the 1877 riots, this emphasis on legitimacy substantially improved police ability to maintain order. The events in Oshkosh make the strongest case for the importance of a local police: 20 men acting in concert and with the authority of law could break a strike that the militia and private guards could only stabilize.

CHAPTER SEVEN

Liquor and the Saloon Question

THE TRANSFORMATION of the American urban police institution from a small watch force to a full-scale, militarized, day-and-night force made possible a "policed society"—that is, a society in which state power could be used on a daily basis to regulate social behavior.[1] Most patrolling hours today are related to this work, as they were 100 years ago. Almost all types of behavior came under police purview, but regulation clearly concentrated in several areas. First, liquor consumption has always been a part of American urban recreational patterns, and a major object of police regulation of workers' recreation concerned their activities while drinking or while socializing in and around places where liquor was sold or consumed—pool rooms, dance halls, vacant lots, and clubhouses, as well as saloons and bars. Second, various forms of working-class morality were also regulated. Working-class sexual conduct in particular offended other classes, and illicit sexual contact among working-class young people excited considerable concern. Other elements of working-class family life also violated conventional middle-class notions of morality, particularly when whole families went to saloons or dance halls, or when young people were allowed to roam the streets with their peers. The fact that whole working-class families worked, reducing the constraints on both women and children when compared with typical middle-class families, further distinguished the working-class family and was a concern to the police.

Even conservative historians of the police agree with this "policed society" model. But they usually refuse to recognize the inherent patterns of class discrimination intended, first, to discipline and, second, to socialize the heavily immigrant working class.[2] An honest examination of these issues must begin, I think, with the recognition that the values that the bourgeoisie and petty bourgeoisie expected the police to enforce were significantly different from those of large segments (but not all) of the working class. That the police were constantly criticized by those same classes for *not* diligently enforcing those values does not prove that officers really sided with the working class, for it is clear that the police could never have adequately enforced the moral standards that were desired.[3] Laxness, to the contrary, gave the police a measure of flexibility in applying a high degree of control. In fact, as I shall argue, the urban police exercised a more pervasive and more effective role in disciplining and socializing immigrant workers than was recognized by the reformers who criticized them. By focusing on the immense range of behavior that the police failed to suppress and on the wide range of shortcomings in the police institution, reformers failed to take adequate note of how much urban behavior the police in fact regulated. After all, a patrolman who spent two to four hours in a saloon would still have eight to ten hours of his shift for monitoring the social life on his beat. Arguably, he was even effective while in the saloon, regulating conduct there and making himself available to persons in the neighborhood who knew where he could be found.

There is little doubt that the values of individual police officers varied substantially from those of middle-class reformers and that these differences account in part for patterns of enforcement that were more lax than the reformers might have liked. But it must also be remembered that the police had much more information about urban patterns of behavior. For example, if the police failed to prevent lewd and rowdy behavior in dance halls and saloons, it was because their experience with the total range of urban recreational behavior and their own values led them to regard such behavior as relatively harmless and not worth suppressing.

However, the values of individual police officers cannot be substituted for the policies of an entire department. The police administrators who decreed departmental policy could indeed make it "hot" for officers who refused to comply. Officers who ignored certain types of conduct did so in accord with official (or unofficial) departmental policy. Those policies in turn were strongly influenced by bourgeois and petty-bourgeois demands and enforced through political channels, including the mayor, the city council, and such interest groups as chambers of commerce and boards of trade, and through such opinion makers as local newspapers. Although the degree of this influence might vary from city to city and from issue to issue, it was generally substantial enough that it could not be ignored.

What is ultimately at issue here is the social meaning of the suppression of working-class recreational activity. Social historians have often romanticized working-class leisure activities, and their analyses usually take two inconsistent positions: on the one hand, that working-class leisure activities deradicalized workers by draining off a large portion of their energy and by providing outlets for class-based hostility; and, on the other, that working-class solidarity and political activity were facilitated by such leisure activities as saloons, picnics, and social and cultural clubs. Both of these views, according to Gareth Stedman-Jones, deemphasize the importance of the workplace as the main socializing agent and as the main factor in disciplining workers' use of leisure time—workers had to regulate their own conduct at leisure so that they would always be ready to work the next shift.[4] Those who wish to celebrate the saloon as a "workingman's clubhouse" and to see drinking, fighting, and carousing as anticapitalist activities, need to look more closely at the evidence.

What forces, then, were behind the effort to regulate working-class leisure time? If the police institution itself was not particularly interested in these types of activities, where did the pressure come from? In the cities of the Great Lakes/Ohio Valley region, three distinct groups generally backed the position that the police should strongly regulate working-class leisure time activity: the employers of labor, both manufacturers and large-scale commercial interests; middle-class and bourgeois residents who lived in fear of their immigrant working-class neighbors (even though their neighborhoods might be miles away); and the religiously motivated temperance forces, drawn primarily from native-born Protestant stock and later including a few Catholic elements. The first group by definition consisted entirely of members of the bourgeoisie. The other two groups, though dominated by bourgeois and petty-bourgeois individuals, included some workers, especially skilled ones. Nativism crossed class lines, and demands for increased police efforts to control immigrant recreational activities was one form of nativism.

Many employers of labor believed that working-class recreational activities, especially drinking, demoralized, enervated, and radicalized their labor forces. In effect, they linked recreational activity with labor productivity and argued that drinking brought them less labor for their wage dollar. Some employers believed that liquor caused brain disease, or at least lethargy, resulting in lower productivity and poorer quality work. Others believed, as did one steel maker, that "today's drinker and debaucher is tomorrow's striker for higher wages"—that is, drinking caused "radical ideas" or dissipated family earnings so that the worker required more money to live. Others simply foresaw trouble when workers spent so much of their time in pursuit of pleasure, thereby undermining their ability to stick seriously to their work. Still others genuinely feared the effects of alcohol on workers who operated heavy machinery or transportation equipment, and they advocated temperance or abstention as a social movement.[5]

A second group, perhaps best described in Richard Sennett's *Families Against the City,* consisted of bourgeoisie and petty bourgeoisie who feared immigrants and the dark, unknowable, increasingly working-class city.⁶ Within one generation, large cities had been transformed from comfortable, secure, homogeneous small towns to sprawling, diverse conglomerates full of unfamiliar people. Large crowds of foreigners gathered on corners all over town, spoke strange languages, shopped in open markets for strange comestibles, hung out in saloons, shops, and vacant lots, and exhibited strange customs and beliefs. Fearful of these new arrivals, and feeling themselves powerless to affect these communities, the old guard expected their newly created social institutions—the police, schools, settlement houses—to discipline and socialize these people to conform to acceptable standards. They directed much criticism at all of these institutions because none of them individually (nor all of them collectively) managed to restore a sense of security in the city.

Finally, the temperance movement included many people from both groups above. Originating in rural areas and small towns, in the cities it attracted the petty-bourgeois class and native-born American Protestants of all classes. The temperance movement saw liquor as the key to an entire range of social problems brought about by the industrial revolution. Immigrant crime and poverty, even class violence and strikes were the result of "demon rum," and the weak people who succumbed had to be saved from themselves by appropriate legislation. In addition to the national program, local prohibition movements sought to raise the cost of saloon licenses, close "low-dive"saloons, restrict the number of saloons, impose local option laws, confine saloons to certain areas, shorten the hours of business, and enforce Sunday closing laws. Once again, the police were constantly criticized for not doing enough to enforce these measures.⁷

In this chapter, I shall examine the pattern of policing working-class recreational activity, beginning with the saloons and liquor consumption and moving on to the related issues of dance halls, sexual morality, and organized gambling and prostitution. The focus will be on patterns of police enforcement (and nonenforcement) and on the political forces behind those patterns.

THE LIQUOR QUESTION IN CHICAGO AND MILWAUKEE

Clearly the single most troublesome issue for the urban police was the liquor question. Perhaps 50 percent of the total population of Chicago and Boston used saloons every day—in effect, practically every working-class male and a good many others besides. In 1905 Chicago reported 7,334 saloons; Milwaukee, 2,134; Buffalo, 1,741; and Pittsburgh, 568. On a per capita basis in 1890 Buffalo had 7.81 saloons for every 1,000 citizens; Milwaukee, 6.44; Chicago, 4.73; Pittsburgh, only 0.41. These figures refer only to licensed saloons. Many purveyors never bothered to get a license due to complex regulations and high fees, especially in Pittsburgh, which accounts in part for its low ratio.[8]

The police were particularly irked by the criticism leveled at them by petty-bourgeois reformers for failing to regulate the closing hours of saloons, discover unlicensed liquor rooms, and prevent the sale of liquor to minors. Ironically, it was precisely these activities, together with the control of liquor-related personal altercations, that consumed most police time and energy and took away from more critical crime control efforts. An analysis of arrest statistics shows that liquor consumption and related behavior was behind 60 to 70 percent or more of all arrests, and at least as many warnings to "move on," "shut up," and "go home" and instances of police surveillance can be assumed. At the same time, workers criticized the police for harassing peaceful drinkers on their way home, for molesting saloonkeepers, and for enforcing antiliquor laws against workers while allowing wealthier people to drink privately or in clubs well protected from police surveillance.

The police were much easier on saloonkeepers than on working-class drinkers. Violations of late hours and Sunday hours, illegal rooms, and unlicensed bars were probably easy for officers on the beat to discover. Though some offenders were closed, others operated with impunity for years. This paradox suggests that saloonkeepers were well integrated into the political life of cities as respected small businessmen, politicians, and power brokers. Moreover, on a day-to-day basis they enjoyed a mutually beneficial relationship with police officers, treating them to free lunches, drinks, and information in return for favors and "looking the other way" occasionally. This was true even when the officers were not directly bribed.

Behind this cat-and-mouse game was the intense social conflict over liquor. The temperance movement united a variety of reformist objectives, fears, and prejudices into a program with a decided antiurban and anti-working-class bias. Although prohibition later attracted support among Scandinavian and British workers, in the cities the temperance movement's leaders were most often Protestant clergymen and manufacturers. The petty-bourgeois reformers who constituted the core of the movement feared the working class and saw liquor control as one means of stabilizing and Americanizing dangerous immigrant communities. Liquor, they believed, inflamed radical tendencies, dissipated limited wages, and undermined the solid socializing influences of the family, church, and work.[9]

Workers usually devoted most of their political energies to organizational priorities, such as union building, strikes over higher wages, and control of the work process. Only on the eve of the First World War did it become obvious that the neighborhood saloon was in trouble. Hence, early battles over licensing and hours seldom involved the participation of the working class. Moreover, the issue caused a split within the working class between older immigrant groups, who often boosted temperance societies to improve the workingman's lot, and newer immigrants.[10]

The liquor interests waged their own battle, financed by the substantial proceeds of their business. Liquor represented 8.5 percent of the total value of all manufacturer products of Chicago in the 1890s. In 1894 alone, Chicago saloons took in about $70 million and paid 10 percent of the city's operating costs through high license fees—a powerful weapon for influencing municipal matters.[11] Although the issue was the "liquor question," it was really the saloon that came to symbolize the enemy. Responding to the charge that the saloon dissipated the earnings of workers, fostered crime, illicit sex, and the breakdown of family life, corrupted youth, promoted disease, laziness, and municipal corruption, and encouraged political radicalism and strikes, saloonkeepers presented their establishments as strongholds of working-class virtue—the "workingman's clubhouse."[12]

The attraction of the saloon for workingmen is not difficult to estimate; even the Anti-Saloon League in its report, *Substitutes for the Saloon,* described the saloon in highly positive terms. Establishments ranged from filthy low dives to huge rooms decorated with mirrors and chandeliers and filled with ornate furnishings. Most were somewhere in between—furnished with a long bar where drinkers stood and with tables and chairs against the back or side wall. Some free food was often present, especially in the Midwest and West; Chicago's saloons were famous for their free lunches. Crowded working-class housing alone would explain full saloons: where families occupied only one or two rooms, most social activity had to occur outside of the home. Yet there was a social function beyond the simple necessity of space. Whole shops of workers adjourned to saloons after work, and often at lunch as well. They discussed work, politics, sports, and family life, played cards, perhaps placed a bet or two, and drank beer and whiskey.[13]

The saloon performed solid utilitarian functions as well. Saloonkeepers cashed checks and made loans to many workers. One coal shipper reported that among his 240-man work force in two cities, 100 percent of his Polish and Hungarian workers in Milwaukee cashed their checks in saloons, as did 77 percent of them in Chicago. For Germans among his work force the proportion was 70 percent in Chicago and 64 percent in Milwaukee; for English and American workers, 61 percent in Chicago and 35 percent in Milwaukee; for Scotch and Irish workers, 74 percent in Chicago and 35 percent in Milwaukee. Saloonkeepers' loans doubtlessly fed many working-class families until payday.[14] The saloon also served as a post office where itinerant workers could collect mail sent in care of the saloonkeeper, who was also a source of information on where to look for work, where to get a bed, and who to see for help. Politically, saloons served as offices and meeting halls for unions, ethnic societies, and work-ing-class cultural organizations. Local politicians and ward orga-nizers used them as headquarters for turning out the vote and brokering political favors.

Given the large number of neighborhood saloons and their so-cial importance to workers' communities, it is not difficult to understand the prominence of saloonkeepers in local politics. One-third of Milwaukee's 46 city councilmen in 1902 were sa-loonkeepers. Bourgeois reformers cited this as evidence of the political corruption of the working class, but the role of the sa-loonkeepers was far more complex. John J. Brennan, alderman of Chicago's West Side Eighteenth Ward from 1891 to 1913, is a case in point. His saloon was adjacent to a police station, and in his secondary role as bail bondsman he saved many workers from nights in jail. He won elections partly by providing free food and lodging to many in his district. According to Raymond Robins, director of the Municipal Lodging House:

> John Brennan comes nearer to living up to the teachings of the scripture than a great many who make greater pretentions to morali-ty. He controls the people of his ward, not because he is base and corrupt, but because he is simple and democratic. He has saved more people from eviction, given more food to hungry men and sent more people to the hospital and kept them there than perhaps any other man in Chicago.[15]

On the other hand, a wide range of criminal activity revolved around saloons. Many low dives fronted for organized gambling and prostitution. Others offered hangouts for criminal gangs and headquarters for criminal enterprises. Saloonkeepers were regu-larly arrested on a variety of charges, including robbing their drunken customers, encouraging drunken customers to write checks for loans, and serving liquor to minors.[16]

These contradictory images simply illustrate that the saloon controversy reflects both the class structure of urban society and the class conflict. Every urban class had its places of recrea-tion, including its saloons. As a service industry in a relatively free market, saloons offered whatever features their particular segment of the market was willing to pay for. Hence, the saloon could stand for solidarity, brotherhood, sharing, and all great working-class virtues, while at the same time it represented all that was evil in urban life.

In analyzing working-class drinking and the policing of working-class saloons, I shall concentrate on the antisaloon movement and the law enforcement patterns it advocated as an anti-working-class effort. Any notion of value-free law enforcement is impossible in the face of a strong bourgeois and petty-bourgeois movement aimed at smashing the saloon and punishing working-class liquor-related behavior. Even if police enforcement of the law in some situations might be regarded as neutral, no individual act of law enforcement can be understood outside of its social context.

For purposes of this discussion, I shall focus on the cities of Milwaukee and Chicago. During the prohibition era Milwaukee's notorious toleration of drinking earned it the label "the most orderly city in America—in every respect except one."[17] Earlier, drinking had been related to the city's reputation as an open town for gambling and prostitution, but this relationship was severed by the Social Democrats when they rode to victory in 1910, pledging to defend the saloon and to end gambling and vice. Chicago, though also tolerant of drinking, witnessed some of the nation's sharpest struggles against the saloon. On one side was a large and well-financed middle-class and bourgeois coalition out to destroy the saloon as an urban institution. On the other side was a perhaps equally well-financed, but much looser, alliance between the liquor dealers and manufacturers and the workers who frequented saloons.[18]

Although Milwaukee easily had more saloons per capita than Chicago, Chicago acquired a national reputation as a corrupt city where the saloon was king. Where the Milwaukee saloon stood for the hard-drinking but hard-working German tradition, the Chicago saloon stood for vice, crime, and political corruption. From the 1890s onward, Chicago's more than 7,000 saloons faced a serious challenge from reformers who aimed at nothing less than the complete abolition of the saloon. Moreover, Chicago's importance as a national center meant that the struggle in Chicago had national impact. Chicago's graft and corruption were famous nationwide, and Chicago was held up as one (if not the major) example of saloon government run wild. The city's police force was perhaps equally famous for its support for saloon government and everything it stood for, but the police performed similar roles in both Milwaukee and Chicago, which in itself tells us much about the role of the municipal police during this period.

The impact of the struggle over the saloon on the police institution can be seen in a number of areas. Most directly, some proportion of police expansion after the 1880s was financed by new license fees for saloons, the so-called high license. Municipal finances were fragile, and police expansion had to be accomplished without substantially increasing the tax burden, especially on the local bourgeoisie and their petty-bourgeois allies. The link between the need for revenue for increased police protection and the desire to restrict liquor consumption was self-evident. If the saloon was responsible for rising crime, violence, and public disorder, then a substantial increase in the license fee could achieve two objectives: it could provide additional revenue for police expenditures while at the same time it could potentially decrease liquor consumption by driving the less profitable working-class saloons out of business and by increasing the cost of each drink.[19]

Enthusiasm for the high-license idea swept the nation in the 1880s. Illinois's Harper High-License Act of 1883 raised the annual license fee for a Chicago saloon from $50 to $500. Fees in Milwaukee increased threefold. In addition to being a simple revenue measure, the reformers argued, these increases would sharply reduce the number of saloons, especially the low dives that propped up their weak business with gambling and vice. Although the actual number of saloons may have dropped somewhat, breweries nullified the social impact of this legislation by purchasing licenses and setting up saloonkeepers, usually for about $50 in front money. Moreover, gambling and prostitution thrived as means of augmenting saloon income to meet the new license fees. In addition, perhaps 5 percent of the saloonkeepers in Chicago continued to be involved in more serious forms of felony crime.[20]

The 1884 election in Milwaukee was dominated by the high-license issue. The Republican bosses nominated Emil Walber, a lawyer of German descent, to split the vote of the traditionally hard-drinking German community and to pre-empt the possibility of a third-party high-license ticket. Walber deliberately equivocated on the issue. Saloonkeepers drew up their own platform advocating equal taxation, better compensation for labor, low license fees, and "city government controlled by the people and not the monopolists." S. Y. Cameron, a representative of the saloonkeepers' association, tried to engage trade-union support for this platform, but trade unionists feared the domination of the saloonkeepers. Workers, however, were not unsympathetic to low license. Knights of Labor organizer Robert Schilling believed that "high license would rob poor women of their livelihood," and he blamed "the gilded saloon as the source of mischief." Milwaukee organized labor took the position that poverty was caused by the unequal distribution of wealth, not drunkenness.[21]

Mayor Walber was unable to push a high-license bill through the city council before the state legislature, as in Illinois, raised the minimum fee from $75 to $200; it also permitted a $500 maximum by local referendum. The Republican *Milwaukee Sentinel* favored the $500 maximum because, it argued, saloons were a "dangerous political influence within the community." Furthermore, the paper editorialized, "the prisons and police should be supported by those who enjoy the pleasure of drinking." Walber took a similar position in his annual message to the city council.[22]

The sharp class opposition to the high-license referendum held in Milwaukee in September 1885, which proposed to raise the license fee from $200 to $500, clearly surprised the city's ruling class. Workers hung "high license" in effigy, and saloonkeepers turned out wagons to haul voters to the polls; but contemporary charges of massive voter intimidation and vote fraud are irrelevant in view of the three-to-one margin against the bill.

High license lost every ward in the city except "Yankee Hill," the best residential district. Whole precincts in the Polish and German wards produced not one vote in favor of high license. Milwaukee workers had risen solidly in defense of the saloon, and bonfires were kindled in celebration of their victory.[23]

Chicago's working class was never allowed an opportunity to defeat high license in a local referendum. The Illinois state legislature passed the high-license statute of 1883 without the local option clause found in Wisconsin. Overnight each saloon's overhead increased by roughly the equivalent of a worker's annual salary, putting a heavy burden on small saloonkeepers without appreciably reducing liquor consumption—and certainly without reducing crime and public disorder.[24] In 1903 and again in 1906, however, petty-bourgeois and bourgeois demands for stronger police protection and their fear of saloons, dance halls, theaters, and other places of working-class amusement resulted in a prolonged high-license fight in Chicago. The saloon question was directly linked to a crime wave, and high license was intended specifically to finance a 1,000-man increase in the police force, new stations, and a 100-man mounted patrol.

Chicago's 1903 high-license fight was set off by charges that a crime wave had followed the important streetcar strike in November. Though there was some clamor for higher license fees, the Chicago council moved toward increased regulation instead, achieving social control objectives without the hated high license. A new saloon ordinance was proposed to transfer the power of license revocation from the council to the mayor. Licenses of low dives could then be immediately withdrawn upon the recommendation of the police. "If the police did their duty," commented Alderman Hunter, "the mayor would be given information which would result in the revocation of about 300 saloon licenses every year." The saloonkeepers responded by pointing out that to give more licensing power to the mayor was simply to offer him more political power, and they feared that revocations would be based on political dislikes, without due process.[25]

A second provision of the saloon reform bill, a measure to outlaw "can rushing," met with a much more emotional response. Can rushing, the practice of sending out a child with a quart "can"—a bucket with a lid—to a local saloon to bring beer home, was as traditional in working-class communities as it was illegal. Illinois and Wisconsin state law formally banned the practice, but the law was not enforced in Chicago or Milwaukee. Reformers in both cities tried to abolish the practice formally via local ordinances. Chicago's attempt in 1903 provoked a stirring defense from former Alderman Rhode: "I went for beer for my father. When a man's a boy he gets beer for his father, and when his boy grows up the boy gets beer for him." M. R. Harris, attorney for the liquor dealers, argued:

> A boy with a can saves money for the family. If the boy didn't go to the saloon for beer the man would go. He would meet other men and be subjected to the great American temptation of treating. He would spend 50 cents or $1. The family needs this money and the boy with a can saves it.[26]

A further measure would have required each saloon to lock its doors at midnight, throw up the shades, and leave the lights on all night—an attempt to enforce the midnight closing laws, commonly evaded by darkening doors and windows and perhaps locking the front door, but keeping a side door open. Saloonkeepers countered that they would become easy targets for bandits.[27]

While these measures were tied up in city council, the Chicago police issued a regulation confining saloons to one room only and ordered all tables and chairs removed from side rooms and the rooms closed to the public. This measure affected both saloons evading closing hours, a practice obviously easier in back rooms, and saloons offering "wine rooms," rooms in back where liquor was served to mixed couples in relative privacy. The police department's motive was suspect, however, because some wine rooms had been recently closed under a "wine room ordinance," and some City Hall politicians argued that the police were protecting their friends in the wine room business by knocking out downtown competition.[28]

The struggle of 1903 far from decided the issue. Increased regulation was not enough: somehow the burden of that regulation had to be passed on to the working class. In 1906, after the brutal rape-murder of Mrs. Franklin Hollister while on a late-morning shopping trip near her fashionable Fullerton Avenue home, a well-organized campaign was mounted for the high license. Three distinct groups can be identified behind the movement: the Board of Trade and Chamber of Commerce, representing the business community; the Chicago Federation of Women's Clubs, representing the wives of the businessmen in the first group; and the Protestant clergy, always behind antiliquor initiatives. They directed their main effort at Mayor Dunne and the city council, demanding that the council double the $500 license fee for the city's 8,000 saloons. It was claimed that the measure would produce a revenue increase of about $2 million and reduce the number of saloons by perhaps 25 percent.[29]

The *Chicago Tribune* made the campaign front-page news for six weeks, in which time the measure went to the city council twice. The coverage included running accounts of daily attacks on women (mostly street robberies), activities in dance halls and saloons on Friday and Saturday nights, arrests of saloon keepers, and police efforts to regulate saloons and dance halls. Front-page cartoons emphasized the need for all citizens to combat the saloon, and the mayor and chief of police were repeatedly criticized.[30]

The first month of this effort led to a tense debate in the city council, which then voted 35 to 32 in favor of high license, one short of the 36 votes necessary to pass the ordinance. The debate illustrates the sharp class divisions in the city. Alderman Kunz addressed the crime issue by arguing that druggists, not saloonkeepers, were behind the cocaine trade that so incensed the *Tribune* and that saloons had nothing to do with the crimes of respectable people. Finally, Kunz hit the class issue directly:

> Now this high license proposition is aimed not at the brewer or the saloonkeeper, but at the poor laboring man who toils ten and twelve hours a day. He is the man who can't pay five cents for a glass of

beer. He sends out and gets a pint for five cents. That's six glasses, enough for a whole family. It's different with the swells, who can afford to keep wine in their cellars, or to belong to clubs which are open all night.[31]

He further argued that saloonkeepers were disproportionately the victims of crime and that they did not get the police protection they paid for.

Alderman Wendling offered a petition:

> I have a petition here from 4,800 workingmen from the strongest workingmen's ward in the city. It asks you not to raise the saloon license to $1,000. Down in my ward the laborer gets $4.50 a week and supports a large family. He gets a little piece of bread and 5 cents worth of beer at the noon hour. He gets a pint for 5 cents. Raise this license and you will wipe out the small saloons and the poor man can buy pints of beer no more.
>
> . . . Now here is a picture in *The Tribune* of a row of saloons—a solid block in Ashland Avenue. It's true all right. But the photographer forgot to take a picture of the row of packinghouses right behind these saloons. Thousands of men pour out of these packinghouses at noon and go into these saloons where they get beer and lunch for 10 cents. There are not too many saloons there for such a crowd. High license may be all right for the rich but not for the poor. The poor have no liquor in their cellars.[32]

Alderman Martin prophetically warned that automobiles were responsible for more deaths than were holdups and suggested taxing automobiles instead of saloons to pay for increased police protection. He further argued that 200 saloons in his ward had been driven out of business by high license in 1883.[33]

The marginal economics of the saloon business became an important issue. Aldermen defending the saloon argued that most establishments produced a profit of only $300 to $500 per year for their owners, who were often the sole employees. Obviously, a $500 license increase would force a sharp rise in the price of a drink. When the antisaloon forces pointed out that three-quarters of the 8,000 saloon licenses were held by 42 breweries and the rest by individuals, the saloon industry responded that the breweries were only acting as agents in buying the licenses and were reimbursed by beer sales, leaving the proprietor responsible for the profit or loss of the business. The *Tribune* maintained that the additional license fee would add only marginally to the costs of operating a saloon and could easily be absorbed in the business of most places. To the liquor industry's claim that high license would drive more saloonkeepers into illegal activities like gambling and prostitution to pay for the license, the antisaloon lobby responded that saloons were dens of vice and corruption already.[34]

Five thousand saloonmen crowded into the council chambers to witness the vote on high license and to cheer on aldermen representing their position. Representatives of numerous churches, womens' clubs, and civic organizations also attended, as did a force of 25 policemen under Captain Gibbons. Joseph Graff, a carpenter, was arrested for disorderly conduct when he, at the head of a large crowd, demanded admission to the closed chambers. The measure's narrow failure sparked a long celebration.[35]

However, the antisaloon forces soon organized a letter-writing campaign aimed at several borderline aldermen, and the measure was again scheduled for committee hearings. The prosaloon forces wavered, possibly afraid of stronger antisaloon actions if they resisted an anticrime measure. The large breweries, particularly Pabst and Schlitz (both based in Milwaukee but doing a huge business in Chicago) only weakly and symbolically supported the small brewers, evidently preferring not to line up against "law and order." Even the small brewers began to talk of a compromise $750 license. Mayor Dunne, who had only weakly supported the measure, seemed to sense that the winds were changing and announced that he immediately needed high license to put 1,000 policemen on the beat, literally the day after the measure passed. The antisaloon forces, encouraged by their need for only one vote, pushed relentlessly, while the *Tribune* increased its anticrime and antisaloon propaganda. When the measure came up three weeks later, it passed 40 to 28.[36]

The political power of the antisaloon forces, when combined

with the powerful social issue of the saloon-caused "crime wave," was enough to carry Chicago for the high license. But this struggle cannot be narrowly understood as a revenue measure. As the saloon forces pointed out, the city needed only just over $1 million for the projected increase in the police force—which worked out to an additional fee of about $125 per saloon, to which the saloonkeepers would have acceded.[37] A strong sector of the city council still resisted both the crime wave argument and the assumptions behind that argument—namely, that working-class people had weak characters and were easily misled into crime and dissipation.

Between March 1905 and June 1906 a weak attempt to raise the Milwaukee license fee from $200 to $350 or $500 was made in conjunction with an effort to deny licenses altogether to the city's worst saloons, usually defined as those that openly permitted prostitution but also including others with significant citizen complaints. The resolution was introduced by City Council President Meisenheimer at the request of attorney Charles Faber, who had polled only a few votes in his campaign for mayor on a high-license platform.[38] Faber had likewise failed to persuade the council to approve a special election on the license issue. At the council hearing, Faber's testimony revealed his financial considerations, which were coupled with a desire to reduce the number of saloons and enforce his notions of public morality:

> Saloon licenses cost $1,000 a year in most of the large cities of the country, and $500 in the second class cities of Wisconsin. Milwaukee now receives from 2,100 saloons $420,000 a year, but with an increase to $1,050,000 a year we could wholly maintain our fire department or pave Grand Avenue and keep all streets well. . . .
>
> The cheaper kind of saloons, and the ones which do most harm to public morality, are those in the residence districts. . . . What morality is learned in ladies' entrances and cheap dance halls. There is one saloon to every 145 inhabitants of Milwaukee. . . . [39]

Joseph Ulhlein, president of the Schlitz Brewing Company, made the case for the saloon:

There is no doubt that the number of smaller saloons in the suburbs which would be compelled to go out of business would be great. And this is where one of the great wrongs would be done. To the poorer classes in the outskirts the beer is food and is purchased regularly twice each day. If the license is raised these small saloons would be compelled to go out of business, leaving the people without their beverage. The poorer and, I might say, evil class of saloons downtown would still flourish.

In a similar statement Charles Henning, vice-president of the Pabst brewery, demanded that the matter be submitted to popular referendum, confident that it would be defeated.[40]

The measure was not referred out of the council committee, for it was obvious that it enjoyed little support in heavily German Milwaukee. The committee adopted an alternative control measure, however, in the form of the "blacklist." This method required the chief of police to prepare a list of saloons that, in his judgment, systematically violated saloon laws. The owners of those saloons then had the right to appear before the council to protest their inclusion on the blacklist. Chief Janssen focused mainly, he explained, on owners who kept rooms in the back or upstairs and received a commission on drinks sold there. Twenty-five establishments appeared on the first list.[41]

The measure provoked hot debate in the council, primarily on the question of the criteria used by the chief. Many councilmen insisted that equally bad dives had been left off the list, and there were accusations that the police were protecting some places. Some saloonkeepers protested that the charges were false. Aldermen Seidel prepared his own list of 17 saloons and demanded that the council add them to the chief's list. Furthermore, Seidel wanted to know why those on his list did not appear on the original Janssen list. In the end, the council sustained Janssen's judgment by denying licenses to the 25 establishments (one additional license was revoked for purely political reasons), and by 1910 the list had grown to 103 saloons. The department, however, invariably left a large number of equally bad dives in operation, and the blacklist issue always brought into question the honesty of Chief Janssen and was central to the police corruption charge in Milwaukee.[42] For better or for worse the impetus of the anti-saloon drive and the burden of enforcing liquor laws was being transferred from city councils to police departments, with all parties fully expecting (though perhaps not approving) the police to use extreme discretion and to enforce liquor laws selectively. In the process they would perhaps make it tougher for the worst dives and perhaps even reduce the number of saloons marginally.

How did the urban police enforce liquor laws? Since all authorities agree on the laxness of enforcement, the real issue is the social meaning of lax enforcement patterns. So much debate about the police and about saloon law enforcement occurred in Chicago that we can construct a good picture of these practices. There can be no question that patrolmen, reflecting official department policy, took no interest in the routine violation of most regulations by ordinary saloons on their beats. Regulations universally ignored included the midnight (later, 1 A.M.) closing law, the Sunday closing law, the serving of older-looking minors (remember that children aged 13 to 18 were often in the labor force), and loud and "riotous" behavior within loose bounds. Except where there were a large number of complaints or where the violations of a particular saloon stood out, officers needed no bribes to overlook such behavior.

Two factors account for this systematic negligence. First, police administrators almost universally agreed that they could not control such behavior in the face of other pressing police problems. Frequently the implication was that "blue laws" were appropriate to a Puritan society but not to a modern urban setting, a view expressed by Chicago's Superintendent Collins during the high-license fight.[43] Second, officers on the beat depended on saloons for information, rest and recreation, shelter—and a few dollars now and then. Police administrators fought hard to control officer relationships with saloons. Since an officer's duty was bound to take him into saloons, the Chicago department's regulations included a prohibition against drinking on duty (often violated) and one against remaining more than 20 minutes inside a saloon.[44]

Major investigations of the Chicago police undertaken in 1898 and in 1904 agree that the department was virtually undisciplined and that many officers were drinking on duty, customarily enjoying free drinks in the saloons on their beats. Captain August Piper, in his investigation of the Chicago police in 1904, listed innumerable incidents of policemen in saloons:

> We walked up the street and found a man of the First precinct at 3 o'clock. . . . He left the south crossing of Van Buren Street and Fifth Avenue where he was on duty, and was found standing at the bar of the saloon on the corner of Van Buren Street and Fifth Avenue, drinking with a citizen. At 3:10 P.M. we saw No. C standing at the bar drinking in the saloon at 86 Sherman Street. . . . At 4:20 P.M. No. F was in the saloon at the southwest corner of Harrison and State Streets. At 5:05 P.M. we found Officer No. I absent from his post, standing at the bar in a saloon on the northeast corner of Wabash Avenue and Fourteenth Street; he went there immediately after pulling the box.

In the Second Precinct that same afternoon, Piper found 15 more patrolmen in saloons and others loitering in restaurants, drugstores, and other places—27 derelictions of duty in all.[45]

Piper asked police supervisors about the practice and was informed that "it would be a poor policeman who would not go into a saloon occasionally, for by going there he can become friendly with the saloonkeeper and obtain information about criminals that he could not get elsewhere." Of 108 cases of patrolmen loitering in some building, 68 involved saloons. Piper asked:

> Who gets the benefit of the loafing in the saloons? The public whom the officer is paid to protect or the saloonkeeper? The officer accepts his beer, whiskey, and cigar, and his hospitality generally, and do you suppose the cop will strictly enforce the 1 o'clock closing ordinance and will keep minors from making purchases and will generally enforce the laws in accordance with his oath where it affects the saloonkeeper, and will the saloonkeeper do his duty as a citizen and drive the cop out on the street where he belongs? Can you rely on a patrolman who is constantly visiting saloons and drinking?

The newspapers obviously agreed with Piper. They regularly carried reports of drunken police officers engaging in misconduct—beatings, shootings, and spectacular errors—that brought great discredit on the force.[46]

For all the revelations of the Piper report, including the reprinting of the names and charges against 85 police officers in the *Tribune*, the findings had little impact on the force. Mayor Harrison and Chief O'Neil announced an immediate drive to improve discipline, but the City Club of Chicago, the bourgeois reform organization that had sponsored Piper's work, announced that Piper would not be available to testify against individual officers:

> The directors are of the opinion that the prosecution of the charges suggested might tend to divert attention from the real purpose of the City Club, which was the investigation and improvement of the discipline and administration of the police department as a branch of our municipal government and not the discovery and punishment of specific derelictions of duty by individual patrolmen. . . .
>
> . . . If such offenses persist, under efficient administration and proper discipline, they can easily be detected and punished.[47]

The department took some disciplinary actions against individual officers, but there is no evidence that the behavior of the force improved overall.

What seems clear is that most officers were permitted to drink on duty within commonly understood limits but that being too drunk, being seen drunk too often, or neglecting other patrol duties led to charges. In a society where large segments of the urban population routinely drank, a few beers or a little whiskey on duty was not taken all that seriously. However, since the effects of excessive consumption of alcohol completely undermined an officer's ability to function, and since alcohol consumption was such a problem, departments still regularly disciplined drinkers. It should also be noted that such action could rid the department of men that a captain or other administrator wanted off the force for other reasons, including political ones, although evidence of this type of action is difficult to locate.

Fig. 1

Chicago Tribune, March 21, 1904

What effect did police misconduct have on public order arrest rates? Chicago police made many more such arrests than did Milwaukee police—40,000 to 50,000 a year between 1900 and 1910, more than three times the Milwaukee rate. Most of these were for an offense simply called "disorderly," which in Chicago was a catchall offense that included both public drunkenness and disorderly conduct. We know little about those arrested except that they were working-class, immigrant, and male. But it is obvious that they were outside the political protection networks afforded most saloonkeepers. Between 1901 and 1908 the Chicago police arrested 324,239 workers for the offense of disorderly alone. Put in larger terms, the arrest of more than a million "disorderlies" in Chicago between 1890 and 1915 surely had a major impact on the public life of the city's working class, particularly on unskilled, immigrant workers.[48]

How does this high arrest rate correlate with the close relationship between the saloons and the machine politicians who controlled much police behavior, and with the close relationships between saloonkeepers and patrolmen on the beat? An *International Socialist Review* editorial in 1913 offers one interpretation. Calling the existing police system ineffective and a "constant menace to the lives of a large portion of the working class," the writer pointed out that most arrests were for drunkenness, with fines of $1 to $100 often worked off at 50 cents a day. Furthermore, police enforcement practices were highly discriminatory:

> The average policeman in the exercise of his discretion is careful not to arrest any one with money or a "pull", and saloonkeepers exercise their "pull" in behalf of regular customers, so that the ordinance fails of accomplishing its normal purpose of suppressing drunkenness in public. But the unfortunate with no money and no "pull" after the perilous night in the police station, is confronted with a jail sentence for lack of money to pay his fine. If he has a wife and children, they are dependent on public or private charity until he has served his time and found a new job.[49]

Thus, the patrolman's arrest power was in effect a commodity to be traded to saloonkeepers.

We have seen that the police departments in Milwaukee, Chicago, and other cities spent a great deal of effort disciplining working-class recreation. The 60 to 70 percent of all urban arrests that were liquor-related were aimed disproportionately at the lowest paid, most heavily immigrant portions of the male working class. The best way to understand these arrests is to see them as having nothing to do with liquor control. Rather, they related to the general police function of regulating the urban class structure.

Milwaukee police, for example, made few arrests for violations of liquor license ordinances (27 in 1899 and 37 in 1900, out of more than 2,000 saloons), but they arrested many workers for liquor-related offenses. In 1900, a typical year, drunkenness and disorderly conduct together accounted for about 60 percent of all arrests—3,295 out of 5,266—while assault and battery, vagrancy, and miscellaneous arrests (most for violations of city ordinances of various sorts) accounted for another 1,356 arrests— together more than 80 percent of the total. We know from occupational statistics that virtually all of those arrested were workers, mostly laborers.[50]

Some measure of the seriousness of these petty arrests in Milwaukee can be seen in the financial havoc they caused among working-class families. Although these offenses were most often punished by small fines—$5, $10, $25 (workingmen's wages averaged about $500 a year in the 1890s)—fully 50 percent of those fined could not pay and were sent to jail to work them off, often at rates of $1 a day or less. Since friends and families often pooled funds to pay fines, these data show how close to the margin of survival entire communities lived. Thus a petty drunk arrest cost a Milwaukee worker at least a week's pay—if he was lucky enough to have access to that kind of money. Otherwise it could cost him from a week to a month in jail.[51]

Still, Milwaukee workers were better off than workers in comparable cities in one respect: fewer of them were arrested for public order crimes. Milwaukee had only about one-third as many public order arrests per capita as did Chicago, Pittsburgh, Buffalo, and other cities in the region, even though Milwaukee was an unusually hard-drinking city, ranking sixth in the nation in number of saloons and clubs (2,134) in 1905, though thirteenth in population. Milwaukee probably had stronger local support for drink than any city of comparable size in America. Even local temperance forces focused on "moderation" and opposed "radical" efforts to bring about prohibition. German cultural traditions alone do not account for this tolerance of liquor and saloons: Cincinnati, St. Louis, and Buffalo, also heavily German, had high public order arrest rates. Rather, it seems that Milwaukee's well-organized working-class political forces made it politically inexpedient for the police to emphasize public order arrests, in spite of a high degree of police independence from local political control and a certain police inclination to enforce public order laws rigidly against working-class recreational activities.[52]

A second factor contributing to Milwaukee's low public order arrest rate was a lower ratio of police officers per thousand population than found in most other cities of comparable size. On the average, Milwaukee employed only 60 percent as many officers as other large cities. Since public order arrests depend entirely on police presence and discretion, fewer police necessarily means fewer arrests. And it should be remembered that this smaller police force was a product of the same strong working-class political movement that defended the saloon.[53]

THE LIQUOR QUESTION IN PITTSBURGH, CLEVELAND, AND TOLEDO

Pittsburgh, Allegheny City, and the company towns in the iron and steel district of Pennsylvania saw a direct and well-planned attempt to use the police institution to control the saloon and to socialize the hard-drinking behavior of "Huns" (Hungarians) and other Eastern European steelworkers. Industrialists in the Pittsburgh region, through a Republican, business-dominated political machine and in alliance with middle-class reformers, had kept the number of saloon licenses small. Only about 250 legal saloons operated in Pittsburgh in the 1890s, fewer than in any other large city in the nation. The result was a large number of illegal sellers of liquor to workers, particularly in new immigrant communities.[54] In the late 1880s and early 1890s the newly reformed and restructured police forces of Pittsburgh and Allegheny City aimed a concerted attack on these illegal liquor sales and on the workers' communities where the sellers thrived. This double purpose can be seen quite clearly in the first annual report of Superintendent Henry Muth of Allegheny City:

> I found, according to your orders given me, that there was a vast amount of illegal liquor selling in our midst, commonly called "Speak Easies," and I wish to call your attention especially to the Hungarian element, or Huns, in our community. They have given the Bureau more annoyance than any other class of people: they are very ignorant and stupid, most filthy in person and habits; having less regard for our laws than any other class; and in proportion of their numbers have caused us more trouble.
>
> In obedience to your command to suppress their frequent disorders and disturbances in the community, where often as high as twenty of them were found living in a small house of one or two rooms, in a most degraded condition, on several occasions I have raided a number of them, and they were brought before the Mayor and fined; sometimes as high as twenty in one room, where we found them in a drunken carousal which had been going on for some time, including the Sabbath Day.
>
> The results of these raids have no doubt convinced them that they must not disturb the peace and quiet of our city, by their lawlessness; and on several occasions the fights among them nearly resulted in murder; and have given our officers a great amount of trouble in bringing the participants to justice. My observation leads me to the conclusion that you must deal severely with them before they begin to realize that our laws must be obeyed.[55]

Allegheny City matched Pittsburgh in its lopsided arrest statistics for public order offenses. In 1892 Muth's 113-man force made 3,730 arrests: 1,911 for disorderly conduct, 956 for drunkenness, and 170 for vagrancy—more than 3,000 public order arrests. Of those arrested, 1,637 paid fines, 658 went to jail, 328 were assigned to the workhouse, 17 were sent to reform school, and 77 were bound over for felony trial. Workers accounted for virtually all of the arrests, including 1,819 common laborers. Hungarians constituted only 235 of those arrested, a high proportion probably, based on their population, but a small number when compared to the 2,413 native-born Americans who were arrested.[56]

The scene was the same across the river in Pittsburgh. Inspector William McKelvey of the Third District, the factory region on the south side of the Monongahela River, echoed Muth:

> The record is a good one, considering the class of people in this part of the city. Besides having many good citizens of the American, German, Irish, English and other nationalities, we have a large number of the worst classes from the lower European states, who if their propensities to vice remained unchecked, would commit all the crimes in the calendar without a quiver of conscience. Vigilance and prompt action is required to curb the passions of these people, and a great portion of the smaller offenses are perpetrated by them.[57]

Inspector Henry Whitehouse of the Second District took the same position:

> I have . . . a large proportion of the middle, the working and the lower class of laborers to watch over. It is hardly necessary to say that the ordinary routine police work of the district, in so far as the preservation of peace and good order is concerned, is confined very largely to the necessary government of the latter class of people in that particular community. . . . Sometime ago the practice was common among certain classes of working men of the lower sections of the city to use the outlying wards for places of resort for the indiscriminate drinking of beer and liquors. These gatherings were productive of disorder, and they were immediately attacked by the police. . . .[58]

In 1890 the Pittsburgh patrol service made 17,508 arrests, including 6,961 for disorderly conduct, 5,905 for drunkenness, 1,124 for vagrancy, 1,226 for suspicious persons (a vagrancy-type catchall for people who could not account for themselves), and 1,391 for "miscellaneous." Of those arrested, magistrates fined 7,174 and committed 3,145 to jail and 2,760 to the work-house. Twenty-seven were sent to reform school, and 152 were bound over for felony trial. The rest were discharged, usually after a night in jail. The New York Bureau of Municipal Re-search, in a 1913 investigation of the Pittsburgh Police Depart-ment, found that more than 41 percent of all arrests for the years 1909, 1910, and 1912 were for drunkenness, suggesting that "ei-ther the policemen were making a great number of unnecessary arrests or that the city of Pittsburgh has an inebriety problem to solve."[59]

The Flinn-McGee Republican machine controlled Pittsburgh. Thirty-six percent of its leaders appeared in the city's blue book, and its two leaders were millionaire businessmen, Flinn in con-struction and McGee in street railroads. Their program was cal-culated to appeal to the city's rich and middle-class citizens, but it won working-class votes as well with city jobs and other con-cessions. Police repression of working-class recreational activi-ties was directed by Public Safety Director J. O. Brown, one of the machine's top men. A "Puritan" by reputation, Brown lim-ited liquor licenses, and his force raided speakeasies and made more prostitution arrests than any department in the Great Lakes/Ohio Valley region. At the same time, however, gambling and prostitution continued under police protection in many parts of the city.[60]

The events in Pittsburgh and Allegheny City were repeated against Slavic and Hungarian workers in mill towns across Penn-sylvania. In Steelton, "Hungarian wedding celebrations," in-volving prolonged drinking and merrymaking by these "so-called Americans," were bitterly attacked, and city councilmen demanded protection from the "disorderly conduct of the for-eigners." In 1901 the town council there "empowered the Burgess to swear in special officers to aid the constables on Saturdays and Sundays when the behavior of Hungarians was dangerous and unsafe." Sundays were a special occasion for workers who had put in six days in the mills, and they celebrated: "The Hun-garians on Hun row were again in a turbulent state on Saturday night," a Steelton editor lamented. A report of a raid on a

Steelton speakeasy doubtlessly describes thousands of similar occurrences:

> Twelve men were sitting around drinking beer and enjoying themselves. When the officers pounced in a general skirmish took place, but all the doors and windows were guarded. A Hun attempted to interfere with the officers and was silenced. Four quarter kegs of beer were confiscated.[61]

Assistant Superintendent Roger O'Meara of Pittsburgh claimed that speakeasies were "carried on principally by widows who have large families of children to keep, and who take chances selling liquor on Sunday that they may provide for them." O'Meara further asserted that 90 percent of his trouble "came from the liquor traffic." Police defense of the Sabbath, a major issue in Pittsburgh, had anti-working-class overtones:

> There is a standing order issued to police officers that they shall arrest all drunken men or women whom they may find travelling the streets on Sunday, and if possible to locate the place where the liquor was bought and drunk, and should they find the owners or proprietors of such houses disorderly or selling intoxicating drinks, that they shall close up the same and immediately arrest the proprietors.

Speakeasy proprietors fought back by taking more precautions: "They ply their work in a very quiet manner, either selling behind barricaded doors or have sentinels placed in the immediate neighborhood to give the signal of alarm at the approach of the officers of the law." Neighborhood support for speakeasies ensured their survival and pitted the police against entire working-class communities. Many speakeasy proprietors were simply workers who had bought large bottles of liquor, divided them up into smaller bottles, and sold them to friends and neighbors at a small profit.[62]

Recognition that it was impossible to eliminate such trade spurred attempts to create more saloons, so that the sale of liquor could at least be open and controlled. Roger O'Meara of Pittsburgh argued for an increase in the number of licensed saloons from 250 to 300 to compete with the speakeasies, but his opposition to Sunday sales would have left much of the speakeasy trade in any case. In Steelton the steel company did an about-face and sent J.V.W. Reynders, a vice-president, to persuade the city aldermen that, although the company opposed all saloons, if an additional license were granted, it should be granted to Martin Kocevar, a Slovene. Reynders suggested that the company could better control drinking if it occurred in one big saloon rather than in many illegal small places all over town. He argued that "the foreigners are socially inclined and fond of music. We believe that if we provide a place where they can rest . . . and if we safeguard them properly, the desired results will be obtained." Challenged by the antisaloon league, the Pennsylvania Steel Company restated its case: after 20 years of opposing drinking, the company now wanted to "police the habit among foreigners" so that drinking could be tempered and less dangerous to the community—and, presumably, less dangerous to the company.[63] J. O. Brown of Pittsburgh agreed; although his force tightly regulated saloons and Sunday closing, he never endorsed the prohibition movement.

Superintendent Henry Muth of Allegheny City took exactly the same view. After proudly announcing his policy of denying licenses for dances to all except "well organized societies composed of reputable citizens"—which excluded immigrant, unskilled workers—and explaining that all gambling in the city occurred in "club rooms" and that no complaints had been received, he described working-class speakeasies as

> another evil, . . . which gives great annoyance to the department. These places being the resort, as an invariable rule, where thieves, prostitutes and vagabonds congregate, they create drunkenness and the lowest type of debauchery, and into them are lured very often the young of our community. While we have suppressed many of them yet before the night is over new ones have started. I attribute their existence to the want of regular licensed houses, and whether the law which requires a large fee is the correct theory I am not prepared to say, but the fact remains they are creatures following the late license law, and the remedy, in my judgment, would be the granting of more licensed houses, distributed in different localities of our city.[64]

We know little about the reactions of immigrant workers to police repression of their recreational activities. In one incident Italian workers in Buffalo drunkenly walking home and carrying a pail of beer were accosted and arrested by two police officers. Neighborhood residents, attracted by the commotion, gathered in the streets, and when the crowd reached several hundred, it attempted to rescue them. The police officers reached an alarm box and sent in a riot call. Patrol wagons arrived and beat back the crowds, saving both the arresting officers and their collars. In Steelton, Meyer Dragovich remembered how "Serbs were kicked around by local police and magistrates." Milwaukee workers knew that the rich could have all the dances they liked without being bothered by the police.[65]

Defense of workers' recreational activities came from two major sources: the saloon and liquor interests, allied with German societies, as in Milwaukee; and the "Golden Rulers,"or "practical" middle-class and bourgeois reformers. The latter were content to leave the saloon alone, both as a means of gaining the working-class political support they needed and because they saw much greater evils in unrestricted corporate power. Samuel "Golden Rule" Jones, mayor of Toledo, exemplifies these reformers and in fact gave his nickname to the movement. One of his innovations was the police practice of taking drunks home rather than arresting them. First, however, the man's name would be entered in a Golden Rule docket so that habitual drunks could be arrested and treated as such, distinguishing them from honest workingmen who got drunk occasionally. Jones was frankly disinterested in any form of moral regulation. Saloons could not be regulated because "the only law that can be enforced is the law that the public sentiment of the community will uphold." Mayor Tom Johnson later adopted the program wholesale in Cleveland, where it was carried out by his chief of police, Fred Kohler. The results in terms of working-class arrests were astounding: in 1908 Kohler's force made 10,085 arrests, down 20,333 from the previous year's total of 30,418.[66]

Though the impetus for the Golden Rule program came from the paternalism of wealthy reformers, there is no question that they aimed for working-class support and took many of their cues from an astute reading of working-class political demands. As Kohler explained in his annual report describing his program: "A great mass of the community do not believe that anyone has a right to prescribe for their personal likes and dislikes and pleasures, especially when they are not interfering with the rights of another." Kohler went on to say that in his years on the police force he had always tried to do his duty and enforce the law, but he concluded that he had wasted valuable police energy that could have been better spent on more serious matters than enforcing public order laws.[67]

The Golden Rule policy was attacked, ironically, by a coalition of temperance supporters and saloonkeepers. Middle-class residents feared that their communities would fill up with carousing drunks. The plan provoked a sharp debate at the 1908 and 1909 meetings of the International Association of Chiefs of Police, where motions to adopt it as official IACP policy were withdrawn. But as more cities embraced it, the police chiefs finally adopted it at their 1910 meeting in Birmingham. The strength of the plan, however, lay in the class of municipal reformers who saw it as an easy solution to part of the police problem. Even when the Golden Rule was in operation, cities like Toledo and Cleveland had difficulty distinguishing between organized vice and saloons and legitimate forms of working-class recreation. In fact, the Golden Rulers were not particularly concerned about vice and never worried about separating it from innocuous working-class activities, making the latter vulnerable to the attacks of temperance reformers. Furthermore, without a foundation in the working class, the plan did not last past the influence of the municipal reformers. Kohler lost his job in a 1913 scandal involving his relationship with a married woman, and by 1915 the Golden Rule was finished in Cleveland.[68]

A summary of the saloon question as a complex issue in police history requires recognition of the distinct elements of the issue. The first involves the saloon itself as an urban location. The license issue, coupled with the tendency of saloons to attract some forms of crime, drew police attention to the saloon, but because most saloons were well protected by the political machines they served or paid bribes directly to the police, saloon-keepers were clearly greatly underrepresented in arrest statistics. Second, the customers of saloons—the workers who drank, caroused, fought, argued, and in general had a good time—were clearly the major object of police attention, but I have argued that police concern was for the most part independent of the saloon question. Working-class liquor-related activities in many cases simply offered an excuse for exercising the power of the state. Finally, the saloon represented a part of a complex power-brokering machine, perhaps best seen as a bridge between the power of corporations and commercial elites and the working class. This is true even if some reformers from those same classes failed to accept the wisdom of this alliance and bitterly fought against it. This split in the ruling class over the most appropriate tactics for the achievement of the domination of the city is certainly significant, but it confounds the issue to set up a false dichotomy between the "saloon" forces and "reform" forces that conceals the class struggle behind the issue.

CHAPTER EIGHT

The Crusade Against Dance Halls, Gambling, Spitting, and Other Recreational Behavior

DANCE HALLS

Class issues were clearly drawn in the campaign against working-class dance halls. By and large, the forces that allied themselves against the saloon found the dance halls objectionable for the same reasons: all-night carousing, they believed, led to social behavior that undermined the work ethic. In addition, they concerned themselves with the issues of sexual morality and the youth of the participants.[1] As in the case of the saloons, the police were expected to stop such evils by enforcing liquor laws, but once again the police, by experience and temperament, were not particularly concerned about drinking or sexual immorality in the dance halls.

Dance halls were almost always adjacent to saloons. Often the hall was a large room directly over the saloon, but with its own entrance. The room was plain, furnished only with a few tables and chairs and a small stage for the orchestra. The saloon sometimes directly administered the dance hall; more often, dances were conducted by clubs, fraternal associations, and labor unions, which rented the room, either on a regular basis (for example, every weekend) or occasionally for special parties. Rents were nominal, since the saloon made most of its return from the sale of liquor. No matter who sponsored the dance, it was open to all at a small admission price. Those in attendance always included more men than women and a large proportion of teenagers.

The class issues were perhaps more clearly drawn in Milwaukee than in Chicago because the Social Democratic party, though a bit "puritan" on questions of vice and immorality, rigorously defended dance halls as legitimate working-class recreation and distinguished them from the organized gambling and prostitution that it vigorously suppressed. Milwaukee in 1912 had approximately 99 dance halls—frequent openings and closings made them difficult to count—where young people drank and danced until as late as 5 A.M. Inevitably, a certain amount of sexual activity followed. The atmosphere was loud, the places were full of cigar smoke, and half-hour breaks between music encouraged heavy consumption of beer—with the women drinking as much as the men, according to one scandalized witness. An atmosphere of familiarity prevailed; men and women held hands, and there occurred other actions "indescribable," in the words of a social worker who observed such places. Reformers shook their heads in dismay over stories of working girls who would come home at 5 A.M. too drunk to go to work a few hours later.[2]

Chief Janssen's supporters introduced a bill into the city council providing for police regulation of dance halls, a midnight closing, and parental chaperones for young people under 18. Extensive public hearings were held, and the city divided on the issue along class lines. Supporting the ordinance, on the grounds of the protection of the city's youth from vice, was the usual coalition of middle-class and bourgeois reform groups: 20 civic clubs and organizations, led by the City Club, Milwaukee's bourgeois civic association; the Catholic and Lutheran religious organizations; the women's clubs; and numerous private social workers and their organizations. Attorney Walter Bender, speaking for the City Club, directly addressed the unions' assertion of class legislation:

They talk of personal liberty being taken away. Why should any man let his personal liberty stand in the way of the good to countless numbers of girls and boys. They say it is class legislation. I say it is the right kind of class legislation.

Rose Perdue, a social worker, concurred:

This is not a fight against the Germans or Poles. It is not a fight against the pleasures of the working class. All we want to do is lift the moral standards of the city. Give our working girls the liberty of a pure city, pure enjoyment, rather than this personal liberty the opposition speaks of.

Dance halls were responsible for the majority of the 300–350 illegitimate children born in Milwaukee, according to Dr. T. L. Harrington, a prominent reformer, who added: "Do you realize that where one girl thus loses her virtue, there are from ten to fifty men and boys who lose theirs." Descriptions of stall saloons emphasized innocent shop girls getting drunk, then being taken to back rooms and seduced.[3]

This denial of the class nature of the dance hall regulation was necessary in the face of a vigorous challenge to it by the trade-union movement, the city's German associations, and the saloonkeepers. A. W. Mance, representing the Allied Printing Trades council, claimed that the ordinance would deprive workingmen and women of their personal liberty and amounted to pure class legislation:

You ought not to close us at 12 o'clock. Why some of us have to work until 7, 8, or 9 o'clock delivering your groceries to you. You don't expect to go out on the boulevards and stop them there.

John Brophy of the Pressmens Union saw in the measure an attempt to deprive workingmen of their personal liberty and to give officials too much power. Henry Mance of the Federated Trades Council charged that the ordinance favored the rich and discriminated against the working class. Mance continued:

Various interfering societies composed of members who live on fine drives and boulevards and have beautiful YMCAs are favoring this ordinance. If they would spend only half the time and energy in opening up the schoolhouses and churches we would not have to go to dance halls for our recreation.

Walter Wolf of the musicians' association protested that the ordinance would effectively take the bread out of musicians' mouths by sharply curtailing their working hours. A socialist alderman predicted that the law would only drive young people to the "grassy areas" around the edge of the city, where they would get into worse trouble. Several saloonkeepers and dance hall proprietors denied that they had trouble keeping order.[4]

The bill finally passed 26 to 11 on a straight party-line vote, with all 11 Socialists constituting the opposition. Again, however, the impact of working-class opposition was felt in two compromises. Most important, the bill removed the power to shut down disorderly dances from police patrolmen, requiring a higher-ranking officer do the job. Second, the closing hour was set at 1 A.M. instead of midnight, and the mayor was empowered to issue special permits for longer dances. Socialist Mayor Seidel routinely granted late permits.[5]

Within the year, the groups that had won the victory over working-class dances had to admit that their newly established church and social center dances were not competing successfully with the dance halls for young workers' recreational hours. The reformers focused on two new evils: the tango and other sensuous dances, and the sale of liquor at dances. A police official kept records of who sold liquor at dances and found that 90 percent was sold not by saloons but by the organizations sponsoring the dances. "Who then are those organizations," asked the reformers. The Milwaukee Social Democratic *Leader* readily presented the answer:

The police records of the four precincts show that nearly one-third of the dancing is done under the auspices of "athletic" and "pleasure" clubs; nearly one-fifth under the auspices of lodges and sick benefit societies; about one-tenth under labor unions; and the rest under dancing academies, musical organizations, political organizations, church societies, individuals, and miscellaneous societies.

The pleasure and athletic clubs are made up almost exclusively of young men, usually American born of foreign parentage. These boys crave companionship. Instinct leads them to get together in groups.[6]

The reformers selected one of these working-class dances, the Waiters' Ball, for public description, presumably to shock, for they described it as a "debauchery" and reported that "unprintable" things happened on the dance floor. Police officers stationed at the door kept out young people under 18, while officers inside the hall prohibited the "suggestive" new dances and broke up fights. Chief of Police Janssen criticized Mayor Bading (Seidel's Republican successor) for granting the 4 A.M. permit, declaring that he would not have allowed the ball to continue past the prescribed 1 A.M. closing hour. Simply put, the fears that Milwaukee's working class had about the impact of police regulation of their recreational activity were borne out.[7]

During Chicago's "carnival of crime" scare of January-March 1906, the *Chicago Tribune* sent out two reporters on a Saturday night to investigate the dance halls. The *Tribune* had long regarded dance halls as "schools of crime," and it accused the police of making "drunkards and thieves and immoral women by the score" for a few hundred dollars' profit each weekend through special $3 dance hall liquor permits, which permitted the sale of liquor between 1 and 5 A.M., after normal saloon hours.[8] The reporters described the revels they had witnessed in lurid detail. The dances had been of the "rough house order"—that is, partners held each other in unconventional ways. The most popular dance, repeated again and again, was the "Indian war dance," in which female dancers were flung about by males. At the Slavia dance hall, where the Illinois Athletic, Social, and Pleasure Club was giving its opening dance, two police officers guarded the room because a shot had been fired there two weeks before when Polish and Irish youths got into a dispute over a prize. At 2:30 A.M. as many as 300 people were present, and the room was so crowded the door would hardly open. The ticket takers abandoned the doorway then, permitting access to 14- and 15-year-old boys who had been waiting outside. Perhaps 60 young girls mingled in the crowd. A drunk lay unconscious on the floor.

The reporters interviewed one of the policemen, who pronounced the revelers "pretty good tonight." When asked what bad was, the officer responded, "When they start shooting." The officer was called away to drive some small boys out of the barroom and returned. "It makes me sick to look at them. If they were mine I would spank all of them and send them home. Look at those girls. What is this generation coming to." The girls he pointed to ranged in age from the mid-teens to 30, with the majority aged 17 or 18. Those who were not dancing were sitting on the laps of men or boys around the edge of the dance floor. One boy dressed as a holdup man pointed a toy pistol at the heads of other dancers—"playing the game for which he was fitting himself," according to the *Tribune*. At the America dance hall nearby, three girls in low-cut red dresses captured the attention of the reporters. In another room three bartenders served whiskey, beer, and occasionally a lemonade.[9]

Responding to the *Tribune*'s prodding, Chief of Police John M. Collins announced that his men would keep boys and girls under 18 out of the halls. He ordered one-third of the night patrol force to supervise the all-night dance halls the next weekend, and the increased police presence led to a number of arrests of minor young women, eight the first evening. Many more were reprimanded and sent home. The first girl locked up was 17-year-old Dorothy Little, turned over to the Des Plaines Street Station by her mother. She was accused of attending dances two or three nights a week, and her mother wanted her institutionalized. The girl admitted to going and said that she saw nothing wrong with it and she intended to continue. She was sent to a house of refuge. "What have you done, Nellie?" demanded Judge Mack of a 15-year-old girl. "Nothing except dancing," muttered Nellie. She admitted to having met a man in the dance hall, to drinking some wine with him, and then to having sex with him. "Another dance hall victim," pronounced the judge as he sent her away.[10]

Not all the young dancers fared as well as Nellie. In December 1906 police arrested a boy in a dance hall for being drunk and creating a disturbance. He was escorted to a police station and locked up. Four hours later four policemen, including the arresting officer, met at the station, and one officer recounted that the boy had been "smart." The four officers then went to the cell where the boy slept. Reaching through the bars, one officer grabbed the boy by the hair while the others hit him in the head; then they dropped him on the floor. The boy woke up and retreated to the far wall of the cell. The officer then apologized and asked the boy to shake hands. When he did so, they hung him up in handcuffs and hit him again in the head with a blackjack. This story only came to light months later, incidental to a city council hearing for a juvenile school.[11]

When massive enforcement proved to be a failure, the department was not accused of inefficiency or lack of determination. Rather, in the judgment of the *Tribune,* whose reporters had been on duty for another weekend, it was simply impossible both to keep order and to watch out for minors. Many young people wore masks or costumes to avoid detection, and word traveled fast about unsupervised clubs; young people turned away at one club kept trying until they were admitted to another. More accounts of the evil of dance halls were offered, including the story of a 17-year-old girl constantly showing off her pretty garter and that of another 17-year-old who had left her husband and taken their baby daughter. Her 18-year-old husband, who worked in a feed store for $15 a week, protested: "We were happy . . . until she began to go to all night dances and stay out until early in the morning. We did not quarrel over it, but I told her not to go and she would. I believe she has been influenced to leave me by some of the friends she has made at these dance halls. . . . She was too fond of a good time."[12]

Reformers next turned to the special liquor permits and demanded that the practice end. Mayor Dunne refused, insisting that "a differentiation between dance halls must be made. There are many kinds. The desire to dance is natural and healthy, and dancing cannot be suppressed." Instead, the police were instructed to suppress "vicious places." Chief of Police Collins defended his policies:

We are not all on the water wagon. Is it not a fact that there are a great many good societies where whole families go to dances, and the babies are given a taste of beer by their parents? You can't stop all this. The bad ones will be taken care of. There is a way to distinguish.

Collins further solicited evidence of any police officer who failed to regulate a dance under his supervision and promised to make it "hot" for the offending man.[13]

The dance hall issue of 1906 came to a head when reformers called Mayor Dunne before a grand jury investigating the legality of the special liquor permits. Dunne caved in and announced that, although the issue should be settled by the courts, he would stop issuing permits. Among those affected was Emil Hoechster, proprietor of the North Side Turner Hall, who was denied a permit for a beer license for the Sunday afternoon concerts of the Bunge Metropolitan Orchestra. Since he could not afford a $1,000 saloon license for such a short occasion, the concerts were held dry. The Deutscher Bund, representing 30 turning societies, 100 singing societies, 17 military societies, and 280 independent clubs with a total membership of 45,000, deplored the "wave of intolerance" that had swept the city and protested the action. The Irish Hibernians also protested the denial of a license for one of their dances.[14]

Although there was undoubtedly a lot of drinking and sexual activity at dances, there is no question that these dances were important forms of working-class recreation. Reformers fought to end them not only because they abhorred the lax morality such places encouraged but also because they believed that these "pleasure" clubs undermined the discipline of the working class. The turning societies were regarded as no better than the street gangs of the stockyards district, and their dances were seen to be just as dangerous to the social order. The police, however, could and did make distinctions. At the same time, given the full range of police priorities in cities, they did not, and could not, apply the kind of patrol energy to dance halls that the reformers would have liked.

GAMBLING AND PROSTITUTION

Two forms of vice incited reformers as particularly reprehensible products of the "wide open town": large-scale gambling and prostitution. Most large cities boasted districts of gambling halls, where slot machines and faro games were standard entertainment, and houses of prostitution, or "stall saloons"—that is, saloons with small stalls upstairs or in the back for prostitution. Some prostitution and some gambling were not uncommon at dances, pool halls, saloons, or even factory gates, and there was not much that the police could do to control it. On the other hand, gambling halls and houses of prostitution were highly visible and easily raided by the police. Accordingly, these places became major sources of bribery and police corruption, and they were confined to large districts—Chicago's Levee district, Milwaukee's River Street, and Buffalo's Canal Street—where the police could proclaim a policy of "isolating" them.[15]

Although these recreational activities were by no means exclusively those of the working class, each class had its own type of establishment, from low dives to members-only clubs. Clearly, though, working-class vice areas received more attention than those of higher classes in the crackdowns that the police repeatedly undertook at the behest of reformers. Milwaukee's Chief Janssen, for example, protected a large vice district while directing a crusade against low dives and stall saloons. Where it was politically expedient for police departments to engage in some antivice activity, most had a wide selection of working-class dives to harass and close.

Between 1901 and 1909 a series of grand jury anticorruption investigations in Milwaukee, led by both Republican and Democratic reformers, and a series of gambling raids in 1905 produced so much evidence of official corruption that the *Daily News* predicted the imminent indictments of Chief Janssen, Mayor Rose, and other officials. The 1905 grand jury in fact indicted 72 individuals, including 53 elected officials, of whom 30 were eventually convicted.[16] The Social Democrats were the ultimate victors in this antivice drive because neither Republican nor Democratic reformers could achieve sufficient control over their parties to reduce vice noticeably. Sherbourne Becker, a wealthy, young Republican reformer, captured the mayoralty from Democratic machine boss David Rose in 1906, only to fail conspicuously to gain enough control over city institutions to do anything about vice. Rose's reelection in 1908 perfectly illustrated the socialists' charge that bourgeois political parties could not, or would not, control vice.

Both the working class and the police avoided the tendency of reformers to place all working-class recreational activities on the same level as organized prostitution and gambling. One important political struggle that turned on this distinction occurred in Milwaukee, where in 1910 the socialists succeeded in preempting the vice and corruption issue and separating it from the saloon question.[17]

As part of their 1910 platform regarding vice, the socialists demanded that "our city shall protect her youth and suppress vice. At the same time we call attention to the fact that prostitution is a part of the capitalist system and will entirely disappear only with capitalism."[18] The socialists' opposition to organized vice even extended to some early cooperation with their archenemy Chief Janssen to clean up vice outside of the official red-light district. When Mayor Seidel later adopted a compromising position on tightening regulation of the vice district, socialist District Attorney Winfred C. Zabel announced that he would abolish Milwaukee's vice district altogether. Seidel and the socialist aldermen did not support Zabel, probably because of his extreme moralism and the likelihood that he would fail (by then the socialists had lost control of the city council, and they had never won control over the police). Instead, they urged a crackdown on the hotels and rooming houses used for prostitution, again putting themselves in temporary alliance with Janssen.[19]

But whereas the socialists, working largely through their trade-unions base, opposed stall saloons, they supported dance halls. The difference turned on their analysis of the class nature of the two institutions. Dance halls, even if some unfortunate behavior occurred there, were major places of working-class recreation. Stall saloons, on the other hand, were tied into a complex structure of organized vice in Milwaukee, centered in the River Street district. Many of Milwaukee's richest land-owners profited from the high rents in the River Street area, and Milwaukee's businessmen were among the major clients of the established resorts there.[20]

Moreover, regulation of the River Street district was a major example in the socialists' attack on the duplicity of the police department. Here a comparison of public order law enforcement and vice enforcement clearly shows that they were two distinct phenomena in Milwaukee. Though nominally "tolerant" of drinking, Milwaukee police made more than 3,000 arrests for liquor-related offenses each year in the 1890s and early 1900s. In 1905 this same police force arrested 18 people for gambling and 84 for prostitution. Obviously, a hard-drinking worker had a very good chance of avoiding arrest if he went gambling in po-lice-protected gambling halls. Arrests were used to regulate the vice industry, not to punish or control working-class recrea-tional activity.

Open gambling and prostitution flourished in Chicago's noto-rious Levee district on the Near South Side (a mile from the Loop) and in other "neighborhood" vice districts in the stock-yards area, the West Side, and the North Side. A wide range of establishments catered to the needs of the different classes, varying from well-known and protected places to operations that changed location and management frequently. Police protection in the districts cannot be assumed. Many places lacked the pro-tection of the more established operations and were closed in periodic reform campaigns; others, taking advantage of the city's size, may well have operated intermittently without pro-tection. Even within a single vice district all kinds of establish-ments operated: expensive saloons catered to the drinking needs of customers for brothels and gambling halls but did not them-selves engage in such practices.

Gambling and vice began to be consolidated into districts in Chicago in the early 1900s, and regulation of this activity was a major source of police graft. Whether Chicago's police were more corrupt than Milwaukee's might be contested, but there is no question that they were much more open about such activities. It was widely known, for example, that Chief Collins and his men were protecting slot machines for $2 apiece. More disturbing to the political machine was the revelation that the police kept a good share of the political contributions from saloonkeepers for themselves. Pervasive police involvement in vice graft obscured the class issue because the war on vice was touted as a war on municipal corruption.

Reform campaigns in Chicago, as in Milwaukee, achieved a marked degree of success, and the Chicago of the early 1900s was noticeably freer of vice than the Chicago of the 1890s. No less an observer than Reverend William T. Stead, author of the famous antivice tract *If Christ Came to Chicago* and an antivice crusader during the 1890s, revisited the city in 1907. Touring the Levee district with saloonkeeper Hank North, Stead marveled at the improvement: "In fact I was almost looking for a halo about Hank's head. Things have changed wonderfully in this part of Chicago. I would scarcely even know my friend North."[21] Obviously, gambling, vice, and corruption lasted well beyond the period of the present study, but the police, despite corruption and inefficiency, cleaned up a portion of it and restructured vice to meet some of the demands of reformers like Stead: it was relocated to discreet and protected "resorts" that did less to attract the reformers' outrage.

Stead was not the only critic to notice the improvement. Captain August Piper's otherwise critical investigation of the department's discipline (1906) was generally positive on the question of gambling and prostitution. Piper reported that, although he had heard numerous reports of connections between the police department and gamblers, he found no evidence of illegal dealings, except in the case of the slot machine. The "slots" were everywhere—even in the front of a hotel in plain view of the Tenth Precinct station house in Hyde Park. One of Piper's men gave a police officer pennies to play a machine in a saloon in another precinct. In the Fourteenth Precinct Piper himself played a machine in the presence of an officer and won a cigar—and the congratulations of the officer. In addition, handbooks—petty bookmaking parlors—were found all over the city.[22]

With regard to prostitution, Piper reported Chicago more free from streetwalkers than New York. In fact, Piper announced, in the two months that he had been on the streets, at all hours and in the worst neighborhoods, he had not been solicited once on the street, though he reported open solicitation from windows and doors of saloons by women "improperly clad." Piper recommended hammering prostitution hard, but not too hard, warning that it might scatter all over the city, as it had in New York.[23]

Piper's aide, Roundsman William F. Maher of the New York City Police Department, wrote more critically that prostitution in saloons run expressly for that purpose was more open in Chicago than in New York. Maher reported seeing women throw their dresses over their heads in front of two policemen and hearing women "tapping on the windows as if they were putting in glass, with thimbles, and as loud as they could, and in view and hearing of a policeman." Maher learned from prostitutes that they had been instructed by the police not to expose their breasts in the act of solicitation because "the crime committee was out." He also reported seeing bookmaking operations run out of saloons and an open crap game attended by 150 black people at State and Taylor streets.[24]

Although Piper and Maher were more concerned with the discipline of the police force than with vice, they noted that the police force was fully aware of these activities and simply regulated them rather than suppressed them. Clearly, the concentration of prostitutes in saloons and their absence from streetcorners can only be attributed to police regulation. Similarly, both Piper's failure to find gambling halls and Maher's discovery that prostitutes had been given explicit limitations for their solicitation tend to indicate that the police had given similar warnings to gamblers and other purveyors of organized vice. In effect, the police issued specific regulations intended to make such conduct less visible and hence less socially offensive. Those who see only a corrupt connection between the police and such activities overlook a complex regulatory function behind the corruption.

In summary, then, large-scale organized gambling and prostitution must be distinguished from neighborhood saloons, dance halls, pool halls, and other forms of working-class recreation. Organized vice catered to all classes and remained quite distinct in most respects from the activities of workers at leisure. Similarly, police work in relation to large-scale enterprises must be distinguished from their control of the day-to-day leisure activities of workers and of the places that workers commonly frequented. The police used vice laws selectively to regulate vice, and they clearly did not assign a high priority to stamping out such forms of behavior. However, enforcement patterns show an anti-working-class bias, for the police focused especially on those establishments patronized by less affluent individuals.

TWO ANTISPITTING ORDINANCES

Police efforts to control working-class leisure-time activities encompassed more than regulation of liquor, dance halls, gambling, and prostitution. Enforcement of the antispitting ordinances in Chicago and Indianapolis in 1902 and 1903 shows how a simple public health measure could become a significant weapon against working-class enjoyment of leisure hours.

In January 1902 the Indianapolis police chief ordered his men to enforce the city's antispitting ordinance vigorously. The *Indianapolis News* reported that the police had received several complaints of "gangs congregating on certain corners and using sidewalks as a cuspidor. . . . The police say that the ordinance serves as an excuse for breaking up gangs as some of the men are sure to spit on the sidewalks sooner or later."[25]

A year later the Chicago Police Department urged the city council to enact an antispitting ordinance that the department itself had proposed. The *Tribune* chided the department, suggesting that its real motive was to draw attention to a highly popular antispitting campaign and away from the department's failure to repress more serious forms of lawbreaking. Further-

Fig. 2

THE POLICEMAN WAS WILLING TO DO HIS DUTY, BUT—

1. The inspector—"Look here, you'll have to do your duty. No favors to anybody hereafter. I'll go with you and see that you do your full duty."

2. "Say, inspector, here's a saloon open after hours. Shall we pull the proprietor?"
"No, he's a particular friend of the alderman."

3. "Now, here's a quiet little game up here. Shall we pinch the bunch?"
"No, the place is run by a friend of the alderman."

4. "Here's a wholesale house obstructing the sidewalk. Shall we arrest the proprietor?"
"No! Great Scott! He's one of the biggest contributors to the campaign fund."

5. "Here's a tough joint. Shall we call the wagon?"
"No, the building is owned by a prominent society lady who wouldn't want her name mentioned."

6. "Here's a man spitting on the sidewalk. Shall we pinch him?"
"You bet! We'll teach him to respect the law."

Chicago Tribune, March 24, 1904

more, the paper charged, the police promulgated "99 out of 100" reforms for publicity and concerned themselves with those reforms only so long as the newspapers provided front-page publicity. The *Tribune* obliged by publishing a cartoon ridiculing police enforcement of the ordinance.[26]

Such a measure served both as a weapon to harass crowds of working-class young people congregated on street corners and as a publicity tool for a police department beleaguered by reformers. The *Tribune,* after all, did not criticize the ordinance itself, only what it saw as the duplicitous intentions of the police department in proposing it. In fact, the *Tribune's* allegation that the Chicago police manufactured crusades to take the pressure off police complicity in diverse forms of corruption mirrors working-class criticism with regard both to public conduct law enforcement and to strikebreaking activities.

CONCLUSION

The criminologist's definition of "public order crimes" comes perilously close to the historian's description of "working-class leisure-time activity." Whereas the policing of working-class strike activity involved the periodic concentration of large numbers of well-organized police units, public order law enforcement was the daily routine of individual officers. Despite charges of indiscipline, laziness, and corruption, rank-and-file officers spent a good deal of time on patrol in working-class communities, and arrests for public order violations invariably constituted 60 to 80 percent or more of all police arrests. Virtually all of those arrested were workers—usually more than half were unskilled workers—and up to half of them went to jail for their public order violations.

Nevertheless, even in cities with high arrest rates, such as Pittsburgh and Chicago, the average officer made only a few dozen arrests a year. In Chicago the 40,000 to 50,000 arrests for disorderly conduct annually in the years after 1900 were made by a force of about 2,500. That amounts to one arrest per week per officer, given that not all of Chicago's police walked patrol. The point is that an officer, then as today, dealt with situations almost entirely by personal discretion. Hence, the impact of the police on working-class communities and recreational activities was greater than arrest data might suggest. The arrest power was a coercive weapon held in reserve.

The officer-population ratio in most major American cities ranged from 1:500 to 1:1,000, putting each citizen in close proximity to an officer in the densely settled working-class areas of the city. This was particularly true of new immigrants, who received a large measure of police attention and who most often remained outside the protection of political machines. The task of bringing these immigrants into conformity with the labor discipline of industrial society was shared among the factory, the school, and social service agencies, but the "public" presence of those groups came under the purview of the police. Buffalo Superintendent Michael Regan's pronouncement that "Italians are a dangerous class, for they break the law" precisely conveys the bourgeois attitude toward immigrants and offers a rationale for the series of confrontations between Buffalo police and Italians between 1905 and 1910.[27] The Buffalo police fully intended to socialize Buffalo's Italian community to "proper" American values. Allegheny City's police sought to do the same with that town's Hungarians. Republican reformers in Chicago attempted to force the police department to do the same with that city's dance-hall-loving Germans but met with less success because the Germans there had achieved a higher community standing than had Italians and Hungarians elsewhere.

Although it is obvious that the police could never adequately supervise so many workers, it is not true that they did not take that responsibility seriously or that they sided with the workers. Obviously, the police disagreed with their critics about the proper role of the urban police institution in regulating this behavior, but within the set of constraints surrounding them, the police exercised great influence on working-class behavior. Moreover, the police institution *as a whole* exercised these socializing functions regardless of the personal beliefs of individual officers. Simple adherence to a system of class-biased laws operating within a class society ensured that the police institution would fulfill many of society's expectations for a well-ordered system. The urban class system generated disorder, just as it generated institutional reflections of the class system to regulate and discipline that disorder.

CHAPTER NINE

The Tramp Acts and Repression of Unemployed Workers

THE "TRAMP ACTS" offer a classic example of class legislation—
that is, laws specifically designed by one class to be used as
weapons in controlling a weaker class. Beginning in the 1870s,
state after state made it a crime for workers without visible
means of support to travel about the country. Though conceptu-
ally related to existing vagrancy laws, the tramp acts differed in
that they had a far more repressive application: standards of
proof were commonly lower, penalties were higher (sentences of
six months or more), and states often subsidized the costs of
local enforcement in order to discourage the practice of "passing
on" tramps from one town to the next.[1]

Enforcement, of course, fell to local police departments.
Again, bourgeois criticism of the police for failing to jail all
tramps cannot be interpreted as evidence that the police sympa-
thized with tramps and unemployed workers. Rather, the police
fully realized the magnitude of the problem in a way that the
bourgeoisie did not and recognized the impossibility of jailing all
tramps. They did jail many, however, and pushed a good many
others out of town.

The role of the police in the class struggle is much clearer in
the area of enforcement of the tramp acts than in other areas
because the working class was fully aware that most tramps
were simply unemployed workers and not criminals. Police ar-

rest practices often drew intense opposition from organized labor, and a political movement, the industrial armies, built up around tramping. Despite bourgeois efforts to characterize the tramps as criminals, murderers, idlers, and bums—in effect to divide the working class over the tramp issue—workers continued to defend the tramps.[2]

The march of Joseph Rybakowski's industrial army from Chicago to Buffalo during the summer of 1894 presents an opportunity to study police enforcement of the tramp acts and the political struggle it provoked. The summer of 1894 was the height of the depression of 1893–1897, and immigrant workers were among the hardest hit. Detroit, Toledo, Cleveland, and Buffalo reported 50 percent of their Poles unemployed. A major riot had already occurred that spring in Detroit's Polish community, and Akron, Buffalo, Chicago, Cleveland, and Toledo experienced Polish riots as well.[3]

In early June, "Count" Joseph Rybakowski, a Polish engineer in his early thirties who edited a Polish-language labor paper in Chicago, organized an industrial army composed of about 140 unemployed Polish and Bohemian canal diggers from the Far South Side of Chicago. Though modeled loosely after Coxey's Army, Rybakowski's group exhibited several important differences. First, it was overwhelmingly immigrant; newspapers reported that only "eight or nine" of the men spoke English, whereas native-born Americans predominated in Coxey's Army. Second, Rybakowski and his followers espoused socialism, as opposed to Coxey's brand of populism. Third, Rybakowski was more ambitious than Coxey. Although the ultimate objective of both armies was Washington, D.C., Rybakowski planned a longer route than Coxey's, deliberately passing through cities with large, uneasy Polish communities in order to maximize the political impact of his march.[4]

RYBAKOWSKI'S ARMY IN TOLEDO AND CLEVELAND

Rybakowski's Army arrived in Toledo on July 15. Police Chief Benjamin Raitz and city officials quickly conferred. Not anxious to arrest 135 men, they decided to allow the army to camp one day in Metropolitan Park, on the condition that no public meetings would be held and that the army would leave town the next morning. When Rybakowski announced that he intended to stay a week and hold public meetings, the police arrested the entire group, marched them to Central Station, charged them with vagrancy, and locked them up. They were handled roughly, and a number of the men were clubbed awake by a squad of 35 police officers.

The next morning the Count announced that he was prepared to leave town in return for the army's freedom. The men were released and given 300 loaves of bread, 20 pounds of sugar, 10 pounds of coffee, and 100 pounds of sausage. At 10 A.M. the entire army was loaded on streetcars and transported to East Toledo to resume their journey. Even as the police were preparing to expel the army from Toledo, Rybakowski's wife, the "Countess," appeared in the Polish district to recruit among the unemployed Poles at the Lagrange Street settlement house.[5]

Ten days later a division of Jeffries's Army from the Pacific Northwest arrived in Toledo. This 50-man group rested for two days, then headed for Sandusky. Its leaders insisted they needed no charity from the city: "We do not ask the city for help. Nearly all of my men have credentials from labor organizations and they are well treated whenever they come to the home of a workingman." Chief Raitz responded negatively to a request from the army to hold a public meeting at the market: "We have too much of this sort of thing, and it is time to put a stop to it. These men will hold no meeting, tonight or any other time." Jeffries's Army was not arrested, however, and in that respect fared better than Rybakowski's.

Individual tramps found a similar response in Toledo. Vagrancy arrests had more than doubled between 1892 (159) and 1894 (357), and represented roughly 10 percent of all arrests. A "tramp room" was established in the East Toledo station house (near the major railroad yards) to provide temporary lodging. This seeming contradiction illustrates a common strategy of the time: since there was no possibility of eliminating tramping altogether, police departments attempted to control tramp move-

ments. Similarly, the food and transportation provided to Rybakowski's Army were conciliatory measures intended to induce
the army to leave town peacefully. Toledo's officials fully recognized that Rybakowski had the capacity to cause a great deal of
difficulty if he so desired.[6]

And it was precisely this threat that Rybakowski attempted to
capitalize upon between Toledo and Cleveland and that he employed successfully in Cleveland and Buffalo. Arriving in Fre-
mont, Ohio, on July 22, the army set up camp in the local fair-
grounds, and Rybakowski demanded food. When it was not
forthcoming, he marched his men on City Hall, threatening to
"turn them loose" if the city did not feed them. The small police
force sent out a riot call to the local militia, which moved the
army out. The next day the process was repeated in Clyde,
where the local militia drove the army out of town at bayonet
point.[7]

Despite these minor setbacks, Rybakowski determined to
push through to Cleveland, where his army arrived on July 28.
In the meantime, however, Cleveland had been the reluctant
host of Jeffries's industrial army. The 275 men had arrived on
July 24 on the Great Lakes schooner *Grampian,* which had been
chartered for them by public subscription in Bay City, Michigan.
Allowed by the police to disembark, the army marched in a
column to the public square in the center of downtown Cleveland. When police ordered the men to "move out," they
marched a few blocks further and "camped out" in the street
while "Colonel" Jeffries sought lodging. City officials sent him
from the mayor's office to the park commissioner, to the chief of
police. In the meantime, the army itself had chosen an old public
market, but the city would not allow the use of it. The army
threatened to take the public square by force, but contented itself with camping in the streets and with holding a rally at which
Jeffries spoke and the army's quartet sang.[8]

The next day Police Director M. J. Herbert finally gave the
industrials permission to use the St. Clair Market, but he continued to withhold permission for rallies in the public square. Some
local working-class supporters urged the army to "go and take

it" and promised local support. The Central Labor Union passed a resolution criticizing the acting mayor, park commissioner, and public safety commissioner for violating the right of workingmen to free speech.

While public officials were debating what to do with the tramp army, Jeffries rushed their deliberation by seizing the public square, despite the presence of a "goodly" number of police caught offguard by the action. Police Director Herbert pondered: "We can order them away, and if they don't go we can arrest them. But we don't want to fill up the prison and the workhouse with these fellows. What the dickens will we do?" The city quickly rejected Jeffries's offer to abandon the square for a fee of $75, to be paid to the army's treasury. Finally, the police gave the order to clear the square, and the army moved to another downtown site. Jeffries addressed gathered crowds several times before the army adjourned to the market for a supper of "punk"—beef heart and bread—donated by local supporters.[9]

The next day the entire 275-man army marched around the downtown business district wearing improvised cloth gags and carrying a banner with the words "Free Speech in Cleveland." The city ordered the police armed with riot clubs and the reserve force brought from Central Station to the public square. But force was not necessary: that night the army hopped a freight for Pittsburgh.[10]

The next morning the Rybakowski Army arrived, flying flags and banners and marching to a drum beat. After refreshing themselves at the St. Clair Market, the army began a five-mile march about the city, ending in the Polish community, where their arrival caused a "sensation" and they were entertained in the homes of some of the community leaders. The next day several hundred workers turned up to hear the army's oratory, although most of the force spent the day foraging for food.[11]

The comparative peacefulness of the army's stay in Cleveland was owing largely to its close connection with the more powerful Jeffries's Army, which had already determined the police department's policy almost by default—there were simply too many of them to arrest.[12] The police simply kept the Rybakowski Army under surveillance. When two members of the army were arrested for stealing apples and throwing some of them at the owner of the tree when he protested, a crowd of several hundred Polish women and children gathered and insulted the officers until they let the men go. Twelve patrolmen, three detectives, and a police captain were then transferred into the precinct quartering Rybakowski's Army for the duration. After spending five days in Cleveland, the army left for Buffalo.[13]

PATTERNS OF TRAMP ACT ENFORCEMENT IN BUFFALO

Rybakowski's decision to march on Buffalo was his army's undoing. Buffalo's well-organized bourgeoisie took a stronger stand on tramps than was found in most cities, and since 1891 the city had vigorously enforced New York's tramp act. As many as 140 workers had been "vagged" in a single day, and at times tramps constituted 80 percent of the inmates in the county prison.

Through 1890, no one was charged for tramping in Buffalo. In 1891, however, 2,110 arrests were made under the tramp act, or about 11 percent of the total arrests for the year (see table 8). Several explanations of these figures are possible. Throughout this period it is clear that the police had freely arrested people for a wide variety of offenses against public order, including vagrancy, and many of these arrests may have involved behavior that was charged under the tramp act after 1891. For example, there were 1,400 fewer vagrancy arrests in 1891 than in 1890, suggesting that behavior previously considered to be vagrancy had been redefined as tramping. One reason for this shift in categorization may have been that the state subsidized the cost of jailing persons convicted of tramping, but not those arrested for vagrancy. Also, 1891 marks the beginning of the administration of Police Chief Daniel Morganstern (1891–1894), a dry goods merchant who was the first of the businessmen-superintendents who administered the force from 1891 to 1904. The shift toward

Table 8. ARRESTS FOR MAJOR PUBLIC ORDER CRIMES BY SPECIFIC OFFENSE IN BUFFALO, 1886–1900

Year	Total arrests	Drunkenness	Disorderly conduct	Vagrancy	Tramps[a]
1886	9,544	2,803	1,876	1,528	0
1887	12,404	4,152	2,513	2,625	0
1888	14,149	5,132	2,572	3,178	0
1889	16,170	5,926	2,532	3,640	0
1890	17,628	6,599	3,210	3,170	0
1891	18,575	6,759	3,160	1,750	2,110
1892	21,383	8,256	3,642	1,779	2,287
1893	19,062	6,144	3,386	1,820	1,925
1894	26,069	6,824	4,014	4,764	4,716
1895	24,889	9,861	3,653	1,690	2,640
1896	22,573	4,139	4,139	1,090	2,423
1897	25,573	10,319	5,085	1,166	3,149
1898	24,489	9,612	4,764	1,118	2,661
1899	23,338	9,971	4,431	1,021	1,622
1900	28,347	12,160	5,121	1,292	1,932

Source: Buffalo Police Department, *Annual Reports* (1886–1900).
[a]Prior to 1891 there were no arrests for the offense of being a tramp.

more businesslike administration of the force led to a greater number of arrests for two reasons. First, the class interests of the businessmen exerted more influence over policing measures; as class conflict increased and the class position of businessmen was threatened, the police became more important as a force for class control. Second, a renewed concern with fiscal efficiency made state financing of imprisonment under the tramp act an attractive means to encourage local police to enforce fully the provisions of the act. The shift in Buffalo's policy at this time, and the increase by 700 in the aggregate of arrests for tramping and vagrancy, were consistent with this policy.[14]

In enforcing the tramp act, Buffalo's police at first used methods common in most American cities. Officers were stationed in railroad yards to arrest tramps, but the large number of tramps necessitated that officers be given a great deal of discretion, and thousands of tramps got through town safely. As antitramp strategy became consistently more repressive, however, these tentative and uncoordinated enforcement practices gave way to a policy of locking up all tramps on sight. Arrest statistics record the impact of this policy: 1894 tramp arrests more than doubled those of 1891. Heightened class conflict, beginning with a major railroad strike in 1892 and culminating with the severe depression of 1893–1894, led to increased repression of the working class, partly through the tramp act. The Buffalo police linked tramp control measures with anti-working-class strike control measures in the railroad switchmen's strike of 1892. As part of a crackdown on workers that included closing working-class saloons and rounding up "troublemakers" on a wide variety of charges, Chief of Police Morganstern ordered that the city be cleared of tramps. On August 20, the first day the order was in effect, Captain Regan of the First Precinct reported that 75 tramps had been arrested. When an *Express* reporter asked Morganstern to explain the purpose of his order, the chief responded:

> The idea is to get as many of these good for nothings as possible out of the way during the present difficulty, as they are apt to hang around with the strikers and incite them, and possibly may do mischief themselves. Besides it reduces the crowds so that it is easier to distinguish the classes of citizens with whom the police and militia have to deal.[15]

A close examination of these arrests shows that the police rarely distinguished between tramps and workers. Harry Drew and William Brady, both railroad men, were arrested as tramps and given 10 days each. Charles Williams and John Baken, scabs who refused to fill switchmen's jobs when they learned there was a strike, were charged and jailed as tramps, along with six other scabs jailed as vagrants. Drunks, loiterers, stone-throwers, and many more scabs were brought in from the First, Second, Seventh, and other precincts and given 10- and 15-day sentences for tramping. Eventually the newspapers stopped reporting individual arrests and noted simply: "A lot of bums and vagrants collected by the police in first precinct got ten days in the Pen," and "A large number of tramps and vagrants locked up in No. 9."[16]

The extensive working-class support that the switchmen's strike received unsettled Buffalo's ruling class. "The whole strike principle is wrong," editorialized the *Express*. "It turns honest men into criminals and upholders of crime." The idea that "bums and strangers and tramps" were responsible for the violence was attractive to all concerned—including the grand master of the switchmen's union, who did not want responsibility for the mass action that was needed to win the union's strike. But they could not distinguish tramps from community residents and railroad men in practice as easily as they did in such statements.[17]

The increase in the number of workers arrested as tramps and the public clamor for strengthened antitramp measures were outgrowths of the bourgeois perception of the tramp as a dangerous troublemaker in local labor relations. Even the doubling of tramp arrests in a three-year period does not reveal the full extent to which the criminal justice system was devoted to the repression of workers under the tramp acts. The 600 to 900 tramps held in the Erie County Penitentiary during the summers of 1893 and 1894 constituted almost the entire prison population. Not all of these tramps had been arrested in Buffalo, but only a few smaller cities, the largest of which was Niagara Falls, sent prisoners to the Erie County Penitentiary. Tramps were routinely given 30- to 90-day sentences, and they were virtually never able to pay their fines. Most other offenders were punished with $5 and $10 fines or 10-day jail sentences. Tramps, then, filled the penitentiary out of proportion to their share of arrests because of the longer sentences they received and their inability to pay fines. They shared the penitentiary with accused men awaiting trial and convicts doing terms for serious assaults or major property crimes.

These prison statistics only hint at the viciousness of the police in dealing with the victims of unemployment and depression. Much of the violence was committed by police officers, but the overall policies originated with the upper echelon of police officials, the mayor, and local businessmen. Local papers encouraged this behavior. "Police in the ninth precinct are furiously in earnest in their attempt to clear their territory of tramps. The morning report to the Sergeant shows 40 arrests on Saturday and every one of them a tramp." If such publicity were not sufficient to indicate its support, the *Express* a month later celebrated the efforts of Niagara Falls police and directly criticized the Buffalo police for throwing tramps out of town rather than following orders and jailing them: "Twenty-one tramps were disposed of in Niagara Falls, most given 60–90 days in the penitentiary. Tramps are flowing into the city in generous and unwelcome numbers. The police have orders to gather them in at every turn. A few are sent to jail and others are given walking papers."[18]

This accusation of softness failed to note that the population of the county penitentiary was reaching new heights almost daily and that most of the new inmates were tramps. A contemporary observer visiting the Erie County Penitentiary found a large number of tramps "unloading a canal boat in the hot sun . . . they worked slowly and sullenly and had to be continually hustled by those who had them in charge." The prison was horribly overcrowded. The "Pen," a stone courtyard with two iron gates, held 50 tramps; 8 were packed in a small cell so closely that only the heads nearest the door were visible.

Jack London, who served 30 days in the Erie County Penitentiary on tramp charges during June and July 1894, described the scene from the inside: "I was forced to toil hard on a diet of bread and water and to march the shameful lock-step with armed guards over me—and for what? What had I done?"[19] London had been taken to the prison in a 16-man chain gang. There he was stripped, bathed, and vaccinated, his hair was cropped, and he was clothed in a striped convict suit. Then he was locked in a small, vermin-infested cell in a large "hall . . . built out of bricks and rising six stories high, each story a row of cells, say fifty cells in a row. . . . A narrow gallery, with a steel railing [ran] the full length of each tier of cells." The daily fare consisted of a ration of bread the size of two fists, along with water in the form of "coffee" made with burnt bread crusts in the morning, "soup" with grease and salt added at lunch, and a purplish "tea" at dinner. The work task was to unload huge stay-bolts from canal boats and carry them over the shoulders like railroad ties under the watchful eyes of guards with repeating rifles on top of the walls.[20]

The spring of 1894 brought conditions that challenged police, charity reformers, and Buffalo's entire bourgeoisie. Large-scale unemployment, coupled with increasing labor militancy, particularly the threat of a nationwide railroad strike, made each of these groups more determined than ever to keep Buffalo free from tramps. Yet the number of tramps continued to increase, and the editor of the *Express* saw conspiracy as the only explanation:

> The cause of the sudden rush to this city appears to be the imminence of a railroad strike hereabouts. Tramps, like all vicious characters, revel in troubled times and a strike is like a picnic to them. Hence it is that whenever a strike is promised the road agents forsake the country and flock to the big cities.
>
> Much of the damage attributed to strikes is really the work of tramps. In nearly every case when a tramp is arrested in a strike he gives his occupation as a railroad man.[21]

William S. Bull, a "good businessman" recently installed as a reform police superintendent, ordered the department to increase its repression of tramps. Rather than simply increasing the number of tramps arrested at railroad yards, the new policy called for a large-scale effort requiring the cooperation of the entire city government. The first victims of this new policy were the industrial armies of Jeffries and Rybakowski.

The Buffalo press had erroneously reported that Jeffries was bound for Buffalo, rather than for Cleveland, where the *Grampian* landed. The much-feared army was described in the press as "the worst looking cargo ever." Two days later an editorial in the *Buffalo Express* offered a plan for preventing their arrival, a plan that the police and public officials later adopted:

> We do not want the expense of feeding them, the trouble of sending them to jail, or the difficulty of keeping police surveillance over them. They must be prevented from landing. This is a problem for authorities to solve in the next few days. Perhaps Dr. Wende will discover he has the authority to quarantine them 20 miles from the port unless they consent to sail away quietly.[22]

The next day the corporation counsel and the police chief's clerk spent a good deal of time "looking up the law," preparing to advise Superintendent Bull as to his duties. But Dr. Wende, the commissioner of health, saved the day:

> Chances are that all of them will have sore legs if they do give the city a call. It may be that the vaccination (that all hoboes will be given) will not be of the ordinary kind. City Clerk Mark Hubbell has suggested that it might be a good idea to vaccinate them on their legs to prevent them from begging. Commissioner of Health Dr. Wende is seriously considering this suggestion.[23]

Superintendent Bull had announced that all the tramps would go to the penitentiary, but he was upstaged by the sadistic suggestion of the health commissioner. Jeffries's Commonwealth Army landed in Cleveland instead of Buffalo. According to the ship's captain, "They were all mechanics, engineers, sailors, cooks, barbers, all sorts, and a good class of men, clean and intelligent. Victims of the played out boom in Seattle. As trustworthy as any."[24]

RYBAKOWSKI'S ARMY IN BUFFALO

Despite the threats against Jeffries's Army, Rybakowski's Army managed to enter Buffalo unmolested, and it received considerable support in the local Polish community and from organized labor. Ultimately, however, the army suffered the roughest treatment ever inflicted on tramps in Buffalo. Two of them were shot by the police with cold-blooded premeditation, 20 were seriously clubbed, and 120 were arrested and jailed for terms of 10 days to six months.

Upon nearing Buffalo, the Countess went ahead to negotiate with the mayor and the police, and city officials held a number of meetings to determine how to respond. Superintendent Bull insisted on "vagging" the entire army, but more moderate voices prevailed. The later decision to control and contain the army resulted from the Count's defiance of authority and his determination to proceed. When the army overran a solitary police chief in nearby Hamburg—in the presence of Buffalo Superintendent Bull and Police Commissioner Charles Rupp—it seemed more expedient simply to let them pass through. On the way to Buffalo the Count told a reporter about a stormy meeting in Bull's office: "He made great threats as to what he was going to do with us. He doesn't like our crowd and we don't like or care for him." Another reporter questioned the Count: "Then the thought of being arrested has no fear for you?" "None whatsoever," he responded. "We are traveling in the cause of justice." The army was met at the city limits by a mounted police patrol and escorted through the southeastern corner of Buffalo to a farm just beyond the city limits.[25]

The army's arrival intensified class feelings within the Polish community. The Polish neighborhood, located along Broadway on Buffalo's east side, numbered about 25,000 in 1893 and was rapidly expanding. Most of the wage earners were common laborers in heavy industry, the docks, and the railroad yards. So severely were the Poles affected by the depression that one newspaper reported that 5,000 were in "imminent danger of starvation." In August 1893 there had been bread riots in the Broadway Market, followed by an orderly meeting of 5,000 Poles demanding public-work jobs. By the spring of 1894 the Polish community was even more militant. In June 500 to 800 Poles marched on the offices of the mayor and the poor department demanding public-work jobs and protesting inadequate poor relief. They had to be dispersed by the police, and local editors blamed the disturbances on "anarchists and socialists" who lived among the Poles.[26] Similar marches occurred within weeks of Rybakowski's arrival.

The Count and his wife paid dozens of calls on community leaders, although some refused to see them. This attention paid off handsomely. The Polish community collected three wagons of clothing and food for the army, including 400 pounds of sausage, 1,000 loaves of bread, 2 cases of whiskey, 4 kegs of beer, cigars, and tobacco. Meetings were held in the Polish community to discuss the social questions raised by the army. An undetermined number of local men joined. Twenty residents of Buffalo were arrested when the army was crushed, but at least 60 members of the army escaped arrest, and persons from Buffalo were probably in a better position to do so.[27]

Police Captain Frank Koehler harassed local Poles who supported Rybakowski. When a four-person committee was formed to feed the army, Koehler sought out one of its leaders and found him loading bread into a wagon at the Broadway Market. "Is that for the hoboes?" he demanded. "It seems to me that food might be distributed to better advantage!" Superintendent Bull prevented the Count from accepting a three-day engagement at a Main Street theater by refusing to permit the speech. Extra police were dispatched to the main roads leading to the hobo camp with orders to prevent Rybakowski's followers from entering the city. Thirteen tramps who sneaked into the city were arrested, given 10 days each, and segregated from other prisoners.[28]

In the meantime, the army undertook to recruit additional members from among the local unemployed. Five hundred Buffalo residents paid 10 cents each for admission to the camp; indeed, since the gatekeepers refused to accept money from "fellow workingmen," the actual number of visitors was much higher. Thirteen tramps were responsible for security, and the entire scene remained orderly. Local socialist orators kept the crowd's attention with speeches in Polish, German, and English, and socialist newspapers were distributed free. The Count was invited to an endless round of local meetings.[29]

The Count and his men were not accustomed to such favorable community response and were somewhat reluctant to leave

Buffalo when the sheriff's deputy served them with an eviction notice on the morning of August 24. The previous afternoon it had been announced that the army would move to Woodlawn Beach, a resort area on Lake Erie just south of Buffalo. William H. S. Otto of the Woodlawn Association announced that the property owners would meet the tramps with shotguns, and he went off to see Erie County Sheriff Isaac Taggert. The series of meetings that followed led to a decision to oust the tramps. The Buffalo police, in consultation with Mayor Charles Bishop, announced that they would carry out the hard-line policy they had proclaimed four days earlier. Superintendent Bull warned: "I won't let them set foot in city limits. I am tired of hoboes." Although Bull, Mayor Bishop, and the city attorney decided that the police could not legally act outside the city limits, a few hours later the Buffalo police led a charge on the army. Police officials, city officials, and businessmen jointly made this decision to smash the tramp army. Three captains leading four companies of officers were dispatched to the city limits. As soon as they arrived, they offered Sheriff Taggert all the support he needed: "I will back you with all my men and I've got enough to kill the whole outfit," promised Captain Frank Killeen, the senior officer present.[30]

The scene immediately preceding the attack is relatively clear. After a deputy served the eviction notice, the Count announced that the army was not ready to leave and would stay as long as it liked. Taggert, in a fit of rage, announced that he was going to "lock up every damned one of those damned tramps as soon as he could get together a sufficient force of men." The qualification was critical because the sheriff, unlike the police, did not command a large, disciplined force. His regular deputies had to be augmented by the 35 to 40 volunteers, mostly small businessmen armed with their own guns and clubs, who flocked to his office for a chance to participate in the excitement of arresting a large force of tramps. This crew, along with an equal contingent of Buffalo police not under Taggert's command, immediately started for the farm in a rented wagon. The half-hour trip was interrupted by a stop at a tavern in the stockyards for "refreshments." Here the sheriff further incited his men to violence:

"Now understand you're going in there for business. Go right in, don't stop for anything, and take that damned Count dead or alive. Handcuff him first and bring him here at once."

When the deputies and police officers arrived at the camp, they found mass confusion. The men were gathered around the Count waiting for some kind of instruction, which was not forthcoming. Some of them picked up clubs from a fallen tree. A Buffalo police officer on horseback rode into the middle of the tramps and announced: "You unwashed dirty devils, you're under arrest, what the hell are you blowing about. Let these boys alone or we'll knock your heads on the other side of the fence." The Count calmed the situation by announcing that he would walk to the court. The men all insisted on standing by the Count and marched off with him.[31]

Along the way the Count and his men learned what lay in store for them, probably from a reporter. Judge Foster was waiting in his courtroom—a little anteroom off the bar in the roadhouse that he owned in Cheektowaga, 100 feet from the Buffalo line— with a clerk, the city attorney, and a pile of commitment forms that had been completed in advance. In fact, the evening papers had already put out extras announcing that the Count and other tramp leaders had each been given 90 days in the penitentiary and the rank and file 10. This revelation enraged the marchers. When they arrived at the court, they refused to enter but banded around the Count in a field across the street.[32]

The Count's refusal to walk inside the court confused the inexperienced sheriff, who deferred to the Buffalo police. Captain Killeen took command and, mindful of the jurisdictional niceties, ordered the sheriff to send his men to take the Count, promising to back them with all the Buffalo police present. It is unclear whether a deputy was sent to get the Count, followed immediately by a rush of deputies, mounted Buffalo police, and foot patrolmen, or whether the mounted Buffalo police actually led the charge. In either case, a well-disciplined, club-swinging charge by police and deputies lasted three to five minutes.

The extent of the gunplay is hard to determine. The newspaper reporters on the scene described bullets flying "like hail." It is clear that most of the shots were fired by Sheriff Taggert's deputies; whether any of the hoboes fired weapons remains questionable. All of the reporters except one claimed that they saw a few revolvers concealed in the hands of the tramps. A bullet grazed the head of a deputy, and the tramp who reportedly fired the shot suffered a shotgun blast in his leg. In spite of all the injuries, no one called an ambulance for 20 minutes. One reporter later described what he called the "Battle of Hobo Run":

> The level green field looked like a place of battle. Groaning men with blood streaming from heads and bodies lay prostrate on the field and the grass was dyed with blood. Miraculous no one killed—a score wounded, ten seriously.[33]

This sympathetic account belies the hostility of the daily papers. They praised the police action and described the tramps in the worst terms they could muster: "The hobo army of embryo Anarchists scattered like sheep after being shot and clubbed and the haughty Count became a cringing coward and begged for his life, crouching on his knees like a whipped cur."[34]

Within minutes Rybakowski's industrial army had been crushed by the Buffalo police and Taggert's deputies. No sooner had the ambulance cleared the scene than the remaining hoboes were lined up and hauled before the judge. The confusion of the battle complicated the commitment process. Because longer sentences were now in order, the judge had to fill out the commitment forms again. Still, it took less than two hours to try all 70 men, and by the time the judge finished with these, the police had brought in 20 more picked up in a massive search of the area. They were also sentenced on the spot. The Count and 10 other leaders received the longest hearing. They were finally bound over for felony indictments for assualt and committed to jail pending indictment.

The sentences of the others ranged from six months (the maximum under the tramp act) to discharge. As the *Express* reported: "It was a puzzle to discover the basis for discrimination in sentencing." The key variables appeared to be whether or not the accused had a family, length of "tramphood," and degree of dirtiness or raggedness. About 10 followers were discharged without punishment; most were from Buffalo and had just joined the army, though a few were family men from Cleveland and Detroit. The jail terms given to other Buffalo residents were illegal because the tramp act applied only to nonresidents of the county. The lengths of the sentences were deliberately staggered so that the men would be released and thrown out of town at different times to prevent regrouping.

There remained the problem of the Count and the 10 other leaders held in jail awaiting charges. Three days later the district attorney decided not to seek felony indictments. He reasoned that an assault charge would not stand up in court because there was no evidence that the accused had assaulted anyone and because no jury would convict a man so popular with local workers. The prisoners were therefore returned to Judge Foster's court in Cheektowaga to be tried as tramps. A heavy guard attested to police fears that supporters would try to rescue the Count. These supporters had hired an attorney for the Count so that he, unlike the others, had some semblance of a trial. The major witnesses for the prosecution were two deputies, who testified that they had seen the Count in the hobo camp and had heard him request more bread from the sheriff. When the prosecution rested, the Count's attorney made a 20-minute speech moving for a dismissal on the ground that the prosecution had not proven that any of the accused were tramps. Twenty members of the audience applauded. The motion was denied, and the Count took the stand. He protested that not one of his supporters was a tramp, that he was employed as a newspaper editor in Chicago and had $45 when he was arrested. Judge Foster convicted him nevertheless and sentenced him to 90 days. The others got from 10 to 90 days, and all were taken to the Erie County Penitentiary.[35] As their sentences expired, each was placed on a train and sent a short distance outside of the county.

The president of the Central Labor Union, who was a machinist working for the Lackawanna Railroad, vigorously criticized the police action. His statement reveals the class consciousness of the Buffalo workers and their solidarity with the tramps:

When I visited their camp they would not accept admission—wouldn't take money from a workingman. I looked around for the vicious, dirty, bloodthirsty tramps our press has been talking about all week but couldn't find any. I found them ragged but they had tried to improve themselves as much as they could with soap and water. I found that fifty of the men had union cards. The sheriff did good by giving them 300 loaves. How is it that he changed his mind so quickly and gave them bullets instead of bread, treating them like criminals instead of hardworking men?[36]

Other Central Labor Union delegates characterized the sheriff's deputies as "vagrants who hung around city hall" and insisted that "there is not a workingman among them." During 1894 the CLU adopted at least three resolutions attacking the police for repression of working people.[37] The strongest of these was a response to the suppression of Rybakowski's Army:

Resolved that we the delegates to the CLU in regular meeting assembled do hereby emphatically denounce the said Sheriff Taggert and Superintendent Bull for the flagrant and high handed manner in which they violated the law and treated a body of heroic and self-reliant poor to imprisonment without cause, without reason, and without a semblance of a fair hearing. The indecent haste with which the aforesaid officials acted proves their unworthiness.[38]

Even such modest support was remarkable, considering the danger the police posed for working-class groups that defended tramps.

POLICE CONTROL OF TRAMPS IN CHICAGO

Of all large cities in the Ohio Valley/Great Lakes region, Chicago saw the largest number of unemployed workers travel through its environs, both because of its size and because of its prominence as the center of the country's transportation system. However, vagrancy arrests in Chicago rarely amounted to more than 1,000 per year—a fraction of Buffalo's annual record in a city more than five times as large. Exceptional circumstances usually account for years of higher arrests—for example, the Pullman strike of 1894 (here as in Buffalo, tramps were accused of instigating the trouble) and the crackdown on tramps ordered by Chief of Police George M. Shippy in 1907. Equally exceptional was 1904, when the Chicago police arrested only 68 vagrants.[39]

Chicago's method of dealing with vagrancy provides a striking contrast to Buffalo's. In 1901 the city established the Municipal Lodging House, administered by the Department of Police. Vagrants traditionally called at police stations for lodging, and by 1901 the problem had gotten out of hand: between 1898 and 1901 a total of 472,337 people had been lodged at police stations. This number was too great to arrest, but the problem of arresting them may have been secondary. The chief of police appears to have been more concerned about placing these vagrants into the labor market, which required the creation of a supplementary social institution. According to the 1903 annual report of the Municipal Lodging House:

> The central purpose of the administration of the Municipal Lodging House has been to provide a clearing house for all homeless men and boys stranded in Chicago. Each morning for the past year, the lodgers for the previous night have been distributed in accordance with their capacity and need. The theory of helping others to help themselves by sending the worthy and displaced laborer and willing but ignorant and discouraged country boy to paid employment, and the sick and disabled to dispensaries, hospitals, and homes, and the criminal to the house of correction, has prevented the exploitation of the unfortunate by municipal authority, or the equally harmful exploitation of the municipality by corrupt loafers and vagabonds.

The 1904 annual report complained of a "slack demand for labor" early in the year but proudly claimed that "during the last six months over 40% of the lodgers have been sent to paid employment. . . ."[40]

In addition to serving as an employment agency, the Municipal Lodging House attempted to regulate the unemployed workers in the city. Cards with directions for referring applicants to
the house were made available to all citizens of Chicago, to be
passed out to beggars instead of money or food. Furthermore,
the Municipal Lodging House was one instrument to be used to
separate the deserving from the undeserving poor. The police
stations continued to take vagrants, but only after 10 P.M. These
lodgers received a card directing them to the Municipal Lodging
House and informing them that they would be arrested if they
ever again sought lodging at a police station. The police took
pride in the great reduction in the number of lodgers under the
house system: during its first four years the house lodged 78,230
men—about 17 percent of the vagrants lodged in police stations
during the preceding four-year period.

Lodging houses tried to dispense discipline along with their
starchy food and hard beds. Expenses were nine cents per day
per man, and, not surprisingly, many poor men preferred the
streets. Dr. Ben L. Reitman, the famous anarchist, disguised
himself as a hobo and applied to the Municipal Lodging House.
His account of the experience indicates why men would "walk
the street all night" rather than admitting themselves to the lodging house:

> I went to the man at the little box office at the head of those dark
> stairs of yours. "Hurry up there, you hobo," was the way he ad-
> dressed me. "Do you think we can keep open all night for you fel-
> lows." Then he asked me if I was drunk. . . . The next thing was a
> bath and a medical examination. They made me stand naked in a
> cold room for an hour.
> Then they gave me a clean bed. I will admit that. But the next
> morning they nearly choked me with sulphur fumes in fumigating my
> clothes. Why they treated me like a dirty beast, just because I was
> poor and had no home. Is that kind and Christian? Then they gave
> me a little coffee and bread and sent me on my way.

Superintendent James Mullenbach of the Municipal Lodging
House plainly did not like the criticism and retorted: "You had
all the coffee and bread you wanted, didn't you?"[41]

Poor men continued to sleep on the floor of police stations rather than in beds at the Municipal Lodging House, indicating that Reitman must have been on the mark. When a crackdown on vagrants doubled the arrest rate between 1906 and 1907, it was further proof that the lodging house could not solve the tramp problem without being backed by police clubs and arrest powers.[42]

Both the Municipal Lodging House plan, as operated in Chicago, and the plan for tramp repression in Buffalo attempted to regulate the labor force through the police. The Buffalo method was suited to small- and middle-sized cities, where a labor force could be locally recruited. Tramps were easily recognized, arrested, punished, and driven off. Chicago's sheer size and location made this method impracticable. But Chicago also was a national recruiting center for all kinds of labor—seasonal labor on railroads, lumberjacks, and agricultural workers all moved through the city. Locally, industrial expansion was fed by a constant supply of new workers on a larger scale than available to any city except New York. The Municipal Lodging House's 40 percent employment record was the result of careful cooperation between employers and local governmental institutions— with the police channeling tramps into the employment network.

CONCLUSIONS

Vagrancy statutes were often intended to accomplish complex and conflicting functions, and thus they often complicated police enforcement patterns. One function was to prevent the erosion of the marginal segments of the working class into the criminal class. Chicago Superintendent John M. Collins put this problem clearly:

> The close and apparently inevitable relation of the great vagrant class to the distinctively criminal element of a community is well known to everyone who has a first-hand acquaintance with the underworld of a large city. From the vagrant class recruits pass into the criminal ranks, and to the vagrant class they return as a refuge from pursuit and detection.[43]

A second function was the policing of the most marginal sector of the working class, one presumably prone to involvement in community class struggles. To the extent that vagrants and tramps were unemployed workers, they had an obvious stake in class struggles carried out in the form of popular strikes or other community actions.

In addition, tramps and vagrants emerged as a political issue, one of many such issues serving to delineate class lines in the late nineteenth and early twentieth centuries. Who more obviously symbolized the exploitation of the capitalist system than unemployed workers, on the rails as a result of the depressions of the mid-1880s, 1893–1897, and 1906–1908. Conflicts such as that between Count Rybakowski's industrial army and the Buffalo police, repeated throughout the nation in the 1890s, demonstrated the repressive potential of the tramp acts to impose severe sentences on large numbers of workers for trivial offenses.

In terms of the entire range of police activity in the late nineteenth century, patterns of tramp act enforcement were not as important as strike control or the general policing of working-class community life, but these patterns are nonetheless an integral part of the total picture of police activity of the period. Whether the tramp was a benign "wandering Willie" just trying to make it through town, or a member of a 300-man industrial army, the police were an important force to reckon with. Although the bourgeoisie might have preferred that the municipal police lock up all the tramps in order to stabilize local class relations, there just were not enough jails or police to discipline wandering workers. Finally, it is important to note that regional labor market considerations also were important. In the West there was a need for a large, mobile labor force for harvesting, lumbering, mining, and railroad building, and cities in this region tended to force tramps "on the road" toward the labor sources. Further east, except for mining, the labor force was much more stable; hence there was no likely market toward which to send the tramps. Eastern cities therefore resorted more frequently to prison terms as the major means of tramp discipline. Whichever strategy was used, the local police department was the institution that implemented it.

CHAPTER TEN

Policing Felony Crime

No ANALYSIS of the development and expansion of the police institution under industrial capitalism can ignore patterns of the
policing of felony crimes—the serious crimes, including robbery, murder, felony assault, rape, and theft of valuable property, punishable by a prison sentence of one year or more. The
image of the police as primarily "crime fighters" dates from the
mid-nineteenth-century and remains with the police today, perhaps to their detriment, as Egon Bittner has pointed out.[1] David
Johnson, in his study of the development of the Philadelphia and
Chicago police forces, cites their crime-fighting role as the most
important reason for the rapid expansion of these forces.[2] Roger
Lane attributes the decline in rates of serious crime after the
middle of the nineteenth-century to the "civilizing effect" of the
new urban police institution.[3] James Richardson, writing about
the New York police, assigns somewhat less importance to the
crime-fighting role, seeing it only as one of several concerns
leading to the early development of the police.[4]

While sociologists of the Chicago school—followed by most
historians of crime and the police—have argued that urbanization "caused" crime by destroying a sense of community and
decaying the moral authority of traditional society, Marxists
have focused on the class relations of industrial society that
have shaped the urban social order. The importance of common

felonies has been overrated, in the Marxist view, to obscure complex patterns of class relations. Common felonies are only one form of criminal behavior and account for a mere 15 percent of all criminal arrests (the remaining 85 percent being misdemeanor offenses) and for an even smaller proportion when offense statistics, including arrests for common ordinance violations, are taken into account.[5] Finally, the data show that the police were relatively unconcerned about *any* form of criminal activity, serious or otherwise—a fact hinted at when we note that the average police officer in the nineteenth century made less than one arrest per week, and then usually for "disorderly conduct."

What, then, is important about felony crime activity in building a better understanding of the late-nineteenth-century American urban police institution? I think that the key elements here are four. First, the police institution capitalized on a legitimate fear of crime that is held to some extent by all classes in an urban community but is felt most strongly by the bourgeoisie and petty bourgeoisie. What the police institution had to gain was legitimation for expansion of the force and for exercise of far more complex forms of social control than it previously attempted. In this view, crime serves the bourgeoisie by extending state hegemony through the police over wider geographic and behavioral ranges of working-class activity.

Second, during the period of rapid industrialization of American cities, class relations were poorly defined. The police institution, through the enforcement of the criminal law, contributed toward socially delineating the boundaries of the working class. The line between respectable and unacceptable working-class behavior was too important to be left to the working class. The police, in effect, became the arbiters of what was working-class. The "dangerous class" of post–Civil War American cities does not overlap with the "lumpenproletariat," a distinction I shall explore at some length.

Third, the police were a social-service institution, expected to render valuable services to some extent to all members of the community, but particularly to the bourgeoisie and the petty bourgeoisie. These classes benefited enormously from the urban social order they created, but they also were made extremely insecure by the violence of the class system that supported that social order. Obviously, confining the dangerous elements geographically was not enough to protect their interests. Quite simply, the expense of private guards was socialized, and working-class taxes were used to help defray the cost.[6]

Finally, the police institution itself was a major influence in structuring urban criminal activity. It often functioned as an arm of the lumpenproletariat, just as it functioned in other contexts as an arm of the bourgeoisie. This obviously represents an enormous contradiction, one that is reflected in the wild cycles of bourgeois reform movements aimed at the police. There can be no question that large segments of American urban police forces spent a good part of their day regulating urban crime patterns for a percentage of the take; at the same time that an officer was judge, jury, and hit man, he was also a partner in crime. This well-documented, quasi-criminal role was very complex, with its own limitations and contradictions. What is most important here is the effect it had on the role of the police institution in the class struggle. I shall argue that these criminal contacts were not inconsistent with the broader role of the police on the side of the bourgeoisie and that, in fact, they contributed a great deal to strengthening it—though not without costs.

CRIME RATES, FEAR OF CRIME, AND CAPITALIST HEGEMONY

Although forms of crime may change to reflect differing modes of production, the phenomenon of crime is a relative constant under capitalism. Thus it is fundamentally incorrect to attribute the development of the police institution to an observable change in patterns of crime. Similarly, though crime rates are obviously an important social phenomena—particularly during periods of socially generated "crime waves"—crime rates in themselves cannot account for changes in the police system over time.

Industrial cities such as Milwaukee, Chicago, Buffalo, and Pittsburgh experienced a great deal of serious crime, especially property crimes, during the late nineteenth and early twentieth centuries. In general, patterns of crime fluctuated from year to year, but the average rates remained about the same between 1870 and 1915. Such statistics would seem to disagree with Lane's argument about the civilizing effect of the early police. To be fair, Lane traces an actual reduction in crime in Boston in the first two-thirds of the nineteenth century, but those rates may well have leveled off later, leaving his data inconclusive.[7] Another way to make the same point is to cite studies like the 1974 Kansas City Preventive Patrol Experiment, which raises serious questions about whether police patrol practices actually reduce serious crime. If this is so in the mid-twentieth century, would it not have been the case in the mid-nineteenth century as well, especially given the much less efficient forms of policing in earlier periods?[8]

Furthermore, nineteenth- and early-twentieth-century crime statistics are *at least* as inaccurate as those from the 1970s, and probably more so. Meaningful comparisons between cities and across time simply cannot be made. The whole period, rather, is characterized by wild fluctuations from one year to the next in many cities and great differences between cities. Some of these data may well reflect actual behavior changes, and some clues on this subject will be discussed later. What is important here is to establish that crime rates in this period were social constructs put to different uses by different groups, depending on the perceived social gain at the moment. Thus, the Buffalo police could report a 20 percent crime increase in one year and argue that crime was actually going down because the police were so efficiently arresting more of the criminals.[9] At other times a smaller increase could be interpreted as a crime wave and incite demands that the police take some kind of action. The major consumers of crime statistics were police departments and the various political factions and their respective newspapers.

It is important to distinguish the phenomenon of "crime waves" from the phenomenon of "crime." The political mobili-

zation of large segments of the population over the law-and-order issue has excited major cities since before the founding of
the American republic. Most commonly, such campaigns exhibit
a strong anti-working-class bias: bourgeois and petty-bourgeois
segments of the working class. Once an issue emerges political-
demand higher levels of repression and control against particular
segments of the working-class. Once an issue emerges politically, it is not uncommon for some working-class elements to join
as well (as in the temperance movement), but their participation
cannot obscure the class interests that law-and-order issues
serve. Even when the working-class raises the issue of greater
protection from crime, it is much less likely to receive police
attention than are the bourgeoisie and petty bourgeoisie. When
workers raise the issue, it is only a "crime problem" requiring
either no police action or limited, ameliorative action; when the
bourgeoisie raise the issue, it is a "crime wave" requiring a major police effort, as well as political action in all arenas of urban
life—"moral training" in schools and churches, legal action to
coerce "responsible" parental action, and tightened controls on
saloons and places of recreation. The "crime wave" became one
additional bourgeois tool to restructure the urban police institution.[10]

The contradiction between the role of the police as crime
fighters and their actual activity was pronounced during the late
nineteenth and early twentieth centuries because of the strong
anti-working-class reputation that the police acquired during
strikes. Workers did not miss the connection. During Chicago's
streetcar strike of 1903 workers repeatedly protested that their
communities were without protection against crime because the
entire police force was engaged in strikebreaking activity. Alderman Bennett expressed the issue in clear class terms:

> While policemen are protecting the property of a corporation, the
> residences of taxpayers are being left exposed to burglars and
> thieves. Policemen are being used as strikebreakers to make it possi-
> ble for a corporation to operate its road.

Alderman Prieb attacked the police chief for his sarcasm in responding to aldermen's charges that he had "stripped the police

stations of men to aid the street railway company." Alderman Moynihan of the Eighth Ward had the data to back up those charges:

> Last night there were nine policemen on duty in my ward. Four of these were on the police ambulance, four on the patrol wagon, and the other was the captain. The ward was left unprotected and there were many robberies.

The *Chicago Tribune,* without approving of these arguments editorially, did them the favor of illustrating them with a cartoon showing a group of stick-up men comfortably settled in a dark alley with furniture, cards, and liquor, amusing themselves as they waited with outstretched guns for a passerby to rob.[11] Although these aldermen were primarily interested in undermining police strike control efforts by demanding that the police return to their neighborhood beats, they made powerful class-based statements about the appropriate functions of the police.

Working-class protests against the failure of the police to protect them from criminal activity were rare, but accusations from the bourgeoisie and petty bourgeoisie were not uncommon. Law-and-order leagues composed of respectable citizens were a regular feature of late-nineteenth- and early-twentieth-century urban life. Such organizations lobbied for tougher police action in eliminating street crime and implicitly supported a wide range of police crackdowns against both the working class and the lumpenproletariat. These law-and-order crackdowns often followed in the wake of strikes or other periods of unrest, when a community's ruling class had some reason to doubt the effectiveness of the police. Whereas attempts to strengthen police forces to increase their strike capabilities were politically touchy, strengthening them to deal with crime waves was politically more acceptable.

The law-and-order leagues in Chicago were probably the largest and politically most important. Not surprisingly, the major one was founded immediately after the streetcar strike of 1903 and the wave of robberies that followed it. The origin of the idea of a crime wave in Chicago in November 1903 stemmed from the removal of police officers from most sections of the city during the strike, but fear did not end with the strike. As the strike was winding down, a spectacular series of police confrontations with a gang of "car-barn bandits" (so named for their most famous robbery), during which several policemen were killed, excited and unsettled the city.

In terms of their level of activity, the gang indeed stood out: eight killings in eight known robberies was quite an infamous record, and later more robberies came to light. But more intriguing was the sociological background of the bandits. They were not lumpenproletarian elements but rather the sons of respectable working-class families. They refused to work, preferring robbery and hanging around pool halls and saloons to working-class drudgery. Nor were they remorseful in the least. Harvey Van Dein and Peter Neidermeier told Mayor Harrison, Chief of Police O'Neil, and 50 other interrogators that they were proud of their five-month crime spree and regretted only that they had been caught. Their arrest, trial, and execution left Chicago's ruling class wondering about the unknown hundreds or thousands of young men who may have made the same choice.[12]

Within a month Chicago was in the throes of a major law-and-order scare. On December 9 the nucleus of a citizens' group met for the first time in the solidly upper-middle-class neighborhood of Hyde Park and immediately determined to hold a citywide meeting five days later. Though the ostensible reason for the initial meeting was a high rate of robberies, the focus quickly turned to liquor-law enforcement, a crackdown on pool halls, and the poor discipline in Chicago's schools. Citizens charged at the meeting that dozens of young boys were imitating the car-barn bandits. A 12-year-old had recently admitted to breaking into 11 houses to get money for cigarettes. Two other youths, aged 13 and 15, had been caught armed with revolvers behind corn shocks in a farmer's field.[13]

The Chicago police seldom misread the political weathervane and immediately took steps to combat street crime. "Flying squads" of officers were formed to move about the city rapidly and hit trouble spots. Their first targets were the pool halls where tough teenagers hung out. Chief O'Neil gave his men orders to root out all forms of street crime, regardless of who was involved. At the same time, police trial boards heard the cases of officers accused of permitting criminal activity through negligence. The police also prepared a list of 114 people robbed during the preceding 60 days; 7 of the 114 had been killed.[14] These highly visible and publicized actions seemed to be intended only to deflect public criticism. The mayor had ordered the robbery list, and Chief O'Neil's men had trouble preparing it. On its first night out a 20-man flying squad raided two pool rooms and held 40 minors until their parents could pick them up. The police obviously picked an easy target and were aiming to amass impressive statistics rather than to use the flying squadrons to catch robbers.

Not surprisingly, public organizations continued their campaign. Ministers in the wealthier sections of the city denounced the crime rate on Sunday mornings, and a good crowd was ensured for a Tuesday meeting to consolidate all of Chicago's "moral improvement and reform" organizations into one city-wide anticrime crusade under the leadership of a "Committee of Twenty-five." Confederation on the crime issue provided these organizations with a more powerful political base for attack on their traditional working-class targets—saloons, pool halls, and other recreational outlets. Although the preamble of the organization referred to the "inability of the police to enforce law and order," criticism of the police was muted. Judge Richard Tuthill, a spokesman for the group, emphasized:

> We intend to assist the constituted authorities in the suppression of crime, not to "knock" them. I have informed Mayor Harrison that our aim is his aim—the betterment of the police service, and, if possible, the increase of the force. The only things this committee is against are crime and the conditions which produce crime in Chicago. . . .

The *Chicago Tribune* reported that the society "blue book" and the membership lists of Chicago's major clubs had been consulted to select members of the Committee of Twenty-five. The

City Club dispatched one of its members to New York City to study police reform there.[15] In January 1904 the City Club committee brought Captain August Piper, a New York City police expert, to Chicago. Accordingly, his study on police discipline, the best-known product of the committee, concentrated on police reform and working-class public order activities (see Chapter 7).

Why did such bourgeois and petty-bourgeois reform organizations intervene in the police system? What was the influence of that intervention? Most often these bourgeois reform movements are explained in terms of weakened ruling-class control over the working-class and the police and of failure of the police as an instrument of class domination. In Chicago, however, the police had just completed a masterful job of breaking the streetcar strike. Thus, the Chicago crime commission represented a ruling-class experiment, an attempt to continue to prod the police in the right direction, to ensure their continued loyalty. In a period when efforts to establish a professional, internal control mechanism on the police institution were weak, these indirect pressures from citizens' groups helped to legitimate and monitor the police institution.

No other single issue could legitimate as much police intervention in the lives of citizens as the anticrime issue. And crime could always be an issue; it was readily available politically to justify a wide variety of police intervention. This does not mean that crime was opportunistically used in ways that members of bourgeois crime commissions knew to be false. The crime issue bolstered a wide range of other social concerns of the bourgeoisie and petty bourgeoisie. The police were pressured to increase their level of intervention into the entire complex of issues concerning the socialization of the working class. The net result of 1,000 additional officers in Chicago, recruited to step up the fight against crime, was likely to be more reprimands for working-class young people and more disorderly conduct arrests than a significant increase in felony arrests.

The working class was not overly concerned about crime and never organized politically to influence the police institution to action in that area. Rather, the working class was concerned about the social use or misuse to which police officers were put. The crime issue deflected the class issue, however. No one could argue against "crime control." This was the one issue on which the police could be effectively exploited in virtually any social context.

EROSION OF THE WORKING CLASS

I have argued that the real object of police activity was the working class, not the lumpenproletariat. Workers are supposed to adhere strongly to a work ethic; yet at the same time they are fully aware that a lifetime of hard work will not raise most of them above the class position into which they were born. Hence, a good proportion of the working class may well reject the work ethic and move downward into the lumpenproletariat—the class of criminals, beggars, and others permanently outside of the economic system.[16] One key function of the police was to maintain the existing class structure by retarding the movement of the working class in the lumpen direction, an effort aimed primarily at the bottom half of the working class. Not surprisingly, this portion of the population was most frequently arrested. In the context of late-nineteenth-century urban America, Charles Loring Brace's "dangerous classes" clearly included the lumpenproletariat. But he also applied that rubric to a substantial proportion of the working class—specifically, to those who were unemployed, who held marginal jobs, who were of "unsavory" immigrant groups (Italians, Poles, and Irish), and to tramps looking for work. More important, there was a marked tendency to fit lumpen terminology around specific types of behavior rather than class. Thus violent strikers, corner loungers, rough teenagers, and vagrants all became part of the "dangerous class," regardless of their work role or their class origin.[17] In effect, individuals, families, and whole communities moved back and forth between the respectable working class and the dangerous class from one day to the next, depending on their behavior. The police institution was thus assigned the heavy burden of combatting the "erosion" of working-class values.

The language of the Chicago crime wave of 1903 is replete with such notions. It has already been pointed out that the "car-barn bandits" were regarded as especially dangerous because they were of respectable working-class background. The story of Emil Roeski, the last of them captured, provides an apt illustration. In his statement to the police he described the process of descending in one day from brewery worker to one of the most dangerous professional criminals in Chicago: "I was working in the Northwestern Brewery when Van Dein and Marx came to me and asked me to join them in holdups. I wasn't getting much wages so I quit my job and they fixed me out with guns. . . ."[18]

Schoolboys in November 1903 aroused the alarm of police, school officials, and reformers by their militancy in the streetcar strike, a role common to teenagers in many mass strike actions. The strike spread to the school system as children refused to attend classes with "scab" teachers who rode the cars to work. Immediately after the strike, police and truant authorities engaged in a major crackdown on truancy and on the informal "clubs" of male teenagers. Chicago Superintendent of Schools W. Lester Bodine expressed the fear of many when he admonished, "This is what makes the Neidermeiers, the Van Deins, the Roeskis, and the Marxs." He did not mean that the boys were lumpenproletariat, but was warning that they were in constant danger of becoming so. Only the concerted action of the police, the schools, and related social agencies could save them.[19]

Strikes, as we have seen, were dangerous not only because the working class could win direct concessions from the capitalist class but also because they encouraged the development of lumpen tendencies inherent within the working class. Workers who learned to fight, block tracks, beat up scabs, and evade the police were learning both real skills and a value orientation that was very dangerous indeed. By attributing strike violence to the worst lumpen elements, capitalists both denied that legitimate workers could engage in such activity and drew a strong line between the working class and the lumpenproletariat. Thus strikes were defined in part as struggles against crime and criminal tendencies in the working class rather than as struggles between labor and capital.

Similarly, saloon laws, pool hall crackdowns, and ordinances controlling working-class dances were regarded by the bourgeoisie not as unwarranted interferences in workers' recreational activity but as necessities to keep the working class from sinking into the lumpenproletariat. Public order offenses defined the thin line between workers who could be counted on and those who could drift, almost at a whim, into the ranks of violent strikers, holdup men, tramps, and drunks.

The ambiguities of the class basis of criminal activity show up especially around the issue of tramping. Most people recognized that widespread unemployment and poverty had at least something to do with tramping. Nevertheless, a strong line had to be held against tramps to maintain the urban working class, and imposing a criminal image on the urban tramp reinforced a fundamentally weak boundary line. Thus, all of the traveling unemployed were potentially "yeggs"—half-tramps and half-criminals who traveled from city to city engaging in burglaries, begging scams, and assorted con jobs. The Pinkerton agency clearly regarded the yeggs as formerly respectable members of the working class:

> Nine-tenths of this class are made up of so-called driftwood of humanity in this country, composed of about one-half natives, one-quarter foreign descent, and one-quarter foreign birth. Most of these are mechanics or have been railroad men, iron workers, or originally in some trade; have lost their places of employment through labor troubles; and in stealing rides on cars, or tramping from one city to another, they have formed the acquaintance of criminals, gradually becoming criminal themselves.
>
> A mechanic who loses his employment through a strike or other labor troubles leaves his native town for larger cities in search of employment, intending at first to find work and continue in it. But being unsuccessful he gradually drifts to lodging houses or to the cheaper class of saloons, until, his money being exhausted, he through pure desperation starts out with some other mechanic simi-

larly situated "on the road," tramping, beating his way from one city to another, begging his meals. And it is while doing this that he forms the acquaintance, in camps, of the yegg, who proceeds to take him in hand to determine what his ability consists of. If a mechanic explains that he is a machinist or has been an iron worker, especially in building construction, he is gradually introduced to other yeggmen and finally becomes a member of a yegg tribe. They may also be recruited from ordinary tramps who are possessed with extraordinary personal courage, and resource.[20]

Some sense of how this class vision operated in day-to-day policing can be gathered from a Pittsburgh policy regarding the control of a sneak thief problem:

The Second District has not been free from sneak thieves and burglars the past year, and there has been quite a number of houses entered. However, I am glad to say, we have been able to capture several good sneak thieves and burglars the past year, and they are doing time in the Work House and Penitentiary. The Second District is a great field for thieves of all kinds, it being the main resident part of the city. The officers are always on the lookout for this kind of people. All suspicious persons and vagrants who cannot give a good account of themselves are very promptly taken into custody and sent to the Work House or Jail.[21]

Such a mechanical image of where criminals came from fit directly with police patterns of class repression. Crime control policies were doubly exploitative of workers: on one hand, workers were not protected from criminal activity aimed at them in their own communities and on the way to and from work; on the other hand, workers were closely monitored by the police as potential criminals. Criminal images followed class lines, and crime control policies paralleled class control policies inherent in other police activity.

SOCIAL SERVICES RENDERED BY THE POLICE

City police rendered a wide range of social services to all classes in the nineteenth century, just as they do today. In particular, all classes received some, though not equal, crime control services. A broad range of services went to working-class communities— probably in the long run the majority of all police services, as sociologist Egon Bittner has suggested. Most important, the police represented a source of resolution for the various small-scale disputes common in working-class communities, from family altercations and neighborhood arguments to petty problems involving bureaucracies such as the welfare department and the school. New immigrants used the police officer on the beat as a resource person to direct them to jobs and social services. Police officers provided medical care, called ambulances, gave directions, and sent other urban services such as sanitation men, street repairmen, and building inspectors to places where they were needed. As the most visible representative of state power, the officer on the beat was a central figure in working-class communities.[22]

Of all these roles, the crime control role traditionally attracts the most attention from historians and sociologists. As Bittner points out, a common thread running through all police roles is the officer's power to use force to settle the problems he encounters, and the crime control role patterns prevalent in the late nineteenth century were not unlike those of the late twentieth century. Although the working class was undoubtedly disproportionately victimized by crime, the petty bourgeoisie and the bourgeoisie received a larger share of police protection against crime. Crime rarely threatened the physical security of the wealthy in the same way that it could devastate a working-class family, but it was a particular fear of the bourgeoisie because of the amount of property they held. Furthermore, any form of social instability, of which crime is but one indication, threatened the delicate social order within which the bourgeoisie and petty bourgeoisie preserved their positions. The evidence shows clearly that the police treated crimes against the propertied and those against workers much differently.

There is no question that the police knew they had a special obligation to look out for the security of propertied middle-class and bourgeois citizens. Inspector John McAleese of Pittsburgh's First District complained bitterly that "even the class of people

most benefited by the administration of vigorous police protect-
ive agencies are the least demonstrative in giving us the poor
credit of commendation for our work." McAleese nevertheless
boasted of his protection of business interests:

> The business section of the city is thoroughly protected; the property
> of our merchants is as thoroughly watched over in day time as at
> night, and the system of observation and patrol is of that character
> which requires an officer to so frequently traverse his beat that no
> daring street robbery could occur at anytime, without almost instant-
> ly bringing the guilty parties under the eye of a pursuing policeman.[23]

Inspector William McKelvey of the working-class Third District
defended his record while excusing a homicide:

> The record is a good one, considering the class of people in this part
> of the city. Besides having many good citizens of the American, Ger-
> man, Irish, English, and other nationalities, we have a large number
> of the worst classes from the lower European states, who, if propen-
> sities to vice remained unchecked would commit all crimes in the
> calendar without a quiver of conscience.[24]

The urban police, then, were charged with crime prevention in
a few select neighborhoods and with discipline and "civilization" in the large, immigrant, working-class neighborhoods. Descriptions of police work in the latter neighborhoods often evoke
images of a colonizing army. Reformer James Forbes, in con-
cluding his discussion of "The Reverse Side" for the Pittsburgh
survey of 1906–1908, painted this picture of the problem:

> The former Mafios gains notoriety by his importation of threat and
> knife, spectacular forms of lawlessness. The Slav drinks, batters,
> and sometimes slays. The Jewish parasite of eastern Europe reas-
> serts his old work relation of panderer, usurer, and liquor seller. Thus
> foreign convict types, no less than native yeggs and pickpockets, add
> their quota to the resident criminals of any American city. But the
> great bulk of those whose strange names find a place on the police
> dockets or are haled to court by constables are recruited from a dif-
> ferent sort. They are the inarticulate rank and file; whose burdens,

being the heaviest, are naturally held to the strictest accounting. Ignorant, uncouth, illiterate, compelled to adapt themselves mercilessly to entirely new conditions of life, labor, speech, and conventions, they blunder into the police net, and receive almost inevitably the meed of their helplessness. Southern Negroes, Italians, Slavs—they clog the courts, crowd the jails, rot and choke in the upper tiers of our prisons, go to the gallows or the electric chair, crazed, screaming, but always inarticulate.[25]

Forbes offered a sympathetic analysis, distinguishing the "ignorant, uncouth, illiterate" rank and file from his ethnocentric characterization of criminal types, but the result was the same: the urban police were given a special set of responsibilities relating to the socialization of immigrants, and crime control techniques were another method of achieving their goal, just as public order law enforcement was. In the area of crime control, however, the stakes were higher. The development of class society required a strong police anticrime effort, no matter how great a proportion of police time went into other activities. Someone had to guard the personal lives and property of substantial citizens, and the municipal police did this much more efficiently—and certainly at less cost to those same citizens— than any other institution.

POLICE AS CO-CONSPIRATORS

Perhaps the most noted feature of the relationship between the police and felony crime was the symbiosis of the police and the criminal class. That is, some members of the police force actually joined the lumpenproletarians as professional criminals in blue uniform. No data document the extent of such behavior, and, ironically, it may not have been as common as the police reformers claimed. But, in any case, it was too common.

How did police complicity in crime affect their role in the class struggle? Here predatory criminal activity must be considered as well. Detectives and patrolmen in effect licensed criminals to victimize workers in certain neighborhoods in return for

a percentage of the profit. These activities were regularly de-
cried in Pittsburgh, Chicago, New York, and other cities. Again,
James Forbes articulates reform sentiments:

> The traditional duty of the police is the protection of property, and
> herein lies the first test of any police department. In whatever city
> habitual offenders with deft fingers "work" unmolested upon street
> or railroad cars, at circuses or fairs; with nimble cards or oily
> tongues in bar or hotel; tap imaginary wires from race track or pool
> room; "hoist" goods from department stores, or with jimmy and
> dark lantern force entrance to office, vault, or dwelling, the premise
> may be assured that they work upon a business basis with the local
> police. In the vernacular, such operations are "percentage" jobs.[26]

Forbes found that although Pittsburgh's 1907 reform administration had largely eliminated percentage jobs in Pittsburgh proper,
many of the objectionable practices had simply migrated to
Pittsburgh's industrial suburbs:

> Take, for example, McKeesport, the largest mill town in Pitts-
> burgh District. This was in 1907–08 commonly reported to be a "per-
> centage burg"; namely, a town where the local police department,
> for a consideration, tolerated raids by outside gun mobs on pay day
> at the mills. The time for the gun mob to work was strictly limited. It
> had to be a case of getting in to town, "tearin' 'er wide open" and
> "blowin' on a rattler," all in the same day. This to "cover" the
> "coppers." Here the locally informed criminal had value to give the
> outsider. He sent the "dope" to the outside "guns", and thus pre-
> pared they utilized every moment of their working time. Such a mill
> paid at a certain hour, for example, or the workmen had to ride on a
> certain car under conditions favorable for "dips" (pickpockets). An-
> other mill had a saloon in its immediate vicinity, the proprietor of
> which could be "reached" to the extent of standing for "strong arm"
> work (hold-ups) or an occasional "peter" (use of knock-out drops).
> In another town a certain class of worker was not wise to confeder-
> ate money.[27]

Holdups and pickpocketing were supplemented by all manner of
confidence games and phoney games of chance:

The operation of a "chuck-a-luck" machine or "wheel of fortune" was for many years a favorite means for separating the workman, especially the foreigner, from his pay. Worthless "prizes" were given out to keep the interest alive, and clever boosters (confederates) were employed who won the more valuable awards. An operator who did not clear $50 to $60 a day with a wheel of this kind was doing poorly. After fixing the local cop, or such substitute for a policeman as the neighborhood afforded, paying his boosters and the rent for the wheel a comfortable income remained for the operator. . . .[28]

What was particularly vicious about this exploitation was the selection of targets: workingmen on payday, streetcars carrying workers home, railroad stations where newly arriving immigrants who showed money for tickets were pickpocketed or induced to deposit their money in tin boxes for "safekeeping." Paths leading away from steel mills were "worked" on payday by thieves and swindlers. Even the generosity and class solidarity of workingmen was turned against them by criminal rings specializing in phoney begging scams. Cripples begging from workers lined the streets from the factories on paydays. Whitey O., who enjoyed the protection of the Allegheny City police in 1908, illustrates this vicious swindle:

Whitey was one of the hard-boiled people who was "in right" with the Allegheny bulls, and could and would fix anything within reason for suitable compensation. His picture was in the Rogues' Gallery in Pittsburgh, and his furnished rooming house was a center for fake cripples like the docket-thrower, M. According to a police authority, this was a real "cripple factory" where young men brought in from other cities were "fixed-up"—furnished with crutches, and their arms or hands bandaged in order to carry out the pretense that they were bonafide workmen who had been injured in the mills.[29]

All policemen had some opportunity to collect under these practices, but detectives profited the most because they were in a unique position to develop a mutually advantageous relationship with the underworld:

It has been this detective element which has tended to give tone to police work as a whole. (An ex-pimp and an ex-thief were two professional "guns" on the Pittsburgh staff in 1907–08.) The tendency to crystallize the work of the department in the phrase "set a thief to catch a thief" is one which has inhibited the natural development of the police department into a modern and scientific agency of society.[30]

The 1913 investigation of the Pittsburgh police department singled out the detective division for special criticism, particularly its practice of rewarding "stool pigeons" by letting them engage in minor crimes under police protection.[31]

The detective's stock in trade was his intimate knowledge of criminals, criminal tactics, and specific crimes and criminal plans. Detectives developed extensive networks of stool pigeons and built complex personal relationships with criminals, often based on exchanges of favors—exchanges that necessarily promoted law violation and made detectives accessories to crime. Moreover, much of a detective's work was not the suppression but the regulation of semiapproved forms of crime, particularly gambling and prostitution. To the extent that payoffs were a major regulating device, detectives exercised underworld functions roughly akin to protection rackets.

Mark Haller describes operations in Chicago that, if anything, were more extensive than those in Pittsburgh. Pickpocket gangs occasionally divided territories under the regulation of police officers, so that if an irate citizen complained, the money could be returned. Similarly, officers occasionally worked the streetcars with pickpockets so that if a citizen "caught" the offender the officer could promptly appear, "arrest" the criminal, and hustle him away. Reportedly, con men in 1914 were required to pay a $20 operating fee to the bunco squad, plus 10 percent of the take if a complaint resulted.[32]

Large gambling losses by the rich occasionally stirred the police to action, even to returning the money (detectives who regulated crime had the advantage of being able to "find" the stolen goods or money and return it—without arrests of course). Milwaukee police staged a series of gambling raids after William Allis, one of the city's leading industrialists, dropped $41,000 on a drunken gambling and sex spree. Although it was common knowledge that the police were in the pay of gamblers and one newspaper was predicting the indictment of the chief, an investigation fell far short of that expectation. Pittsburgh confidence artists took a Marietta, Ohio, banker to New York and swindled him out of $100,000 in a bunco card game, again causing a major scandal when the banker went to the police.[33] Workers had no such ability to protest the activities of gamblers, swindlers, and their protectors, and the money that went to the police this way is best seen as one more form of exploitation inflicted by the police.

SUPPRESSING FELONY CRIMINAL ACTIVITY

In considering the interrelationships among the police, class, and crime, it is important not to obscure the police suppression of a great deal of urban crime. The practice of crime suppression through preventive patrol—still the major crime prevention technique—originated with the night watch systems. Most police officers in the period under consideration here worked the traditional afternoon or midnight shift. Most shifts passed uneventfully; routine confrontations with potentially criminal situations could be ended with a simple order to "move on."

The Milwaukee police employed a particularly effective preventive technique that may have accounted for the low felony crime rate in Milwaukee (about half that of Buffalo, an industrial city of about the same size). At the same time that the Milwaukee police protected organized gambling—and shared in its proceeds—they also maintained a rigid policy of arresting potential criminals on "suspicion" and running them out of town. Although this tactic appears to resemble public order enforcement, suspicion arrests were distinct from class-based vagrancy arrests. Milwaukee arrested many more people for suspicion than most other cities, although the practice was common everywhere. At times, arrests for suspicion equaled the official property crime arrests, and they seldom fell below 50 percent of the property crime arrest rate. Furthermore, suspicion arrests probably account for Milwaukee's low property crime rate: where a property crime charge could not be proven, the offender was charged with suspicion, locked up while the police investigated the case, and then ordered out of town. Suspicion arrests were also used in connection with gambling. Professional out-of-town gamblers were arrested, to the benefit of local gambling houses. Milwaukee's Chief Janssen was proud of his department's vigorous policy: "The city has been remarkably free of crime. . . . I attribute this gratifying state of affairs largely to the vigilance and activity of the detective force who have arrested and driven from the city 234 criminals and dangerous persons."[34]

Suspicion arrests may have performed an additional function for detectives and patrolmen on the take. The identification and persecution of a "criminal class" is a simple matter that can be delegated to a few detectives each day. Assigned to the major railroad stations and downtown hotels and hangouts, they could easily note the arrival of "suspicious" characters, particularly with the aid of a "rogues' gallery" of photographs of offenders known to operate in the region. Local stool pigeons also must have helped. Obviously, such arrests were highly subjective. Furthermore, they may well have provided a cover for bad police work and the protection of gamblers. They demonstrated that the police department was alert and efficiently protecting the public from criminal predators.[35]

The standard method of staking out railroad stations, hotel lobbies, and other hangouts of professional criminals later gave way to more sophisticated methods as specialized detective bureaus developed during the 1880s and 1890s. The circulation of rogues' gallery photographs between cities did much to combat the increased mobility of criminals. The telegraph facilitated police contacts between cities, and detectives were detailed around the country on various police business. For example, 19 detectives from Baltimore, Buffalo, Chicago, Cincinnati, Detroit, Milwaukee, New York, Philadelphia, St. Louis, and Toledo assisted the Pittsburgh police in catching thieves at the Grand Army of the Republic Annual Encampment in that city in 1894. Contacts made at gatherings such as this led to the first attempts at nationwide cooperation among police departments.[36]

When detectives chose to be crime fighters, they could be very effective. Nineteenth-century methods emphasized crime control at the expense of human rights, as exemplified by Superintendent William F. Byrnes's famous order to New York police to arrest all known thieves found south of Fulton Street in order to stop a wave of bank robberies. The widespread use of suspicion arrests, again a violation of human rights, was also apparently effective to an extent. Perhaps no police practice has received as much attention as the infamous "third degree," or regular practice of brutality to obtain confessions (as opposed to the more routine clubbing of workers while making arrests on the street). Third-degree tactics were widespread and effective in forcing confessions and solving crimes. But, like other police abuses, occasionally these tactics backfired and fueled demands for change. Chicago in the winter of 1905–1906 saw a major scandal over extensive police brutality. The police, in trying to solve a series of murders of wealthy people, used the third degree to pry confessions from suspected murderers of better-than-average social background. A wave of protests against police brutality followed. The police, however, following a pattern perhaps too familiar even today, vigorously denied that such practices ever existed.[37]

CONCLUSIONS

Municipal police departments of the late nineteenth and early twentieth centuries faced crime problems not unlike those of today, and their methods of dealing with crime would be recognized by modern departments: emphasis on preventive patrol, with a specialized detective bureau that tried to match new crimes to the crime patterns of known criminals. Then as now, the need to suppress crime was overemphasized to the point of legitimating police intervention in the social lives of working-class communities.

High crime rates are a predictable feature of class society, a hypothesis made by Engels in *The Condition of the Working Class in England* and clearly borne out in societies, developed and underdeveloped alike, that exhibit sharp class distinctions.[38] Merely showing that the urban police had a role in combatting crime begs the question of the class basis of both crime and crime fighting. Clearly, the police fought crime along predictable class lines. But perhaps the most important function of the crime-fighter role of the police is ideological. The repressive police institution, so necessary for the maintenance of capitalism, simply could not perform any social functions at all without its legitimating crime-fighter role.

CHAPTER ELEVEN

Conclusion

THE AMERICAN POLICE INSTITUTION and its role in American society cannot be understood outside class relations and the class struggle. The fluctuating industrial economy of the late nineteenth and early twentieth centuries produced a complex set of rapidly changing class relations, and the social institutions that developed to deal with this shifting situation assumed a variety of forms. The paradox of the "friendly corner cop" who, on the one hand, directed immigrant families to local sources of welfare assistance, brought home lost kids and drunk husbands and wives, and called the ambulance when a friend fell and broke an arm, but who, on the other hand, broke strikes, locked brothers and sisters in jail, and beat friends is but one of the contradictions of the period. The police officer's role appears less contradictory, however, when viewed in terms of the necessity of legitimating state force and having relatively easy access to workers' communities. This necessity demanded a friendly, nonaggressive approach much of the time. Most workers undoubtedly learned to distinguish between the local cop and the police institution in general. Thus one could have some kind of genuine respect for, if not always complete trust in, the officer on the beat while still having no illusions about whose side the municipal police were on.

Similarly, the bourgeoisie faced its own set of contradictions concerning the police. Their completely unrealistic expectations that the municipal force could in fact effectively control urban class society led to great frustration over the failure of the police to carry out this mission. The limits of the police institution became apparent precisely as the bourgeoisie also had to respond to the first major working-class challenge to its domination of urban politics. There was confusion and disarray in the ranks of the bourgeoisie over proper courses of action in every area of urban politics, including the police issue. Massive shows of violence by both the public police under bourgeois domination and the private police of the major corporations were one response. Another was a move toward "reform" and "professionalization" in order to insulate the municipal police from the rough-and-tumble of an urban politics that was becoming increasingly difficult to dominate. Although the bourgeoisie often criticized the police severely for a number of reasons, they still called on the chief and his men for help during strikes, applied for private keys to patrol boxes, demanded heavier patrols for their own residential districts, and easily induced the cop on the beat to keep rough-looking juveniles away from their shops.

The conception of a "policed society" emerged from the requirements of the ruling class of an increasingly complex urban society. The forms of policing cannot be understood as value-free and inevitable; rather, they were structured by class requirements. The police departments designed by ruling-class civic activists of the mid-nineteenth century were altered by the necessities of the actual policing of the class struggle. The earlier forces dominated (in fact, virtually run) by members of the ruling class gave way to forces dominated by political machines that only partly depended on ruling-class support and that operated, at least in part, according to legal-bureaucratic procedure. These forces were clearly more than simple adjuncts of political machines. When, beginning in the late nineteenth century, the political machines proved to be uncontrollable, "reform" movements shifted further toward legal-bureaucratic organizational forms, completing the shift to the police force we know today.

From the standpoint of the police institution itself, there is an amazing continuity over the past one hundred years. Central to this continuity is the term "professionalization"—now closely associated with the transformation of the police image in the 1960s and 1970s but actually referring to almost exactly the same changes vigorously supported by the chiefs who originally formed the National Chiefs of Police Union in 1893, the direct forerunner of today's International Association of Chiefs of Police. The police chiefs of the 1890s thought that policing should be a full-time career choice, free of control by the ruling political party (meaning also independence from all forms of popular control), requiring some level of skill and training, abiding by institutionally imposed standards of professional behavior, and enjoying job tenure and promotion based on merit. The major difference between the 1890s and 1970s is that the ideal of professionalization has now been thoroughly inculcated into the supposedly value-free ideology of policing. Rational-legal forms have assumed increasing dominance in all areas of the public sector as well.

Police professionalization is properly understood as simply one small part of the total process of rationalization under advanced capitalism. Consistent with the trend toward increasing domination of what sociologist Max Weber called the "rational legal" form, social expectations of the police institution have changed greatly since 1915. Much of the early criticism of the police, as we have seen, was for not doing effectively that which, we know now, could not be done. No one was fully aware of the potentialities of the police institution in the late nineteenth century, and it seems clear that much more was expected of it than it could reasonably have delivered. In the 1980s few citizens expect that the police institution alone can restructure urban life—ironically, an urban life beset by many of the same social problems, caused by the same social forces. Some of the issues have changed; for example, there is little police strike control activity, and standards of urban working-class morality are only minimally determined by police action. Though the social form known as tramping has all but disappeared, the urban unemployed attract a large portion of police attention. Police crime control activity may well be the least changed: virtually the same crimes are of social concern, committed by virtually the same people, and producing the same police response as 80 years ago, including a heavy emphasis on preventive patrol coupled with efficient response to citizen calls for assistance. Not surprisingly, this adds up to essentially the same police function in class society.

Perhaps the most notable change since 1890 is the high level of legitimacy that the police institution today enjoys. Again, this is part of the tendency toward rational-legal forms in the society at large, a tendency that has benefited many public agencies. But it also represents a vigorous job of law-and-order salesmanship, with the bourgeois mass media rather successfully convincing a large proportion of the population that society is a jungle and that only the police can save our civilization. This argument is at least 100 years old, but the social order is more taken for granted today. This transformation in social consciousness is itself a product of the tendency toward rational-legal forms and the intense domination of popular ideology by the state and the bourgeoisie directly. Police success is no longer measured in terms of the absence of conflict, as it was in the nineteenth century. Now the meager police efforts to keep violent crime in check are lauded without any expectation of success.

Marxists have long noted a central contradiction in capitalist development between the demands of the process of capital accumulation and the necessity of maintaining some level of legitimacy for a highly stratified, inherently unjust social order—class society by definition. The process of capital accumulation—the capitalists' continued expansion of power and wealth—historically breeds working-class struggle. Legitimation is the more complex and much less analyzed process whereby the capitalist class socializes the members of all classes to accept the status quo, to see class society as both natural and in the best interests of all classes.

The hypothesis that the police institution is one of the important institutions of capital accumulation stems from Marx's own observation. Stripped of its subtler elements, it argues that the capitalist class was able to accumulate capital at the expense of the working class because, at least in part, it was backed by the coercive power of local police institutions. Without the ability to call on local police for a wide variety of both direct and indirect coercive services, at least some aspects of capitalist development would have necessarily been restructured or slowed down. Restated in the strongest terms, capitalist accumulation is an inherently violent process that would be impossible without the backing of coercive power. This coercion need not be *state* power, although it universally came to be state power in late-nineteenth-century Western industrial societies. The precise reasons for this could be disputed, but will not change the course of the argument here.[1]

More complex is the whole question of the nature of the capitalist state and its municipal-level public institutions. Marxist theorists of the state have formulated numerous hypotheses to explain the complexities of this relationship, all of which deal with essentially the same problem: on one hand, the bourgeoisie clearly have been able to dominate these institutions historically; on the other hand, these institutions have seldom been *completely* dominated by the bourgeoisie and have in fact served to limit some of the powers of the bourgeoisie. This is a difficult problem, and one on which there is no general agreement. Some Marxists pose a theory of "relative autonomy," which emphasizes the partial autonomy of legal and other public institutions. But they do so at the risk of overemphasizing the quality of autonomy, forgetting that it is often an autonomy that the bourgeoisie grant under pressure at some points and then struggle to withdraw at other points. No less a historian than E.P. Thompson highlights the importance of the law to the working class as a *limiting* force on the power of the bourgeoisie.[2]

My analysis has tended toward the opposite position. Although I recognize that the capitalist class was limited by the class struggle and the democratic state form, I see the state and its municipal institutions, including the police, as instruments of the capitalist class. It is now very common for Marxist theorists to be critical of "crude" instrumentalism, but they often make the error of minimizing the extent to which the capitalist state *is* an instrument of the ruling class. I am suggesting instead that we need to focus on theoretical models that explain the limits of ruling-class domination of democratic institutions. One approach is the "class struggle" model, which regards the class struggle as the ultimate limitation on the use of the state as an instrument of the ruling class. To the extent that other classes— primarily the working class, but also the middle class—can mobilize their own power to demand concessions from the state, the ruling class must give way at certain points, sometimes much more willingly than at other times. Similarly, another approach to the limitations of the instrumentalist conception of the state is simply to recognize that there are inherent limitations on the capacity of state power. This is particularly obvious in the area of social control. Even given maximally favorable circumstances (which was never the case in America in the period under study), how much more successful could the police institution have been? Had there been larger, better-organized, professionalized, honest, well-equipped police departments from the 1880s onward, how would social control in the teeming slums of Chicago's Near West Side have differed? We have seen enough of these departments in action in the late twentieth century to know the answer.

It seems clear that, with regard to the municipal police, the relationship between the process of development and the class struggle is rather straightforward. Whatever the origins of the police (and some capitalists opposed early police forces on economic grounds), once departments were established, the importance of the police as a social control force was obvious to the capitalist class, and in city after city the police institution was reorganized and strengthened as part of a more general effort to control and stabilize potentially explosive class violence in rapidly developing cities. This police power became an important element in keeping the cities livable, orderly places for the accumulation of capital. But both the weakness of the bourgeoisie and the inherent impossibility of maintaining desired levels of control meant that contradictions developed within the police institution, including corruption and political domination as concessions to various segments of the petty bourgeoisie and a certain tolerance for prostitution, gambling, and drinking among police officers that infuriated many segments of the population (including some within the working class). This simply reflected the operational realities of controlling huge, populous areas with limited resources that were needed for "more serious" problems. Conflicts with various groups of self-styled reformers emerged from this contradiction as different segments of the population with political power came to identify distinct problem areas that differed from police concerns. Similarly, class violence was not as well controlled by the police as the bourgeoisie originally expected or hoped that it might be, and this failure can be seen as one reason for the turn toward "progressive" or "reformist" methods of controlling the class struggle, now identified with the welfare state. The police institution, in keeping with the social role to which it was assigned, moved more toward emphasis on crime control, both downplaying and obscuring the issues of overt class domination originally associated with the rise of police forces. All of these focusing points are ideal types: crime control was always associated with the police institution and always used to legitimate class repression on the part of the police; the social services performed by the police were probably proportionately as many in the 1840s as they are today, although now they are clearly less emphasized.

In this analysis of the police function it is important to note that we are not concerned with the *origins* of the police institution. The development of the early municipal police departments probably reflects all of the changing demands of rapidly expanding cities that contemporary police historians have noted: spatial complexity, growing crime rates, riotous disorder, ethnic and racial tension, expanding public services. The thesis here is simply that all these factors need to be understood in the context of the making of a class society dominated by capitalists seeking above all else conditions favorable to the expansion of capital, and that whatever the competing forces behind the *origins* of the police, the capitalist class seized the opportunity to *transform* the late-nineteenth- and early-twentieth-century departments into very effective participants in the class struggle on the side of the capitalists.

We have seen that this transformation was not a simple process. Under a democratic framework, control of any public institution is not automatic but must constantly be refined and developed, with gains and losses along the way. In the last third of the nineteenth century, municipal government grew on a scale that was unprecedented in American history. Considering the lack of models, it is to be expected that there was considerable debate and confusion in all classes concerning the most efficient kinds of political action. But the central tendency was for municipal government to socialize a portion of the costs of the accumulation of capital: the training of workers; the provision of physical facilities, streets, sewers, water; fire protection; public health services (especially important in an era of disease epidemics); public welfare services; and, of course, police services. The class basis of these functions has been established in a long line of historical research. The police are properly seen as only a part of this broader process, but one fully reflecting other developments in municipal government.

Yet we also know that the police institution was different, distinguished by its unique monopoly on the domestic use of force. It is clear that force was often used and *always* potentially usable. It is this *capacity* for force that is the full measure of the violent foundation of the police institution, and in my analysis of the police I have regarded this capacity for violence as the core of the police function, not as an incidental problem area. This is not to overestimate the amount of physical coercion that the police employed, but only to emphasize that the police function is violent at its core. The arguments in the preceding chapters have aimed to show that this capacity for violence is not random; nor is it the product of unique local factors. Rather, it is systematic, performing clearly understood functions for the capitalist class. This does not mean always, but refers to dominant tendencies.

The major opposing tendency, the wide range of nonviolent social services of the police, follows from two sources. The first is simply the legitimation function. As capitalism developed, more effort was made to legitimate the various social institutions that bolstered class society. The wide range of services that police officers rendered in working-class communities served this function at a steadily increasing rate after 1900 until the current period, when many police professionals are arguing that those functions have become dominant. The second source of the social-service tendency derives from the police institution's relation to the other public institutions in class society: the range of services is so broad that the police, largely because of their capacity for violence, must serve in a catchall capacity, both protecting the operation of other social services and taking on directly some social-service functions. For example, workers have often resisted participating in public health measures, public education, welfare benefits such as public shelters and workfare schemes, but the police institution has the coercive capacity to make such schemes mandatory. Thus, even charity under capitalism must have the coercive power of the state behind it. The capacity of the police to intervene in family problems, settle informal disputes on the street, and direct those in need of help to proper institutions all turns on the capacity for violence. The police officer's recommendation that an alcoholic report to a shelter for treatment and lodging is not just another friendly suggestion: the officer has the option of arrest the next time he sees the person. This point is completely missed by those sociologists of the police institution who emphasize the social-service function of the police. Egon Bittner's "Florence Nightingale" model of the police officer confused by the institution's emphasis on pursuing "Willie Sutton" misses the point: Florence Nightingale did not need a gun, a club, mace, and handcuffs to serve her clients. The social-service role of the police requires coercion because social services in class society are unpopular and often resisted. A police officer cannot intervene in family disputes without a gun and the threat of arrest.[3]

All historians of the police agree that the police in America have a somewhat checkered history. Where differences emerge is over the question of the meaning of such phenomena as political control, brutality, corruption, inefficiency, and the like. Here I have glanced over such phenomena, seeing them as endemic in all institutions of municipal government and not particularly as "police" problems. Undeniably, such factors are a part of the American police experience, and they explain a great deal of day-to-day police activity. But all of these activities occur in a particular social context—the class society—and their full meaning can be understood solely in that context. At the outset many of these police problems can be understood as indications of the low level of legitimacy accorded the police institution, government institutions generally, and capitalist institutions themselves. It is some indication of the level of the class struggle that measures to obtain that legitimacy, such as the move toward professionalization, were reserved until well into the twentieth century. The capitalists' ability to protect their interests in spite of low levels of legitimacy necessitated high levels of class violence.

My central thesis—that it was the necessity of policing this class struggle that best accounts for the transformation of the police institution in the late nineteenth and early twentieth centuries—uses this class violence as a central organizational concept, but I am not trying to imply that no other social processes were occurring or that they did not have an impact on the police. We have seen that the transformation of the police institution can be explained in part as one aspect of the familiar process of rationalization that all social institutions went through: bureaucratization, technological innovation, Taylorization, and professionalization. But these processes as well reflect the complex array of social changes occurring in the context of intense class struggle. Rationalization is in many ways the handmaiden of legitimation. A professional police force that accomplishes class control by adhering to an apparently neutral law-and-order ideology is clearly much more efficient than a corrupt or untrained force. Rationalization alone does not offer an alternative explanation of the rise and expansion of policing; it is another aspect of the same class struggle.

The move toward the welfare state, already well under way by

1900, provides a clear and well-documented illustration of another means of social control, one that transformed a part of the police function after 1915. Intense class struggle in American society was gradually reduced by a welfare state, and this required the restructuring of some police activity. Overt violence as a tool to maintain the boundaries of class society has now been largely replaced by other social institutions, but the police will still use considerable violence to maintain those lines whenever necessary. Direct police efforts to regulate working-class activity have been largely eliminated by state and federal policy makers. "Legal" strikes have been institutionalized; companies build up huge stocks and workers set up symbolic picket lines while collective bargaining goes on. During illegal strikes, however, or strikes in areas where unionization is resisted by capitalists, the police still impede union organizing and still arrest strikers and protect company goons. Tramping and vagrancy have declined as a result of welfare state measures and are no longer serious concerns of the police.

The policing of working-class communities in the 1980s is a complex process that many observers assume is accomplished with a broad concensus. However, it is clear that young people and minorities are highly critical of police patrol practices in their communities, a criticism that has transcended the law-and-order politics of the past decade and a half. Even blacks who fear crime criticize the police activity in their communities, which is often seen as racist, unnecessarily rough and abusive, and ineffective at controlling crime. Race and class are intermingled in complex ways; complaints from blacks, who constitute a large segment of the unskilled working class, roughly parallel those of the immigrants of the 1880s. Even in the white working-class communities that approve of law-and-order political candidates, there is a tendency for parents to support children prone to frequent run-ins with local police, most often over the policing of young people's recreational activities, which now often takes the form of traffic law enforcement, since the automobile has assumed the role of the corner hang-out of 50 years ago as the scene of teen-age recreation.[4]

This is not to say that the relationship of the police institution to the class struggle is the same today as it was 80 to 100 years ago. Rather, this relationship has changed considerably because the requirements for the reproduction of capital have changed. The complex class-control requirements of the late nineteenth century that necessitated violence because of low levels of legitimacy and the relative weaknesses of other public institutions gave rise to a strong police force, willing to use violence frequently in the class struggle. The current police institution is only marginally relevant in this process; a host of other public and private institutions now have a much greater impact. Capital is today largely secure without the assistance of the police, something that was not true even as late as the 1930s, when the police had to try (futilely) to recapture General Motors plants occupied by organized and angry workers.[5] The removal of the police from overt intervention in the class struggle to full attention to more popular crime control and social-service functions has transformed the image of the police, but, I would argue, not the institution's core role. *Potentially* the police institution is still available for the same kinds of purposes that it served 100 years ago. These overt class control functions have simply been made obsolete *at this particular period of capitalist development* by the expansion of nonviolent (or, perhaps more accurately, *less* violent, since the public welfare system does much violence) control mechanisms. The importance of a relatively nonviolent police institution as a part of this entire welfare state complex cannot be underestimated: the system has a coercive *core*.

Any study of the policing of class society in America in the 1980s must focus on the area where policing intersects with the social-service sector of the welfare state. The overt class conflict of the late nineteenth and early twentieth centuries has changed and now occurs in workplaces (which are privately policed) and in the allocation of public and private services. Social class has as much to do with the allocation of social resources in the 1980s as it did in the 1880s, and cities today are equally class stratified. An official American ideology that denies the significance of this class stratification does not change this reality.

NOTES

CHAPTER 1. INTRODUCTION

1. Maureen Cain, "Trends in the Sociology of Police Work."
2. See, for example, the discussion of the relationship between social class and policing in Roger Lane, "Urban Police and Crime in Nineteenth Century America." This denial of the significance of social class has been taken to extremes by some American sociologists. See, for example, C. R. Tittle, W. J. Villeme, and D. A. Smith, "The Myth of Social Class and Criminality: An Empirical Assessment of the Empirical Evidence," *American Sociological Review* 43 (1978): 643–656. Legal historian Lawrence Friedman goes even further, denying not only the importance of social class in understanding the police and the criminal justice system but also the utility of any other theoretical explanation; see Lawrence Friedman and Robert Percival, *The Roots of Justice: Crime and Punishment in Alameda County, California, 1870–1910,* pp. 15–16.
3. For example: Egon Bittner, *The Functions of the Police in Modern Society;* Herman Goldstein, *Policing a Free Society;* Jerome Skolnick, *Justice Without Trial;* James Richardson, *The New York Police: Colonial Times to 1901;* Samuel Walker, *A Critical History of Police Reform.*
4. Karl Marx and Frederich Engels, *The Communist Manifesto.* Maureen Cain and Alan Hunt, *Marx and Engels on Law,* chap. 5, "The State, Law and Crime."
5. Edward P. Thompson, *The Making of the English Working Class,* pp. 9–11. See also Henri Lefebvre, *The Sociology of Marx,* chap. 4, "Sociology and Social Classes"; Ralph Miliband, *Marxism and Politics,* chap. 2, "Class and Class Conflict."
6. On the class structure of the late-nineteenth-century United States, see Gabriel Kolko, *Main Currents in Modern American History,* esp. chaps.

1 and 3, and Mike Davis, "Why the U.S. Working Class Is Different." Davis is especially good at sorting out the interaction between class and the complex of racial, ethnic, and cultural factors that make class politics in the U.S. distinctive. See also Leon Fink, "The Figure and the Phantom: Class Conflict in the Gilded Age."

7. In the past decade a number of young labor historians have generated dozens of important community studies that make clear the class consciousness of American workers in the late nineteenth century and have important implications for historians of the police and crime. See, for example, Alan Dawley, *Class and Community: The Industrial Revolution in Lynn;* John T. Cumbler, *Working Class Community in Industrial America;* Leon Fink, "Workingmen's Democracy: The Knights of Labor in Local Politics, 1886–1896."

8. Good discussions of the issue of class consciousness can be found in R. J. Morris, *Class and Class Consciousness in the Industrial Revolution, 1780–1850,* and John M. Merriman, *Consciousness and Class Experience in Nineteenth Century Europe* (New York: Holmes & Meier, 1979).

9. V. I. Lenin, *State and Revolution;* David Gold, Clarence Lo, and Erik Olin Wright, "Recent Developments in Marxist Theories of the Capitalist State."

10. Probably the best of the studies showing this process is Samuel Bowles and Herbert Gintis, *Schooling in Capitalist America.* In general, the extensive literature on the class nature of public education (cited in Bowles and Gintis) has not been matched for other areas of social service. On the general expansion of the state sector and its role in the reproduction of private capital, see James O'Connor, *The Fiscal Crisis of the State.*

11. Steven Spitzer, "The Rationalization of Crime Control in Capitalist Society."

12. The now classic modern study that has redirected much Marxist research on the organization of the capitalist work process is Harry Braverman, *Labor and Monopoly Capital.*

13. A Marxist literature on urban sociology is just beginning to emerge. See, for example, Manuel Castells, *The Urban Question: A Marxist Approach;* C. G. Pickvance, *Urban Sociology* (New York: St. Martins Press, 1976); Lynda Ann Ewen, *Corporate Power and Urban Crisis in Detroit;* William Tabb and Larry Sawers, *Marxism and the Metropolis.*

14. My analysis of the functions of the capitalist city draws heavily on Patrick O'Donnell, "Industrial Capitalism and the Rise of Modern American Cities," and David Gordon, "Capitalist Development and the History of American Cities."

15. There are many sources on working-class living and working conditions at the turn of the century. The most complete is Paul U. Kellogg's six-volume *Pittsburgh Survey,* especially vol. 6: Margaret Byington, *Homestead: The Households of a Mill Town.*

16. This physical evidence of the class composition of late-nineteenth-century cities is still to be seen in the inner-city areas of major metropolises, including Buffalo, Milwaukee, Chicago, and Cleveland.

17. Richard Sennett, *Families Against the City: Middle Class Homes of Industrial Chicago, 1872–1890.*

18. David Montgomery, "Gutman's Nineteenth-Century America." Alexander Callow, Jr., *The Big City Boss in America* (New York: Oxford University Press, 1975), is a good introduction to conventional work on the problem of the big-city boss and the urban political machine. For an alternative view, see Martin Shefter, "The Emergence of the Political Machine: An Alternative View," in Willis Hawley and Michael Lipsky, eds., *Theoretical Perspectives on Urban Politics* (Englewood Cliffs: Prentice-Hall, 1976), 14–44; and Shefter, "The Electoral Foundations of the Political Machine: New York City, 1884–1897, as a Test Case," in Joel Silbey et al., *American Electoral History: Quantitative Studies of Popular Voting Behavior* (Princeton: Princeton University Press, 1976).

19. Karl Marx, *Das Kapital,* 1:742; Freidrich Engels, *The Condition of the Working Class in England.*

20. Bowles and Gintis, *Schooling in Capitalist America,* pp. 53–101, make this argument in relation to public education.

21. For a discussion of the role of the capitalist state and its institutions in the acceleration of the accumulation of capital, see Bowles and Gintis, *Schooling in Capitalist America,* chaps. 3 and 9. On capitalist domination of the organization of work, see Braverman, *Labor and Monopoly Capital.* On capitalist work discipline, see Edward P. Thompson, "Time, Work Discipline and Industrial Capitalism."

22. On police violence against the working class in America, see Phillip S. Foner, *History of the Labor Movement in the United States,* and Jeremy Brechter, *Strike!* (San Francisco: Straight Arrow Books, 1972). These are only the broadest of surveys. A vast literature details police assaults on the working class. For examples of the failure of police historians to come to terms with this literature, see Walker, *Critical History of Police Reform,* p. 17; Eric Monkkonen, *Police In Urban America, 1860–1920,* pp. 8–9; Robert Liebman and Michael Polen, "Perspectives on Policing in Nineteenth-Century America"; and Lane, "Urban Police and Crime," pp. 15–16. Lane criticizes some of my earlier work as being "overgeneralized from insights or evidence limited in time and space." I might respond that he "undergeneralizes" from similar insights, but I think the parameters of our disagreement are nonetheless very clear.

23. Here it must be clear that I take a view diametrically opposed to that of sociologist Bruce Johnson who argues in "Taking Care of Labor: The Police in American Politics" that the police have been on the side of the American working class. Both Lane, "Urban Police and Crime," and Monkkonen, *Police in Urban America,* cite Johnson's argument in some-

what favorable, although not uncritical, terms and point to it as an example of a Marxist interpretation of the police. They then use the fact that Johnson and I are diametrically opposed to attack the credibility of a Marxist interpretation of the history of the American police. This is a false issue. Johnson's interpretation is so flawed empirically as to be unbelievable. He uses Herbert Gutman's well-known studies of small mining towns in the early to mid-1870s as evidence of police behavior on a national basis over an eighty-year period. Furthermore, Johnson fails theoretically: there is nothing at all Marxist about his interpretation; hence it cannot be an example of a Marxist work. I suspect that Lane and Monkkonen give it such attention because it inherently supports their own positions. That is, it supposedly weakens a major opposing position and represents a "pluralist" position, ascribing to workers an inordinant influence over the police to counter-balance their political weaknesses in other areas.

24. Allan Silver, "The Demand for Order in Civil Society," discusses the development of the "policed society."

25. We do not currently have good analyses of the development of the police institutions under socialism. These institutions exist, but their functions differ significantly in at least two ways: first, there is a much greater emphasis on social service functions at the expense of crime control; second, police activities are directed *by* the working class and aimed at their class enemies. Obviously, the evolution of different "socialisms" and the complex developments in individual socialist countries since 1917 make a full analysis beyond the scope of this study.

26. See, for example, James Richardson, *Urban Police in the United States,* and Samuel Walker, *Popular Justice: A History of American Criminal Justice.*

27. Stanley Diamond, "The Rule of Law Versus the Order of Custom."

28. Egon Bittner, "Florence Nightingale in Pursuit of Willie Sutton: A Theory of the Police"; chap. 17 of Bittner, *The Functions of the Police.*

29. Wilbur R. Miller, *Cops and Bobbies: Police Authority in New York and London, 1830–1870.*

30. On the problem of legitimation under capitalism, see Alan Wolfe, *The Limits of Legitimacy.*

31. Mark Haller, "Historical Roots of Police Behavior: Chicago, 1890–1925."

32. Douglas Hay, "Property, Authority, and Criminal Law."

33. Walker, *Popular Justice,* pp. 103–104; Monkkonen, *Police in Urban America,* pp. 8–9.

34. Montgomery, "Gutman's Nineteenth-Century America"; Montgomery, "Labor, Radicalism, and the State in Late Nineteenth-Century America."

35. Gosta Esping-Anderson, Roger Friedland, and Erik Olin Wright, "Modes of Class Struggle and the Capitalist State," *Kapitalistate,* 4/5 (1976): 186–220.

36. This is precisely the point that Eric Monkkonen misses in his analysis of police work in relation to "Tramps and Children." See his *Police in Urban America,* chap. 3.

CHAPTER 2. THE URBAN POLICE INSTITUTION

1. On the Marxist analysis of the social changes of the Civil War era, see Saul Padover, ed., *Karl Marx on America and the Civil War* (New York: McGraw-Hill, 1972). The best contemporary work is Eric Foner, *Politics and Ideology in The Age of the Civil War,* esp. chaps. 1 and 2.

2. These data are computed from various charts in the U.S. Census for 1900 and 1910.

3. From the Marxist standpoint, this process is best described in Karl Marx, *Das Kapital,* vol. 1, and in Engels, *The Working Class in England.* For the United States, the best description of the process is in Kolko, *Main Currents,* chaps. 1–3. The data on foreign-born and foreign-stock populations are taken from the U.S. Department of Commerce, *12th Decennial Census of the United States,* vol. 1, pt. 1, *Population* (Washington, D.C., 1901), table 58, p. cxxii.

4. Kolko, *Main Currents,* chap. 3; Byington, *Homestead.*

5. P. Foner, *Labor Movement in the United States,* vols. 1 and 2.

6. Robert Fogelson, *Big City Police,* p. 13.

7. *Proceedings of the International Association of Chiefs of Police,* Third Annual Convention (1896), p. 27; Tenth Annual Convention (1903), p. 67. Numerous statements of police chiefs from all over the country can be found in the *Proceedings of the International Association of Chiefs of Police* for the period 1893–1915. The IACP was founded in Chicago as the National Chiefs of Police Union on May 18, 1893, by 51 chiefs of police, 36 of them from the Great Lakes/Ohio Valley region and the states immediately to the west. Thereafter the IACP was an important force in the development and diffusion of police innovations.

8. Bowles and Gintis, *Schooling in Capitalist America;* David Hogan, "Education and the Making of the Chicago Working Class, 1880–1930," *History of Education Quarterly* 18 (Fall 1978): 227–270.

9. Henry Mann, *Our Police: A History of the Pittsburgh Police Force under Town and City,* p. 302; U.S. Census, *Urban Social Statistics,* 1905.

10. Monkkonen, *Police in Urban America,* pp. 49–64.

11. George Ketchum, "Municipal Police Reform: A Comparative Study of Law Enforcement in Cincinnati, Chicago, New Orleans, New York, St. Louis, 1844–1877," chap. 5.

12. Richardson, *The New York Police;* Ketchum, "Municipal Police Reform," chap. 4.

13. Ketchum, "Municipal Police Reform," pp. 118–130.

14. John Flinn and John Wilkie, *A History of the Chicago Police,* chaps. 4–6; Ketchum, "Municipal Police Reform," pp. 130–141.

15. George M. Roe, *Our Police: A History of the Cincinnati Police*, chaps. 1 and 2; Ketchum, "Municipal Police Reform," pp. 152–159.

16. Mark S. Hubbell, *Our Police and Our City.*

17. John C. Whitaker, *History of the Police Department of Dayton, Ohio*, pp. 57–59.

18. Ray Allen Billington, *The Protestant Crusade, 1800–1860;* Eric Foner, "Class, Ethnicity & Radicalism in the Gilded Age: The Land League and Irish America," *Marxist Perspectives* 1 (Summer 1978): 6–55; John C. Schneider, "Mob Violence and Public Order in the American City" (Ph.D. diss., University of Minnesota, 1971), chap. 1; Michael Feldberg, *The Turbulent Era: Riot and Disorder in Jacksonian America* (New York: Oxford University Press, 1980); Flinn and Wilkie, *Chicago Police*, pp. 73–79; Roe, *Our Police*, pp. 35–39; Ketchum, "Municipal Police Reform," pp. 153–154, 134–135, 121–122. The Know-Nothing movement, like many similar ethnic movements, combined class forces with ethnicity, but this does not obscure the class basis of the movement.

19. David Montgomery, "The Shuttle and the Cross: Weavers and Artisans in the Kensington Riots of 1884," *Journal of Social History* 5 (Summer 1972): 411–446; Stephen Thernstrom, *Poverty and Progress: Social Mobility in a Nineteenth Century City*, chap. 2; Dawley, *Class and Community.*

20. Henry Mann, *Our Police*, p. 101.

21. *Wisconsin Evening News*, January 14, 1896.

22. Buffalo police turnover rates are computed from the *Annual Report of the Superintendent of Police* for the years 1873–1900. James Francis Caye, "Pittsburgh Police and the Roundhouse Riot," chap. V, found a 70 percent turnover in the Pittsburgh police in the years immediately preceding the 1877 riot, reduced to a 57 percent turnover in the years immediately following, reduced to a 47 percent turnover in the period 1889–1896—that is, about 7 percent per year in the 1890s, half or less the earlier rate, since the 47 percent level is for longer periods of time than the 57 percent and 70 percent levels.

23. Fogelson, *Big City Police;* Walker, *A Critical History of Police Reform*, a study that is not critical and takes the rhetoric of the self-styled reformers at face value; and Richardson, *Urban Police in the United States.*

24. Samuel Hays, "The Politics of Reform in Municipal Government in the Progressive Era," makes this point most clearly. I am indebted to Ted Ferdinand for insightful comments clarifying distinct forms of police "reform."

25. Robert Ozanne, *A Century of Labor-Management Relations at McCormick and International Harvester* (Madison: University of Wisconsin Press, 1967), pp. 20–24; Flinn and Wilkie, *Chicago Police*, chap. 15.

26. *Milwaukee Free Press*, January 26, 1911; Kathleen M. Carlin, "Chief Janssen and the Thirty-Three Year War: Law Enforcement in an Urban

Society: The Concepts of Police Chief Janssen," chap. 5. *Proceedings of the International Association of Chiefs of Police* (1908), pp. 31–35, contains Cleveland Police Chief Fred Kohler's original statement of his "Golden Rule" policy. Cleveland Police Department, *Annual Report of the Chief of Police* (1908), pp. 13–16, contains both a defense of the policy and data showing a 68 percent decline in arrests after the adoption of the policy. Succeeding Cleveland *Annual Reports* through 1914 show further the impact of the policy. The experiment did not last much longer, probably because the loss of this measure of class control was found to be insupportable.

27. Mark Haller, "Historical Roots of Police Behavior," p. 307; August Piper, "Report of an Investigation of the Chicago Police"; *Chicago Tribune,* March 20–25, 1904.

28. The idea of a professional police force, taken by a generation of academics uncritically as a goal in police development, has recently become a major issue in the literature of policing. The two most recent histories of the police, Robert Fogelson's *Big City Police* and Samuel Walker's *Critical History of Police Reform* are primarily histories of police reform. I do not agree that the history of the American police can be written as the history of police reform or professionalization. These ideas have always pertained more to the realm of intellectual history—that is, to what we have thought about the police—than to the actual impact of the police on American social life. Although the idea of professionalism is by no means irrelevant to a study of the police, its importance has been exaggerated.

29. The best current research on the effectiveness of police patrol practices is George Kelling et al., *The Kansas City Preventive Patrol Experiment* (Washington, D.C.: The Police Foundation, 1974).

30. Lawrence Friedman and Robert Percival, *The Roots of Justice*, p. 75.

31. U.S. Department of Commerce, Bureau of the Census, *Social Statistics of Cities*, 1890, pp. 128–132.

32. U.S. Department of Commerce, Bureau of the Census, *Urban Statistics*, 1905.

CHAPTER 3. THE PATROL WAGON AND SIGNAL SYSTEM

1. Flinn and Wilkie, *Chicago Police,* pp. 398–399.

2. Ibid., p. 400; Chicago Police Department, *Annual Report* (1881).

3. Flinn and Wilkie, *Chicago Police,* pp. 403–407.

4. Ibid., p. 405.

5. "Municipal Electric Fire Alarm and Police Patrol Systems," U.S. Department of Commerce, Bureau of the Census, *Bulletin 11* (1904), p. 4; Saginaw Police Department, *Annual Report* (1896), pp. 6–7.

6. Roe, *Our Police,* pp. 284–285.

7. Buffalo Police Department, *Annual Report* (1886), pp. 9–22.

8. "Municipal Electric Alarm and Patrol Systems," p. 4.
9. Buffalo Police Department, *Annual Report* (1884).
10. *Buffalo Courier,* August 26, 1893.
11. Mann, *Our Police,* p. 338.
12. Flinn and Wilkie, *Chicago Police,* pp. 397–398.
13. Howard C. Sprogle, *The Philadelphia Police: Past and Present,* p. 396.
14. Buffalo Police Department, *Annual Reports* (1886–1889); Milwaukee Police Department, *Annual Reports* (1884–1888).
15. Flinn and Wilkie, *Chicago Police,* p. 415.
16. Milwaukee Police Department, *Annual Report* (1881), p. 3.
17. Buffalo Police Department, *Annual Report* (1886); Roe, *Our Police,* p. 238.
18. Saginaw Police Department, *Annual Report* (1891–1892).
19. Sprogle, *Philadelphia Police,* p. 395; Eugene Rider, "The Denver Police Department: An Administrative, Organizational, and Operational History, 1858–1905" (Ph.D. diss., University of Denver, 1971), p. 307.
20. Saginaw Police Department, *Annual Report* (1896), pp. 6–7.
21. Jonathan Rubinstein, *City Police,* pp. 17–18.
22. Flinn and Wilkie, *Chicago Police,* p. 401.
23. *Milwaukee Sentinel,* April 22, 1888.
24. Flinn and Wilkie, *Chicago Police,* pp. 415–416.
25. Buffalo Police Department, *Annual Report* (1894), pp. 7–13.

CHAPTER 4. THE BUFFALO POLICE, 1865–1900

1. Buffalo Police Department, *Annual Report* (1907), p. 35. Several similar letters are included in Sidney L. Harring, "Police Reports as Sources in Labor History," *Labor History* 17 (1977).
2. Hubbell, *Our Police and Our City,* chap. 7. This is the only "house history" of the Buffalo police, written by the clerk of the Police Board.
3. Niagara Frontier Board of Police Commissioners, *Annual Report* (1866).
4. Buffalo Police Department, *Annual Report* (1873).
5. These data on departmental turnover are reported in the Buffalo Police Department *Annual Reports* for the years beginning 1873.
6. The two major works on Buffalo politics in the 1880s and 1890s are Brenda Shelton, *Reformers in Search of Yesterday: Buffalo in the 1890s,* and John Palmer, "Some Antecedents of Progressivism in Buffalo," (Ph.D. diss., State University of New York, Buffalo, 1967).
7. The data on the occupations of mayors and police commissioners are taken from the *Buffalo City Directory* for the years 1870–1915.
8. Beginning in 1893 the number of annual meetings of the Board of Police Commissioners is reported in the Police Department's *Annual Reports.* See also Buffalo Police Department, *Annual Report* (1885).
9. Palmer, "Antecedents of Progressivism in Buffalo," chap. 3.

10. Hubbell, *Our Police and Our City,* contains short career profiles of all the high-ranking officers on the police force. Data on dismissals and resignations are found in the annual reports.
11. Buffalo Police Department, *Annual Report* (1888).
12. Shelton, *Reformers in Search of Yesterday,* chap. 3; Buffalo Police Department, *Annual Reports* (1891, 1894). A detailed description of the class origins of Buffalo mayors and police commissioners is found in Sidney L. Harring, "The Buffalo Police—1872–1915: Industrialization, Social Unrest, and the Development of the Police Institution," chap. 4. See also Shelton, chaps. 2–4.
13. Cyril Robinson, "The Mayor and the Police—The Political Role of the Police in Society," in George L. Mosse, ed., *Police Forces in History* (Beverly Hills: Sage Publishers, 1975).
14. See Buffalo Police Department, *Annual Reports* (1892–1900), for Superintendent Bull's self-authored list of accomplishments.
15. Virginia Yans McLaughlin, "Like the Fingers on the Hand: Family and Community Life of First Generation Italian Americans in Buffalo, New York, 1880–1930" (Ph.D. diss., State University of New York, Buffalo, 1971), pp. 192–197.
16. Rorie MacTeggart, "A History of Buffalo," (M.A. thesis, Canisus College, 1940), pp. 67–71; *Buffalo Courier,* July 24–26, 1877.
17. Buffalo Police Department, *Annual Report* (1884), pp. 6–8.
18. Buffalo Police Department, *Annual Report* (1890), p. 6.
19. Buffalo Police Department, *Annual Report* (1892), p. 7; (1899), p. 10. See also Hubbell, *Our Police and Our City,* on changes in organization prior to 1893.
20. Buffalo Police Department, *Annual Report* (1887), p. 9.
21. *Buffalo Express,* August 13, 1892; Brenda Shelton, "The Grain Shovellers' Strike of 1899."
22. *Buffalo Express,* August 25–30, 1893; August 23–27, 1894; June 16–17, 1897.
23. Virginia Yans McLaughlin, *Family and Community: Italian Immigrants in Buffalo, 1880–1930* (Ithaca: Cornell University Press, 1976), chap. 4; idem, "Like the Fingers on the Hand," pp. 165, 192–195.

CHAPTER 5. THE POLICE IN MILWAUKEE

1. Roger Simon, "The Expansion of an Industrial City" (Ph.D. diss., University of Wisconsin, Madison, 1971); Michael Soref, "Family Capitalism and Sewer Socialism in Milwaukee 1850–1910" (M.S. thesis, University of Wisconsin, Madison, 1973); Kathleen Conzen, "The German Athens: Milwaukee and the Accommodation of Its Immigrants, 1836–1860" (Ph.D. diss., University of Wisconsin, Madison, 1972).

2. Robert Rice, "The Populist Party in Milwaukee" (M.A. thesis, University of Wisconsin, Milwaukee, 1967); Theodore Mueller, "Milwaukee Workers," unpublished manuscript in the Milwaukee County Historical Society Library; Roger Simon, "The Bay View Incident and the People's Party in Milwaukee."

3. Frederick I. Olson, "The Milwaukee Socialists, 1897–1941" (Ph.D. diss., Harvard University, 1952); Harvey Wachtman, "History of the Social Democratic Party of Milwaukee, 1897–1910," *Illinois Studies in the Social Sciences* 28, no. 1 (1945).

4. Soref, "Family Capitalism and Sewer Socialism"; Barbara Howe, "The Urban Upper Class in Milwaukee and Cincinnati" (M.A. thesis, University of Wisconsin, Milwaukee, 1970); Thomas Cochran, *The Pabst Brewing Company: The History of an American Business* (New York: New York University Press, 1948); Margaret Walsh, "Industrial Opportunity on the Urban Frontier: Rags to Riches and Milwaukee Clothing Manufacturers, 1840–1880," *Wisconsin Magazine of History* 57, no. 3 (Spring 1974): 175–194.

5. Wisconsin Statutes, 1885, chap. 378; Daniel Hoan, *City Government* (New York: Harcourt, Brace, 1936), p. 198.

6. Milwaukee City Directory, 1865–1910.

7. Wachtman, "Social Democratic Party of Milwaukee"; Bayrd Still, *Milwaukee: The History of a City* (Madison: Wisconsin State Historical Society Press, 1948); Mary Clare Fabishak, "The Rhetoric of Urban Reform: Milwaukee during the Progressive Era" (M.A. thesis, University of Wisconsin, Milwaukee, 1974).

8. Dan Rumelt, "Milwaukee Police Department Chiefs of Police," *Milwaukee Badge,* October 1976; Herbert Rice, "Know Your Mayors," *Milwaukee Historical Messenger* 15 (1958).

9. Rumelt, "Milwaukee Chiefs of Police"; Milwaukee *City Reports* (1884–1885); *Wisconsin Evening News,* January 29, 1884; February 2, 11–14, 1885; September 28, 1888; *Milwaukee Sentinel,* February 11–16, 1885.

10. Thomas Gavett, *The Development of the Labor Movement in Milwaukee,* p. 45.

11. Wisconsin Statutes, 1885, sec. 378; Milwaukee City Documents, 1883–1884.

12. Carlin, "Chief Janssen."

13. This historical process is best described in Hays, "The Politics of Reform."

14. Current observers who uncritically laud the high level of autonomy of the Milwaukee police miss this point. For example, Berton G. Braun says approvingly, "In some cities the existence of a police commission has meant the diffusion of responsibility and command, the commission in effect acting as a controlling force, and setting department policy. In Milwaukee the Chief has full and unquestioned command of his depart-

ment." Braun, "The Milwaukee Police Department: A Case Study in Police Organization" (Ann Arbor: Institute of Public Administration, University of Michigan, 1955), p. 6.

15. Gavett, *Labor Movement in Milwaukee*, pp. 111–112; Carlin, "Chief Janssen," p. 58; *Milwaukee Sentinel*, December 7, 10–11, 1910.
16. Milwaukee City Directories, 1885–1914.
17. Milwaukee Police Department, *Annual Report*, (1893), p. 4.
18. *Wisconsin Evening News*, September 28, 1888.
19. Milwaukee Police Department, *Annual Reports* (1884–1914); Rumelt, "Milwaukee Chiefs of Police"; Milwaukee Legislative Reference Bureau, "Milwaukee Police Department: The First One Hundred Years" (1955), typescript in files; "Milwaukee's Eight Police Chiefs," *Milwaukee Journal*, April 2, 1933; Hoan, *City Government*, pp. 197–204.
20. *Evening Wisconsin*, June 2, 1890.
21. Milwaukee Police Department, *Annual Reports* (1888–1914); Carlin, "Chief Janssen," chap. 5.
22. *Proceedings of the Annual Meetings of the International Association of Chiefs of Police* (1897–1899).
23. John R. Commons, *History of Labor in the United States*, 2: chap. 9; *16th Annual Report of the U.S. Commissioner of Labor* (1901), p. 29.
24. Commons, *History of Labor*, 2: chap. 9; David Montgomery, *Beyond Equality: Labor and the Radical Republicans* (New York: Random House, 1967).
25. Simon, "The Bay View Incident," pp. 31–32.
26. Carlin, "Chief Janssen," pp. 54–57.
27. Ibid., pp. 56–57.
28. *Milwaukee Common Council Proceedings*, August 29, September 26, 1910.
29. *Evening Wisconsin*, August 12, 1907; *Wisconsin Evening News*, December 1, 1909; *Milwaukee Sentinel*, December 1, 1909; *Milwaukee Free Press*, November 27, 1909.
30. *Milwaukee Sentinel*, March 26, 1912, December 6, 1911; *Evening Wisconsin*, October 28, 1910.
31. *Milwaukee Journal*, September 26, 1911; *Milwaukee Sentinel*, April 22, 1911; *Milwaukee Free Press*, December 3, 1910.
32. *Milwaukee Sentinel*, March 5, 1911; Wisconsin Statutes, 1911, chap. 586; *Evening Wisconsin*, March 11, June 17, 1911.

CHAPTER 6. COPS AS STRIKEBREAKERS

1. For the prevalence of strikes and lockouts during this period, see U.S. Department of Labor, Bureau of Labor Statistics, *Strikes and Lockouts in the United States, 1880–1936*, Bulletin 651 (Washington, D.C., 1938). The data on strike deaths are very incomplete. Rhodri Jeffreys-Jones, *Violence and Reform in American History*, reports 308 during the years

1890–1909 for the entire country. This number, largely gleaned from his research through newspapers, must be seen as a minimum statistic, since we cannot be sure all were reported at the time or uncovered by Jeffreys-Jones. Furthermore, there is no agreement as to what constitutes a strike death. I have found, for example, that Jeffreys-Jones undercounted street railway strike deaths during this period by about 20, both missing some and also failing to count deaths due to careless operation of the cars by scab motormen.

2. For evidence that current histories of the police ignore strikes and labor protest, check the extensive indexes of any of the major police histories: Walker, *Popular Justice* and *A Critical History of Police Reform;* Monkkonen, *Police in Urban America;* Fogelson, *Big City Police;* John C. Schneider, *Detroit and the Problem of Order, 1830–1880: A Geography of Crime, Riot, and Policing* (Lincoln: University of Nebraska Press, 1980); Richardson, *Urban Police in the United States* and *The New York Police;* and Lane, "Urban Police and Crime" and *Policing the City: Boston, 1822–1885.* Although Lane and Richardson briefly refer to strikes in their influential first books on the Boston and the New York City police, respectively, only Richardson substantively (and inadequately) discusses the police role in strikes in his later work (he correctly assesses that they were antilabor). Monkkonen, Walker, and Lane (in "Urban Police and Crime") mention strikes only briefly in the context of objecting to some of my early work.

3. David Montgomery, "Strikes in Nineteenth-Century America," and "Labor, Radicalism, and the State in Late Nineteenth-Century America." Among Gutman's works, see "Class, Status, and Community Power in Nineteenth Century Industrial Cities—Paterson, New Jersey: A Case Study"; "The Buena Vista Affair, 1874–1875"; "The Braidwood Lockout of 1874"; "An Iron Workers' Strike in the Ohio Valley, 1873–1874"; "Two Lockouts in Pennsylvania: 1873–1874." Students of Gutman and others influenced by him have compiled community studies that contain important perspectives on the local police. See, for example, Daniel J. Walkowitz, *Worker City, Company Town: Iron and Cotton-Worker Protest in Troy and Cohoes, New York, 1855–1884,* and Dawley, *Class and Community.* Other work on the importance of the labor strike has been done with reference to other countries. See Craig Heron and Bryan Palmer, "Through the Prism of the Strike: Industrial Conflict in Southern Ontario, 1901–1914," *Canadian Historical Review* 58 (December 1977): 423–458; Ronald Aminzade, "French Strike Development and Class Struggle," *Social Science History* 4 (February 1980): 57–79; Robert Liebman, "Repressive Strategies and Working Class Protest," *Social Science History* 4 (February 1980): 33–55; John Foster, *Class Struggle and the Industrial Revolution;* and Alf Ludtke, "The Role of State Violence in the Period of Transition to Industrial Capitalism: The Example of Prussia from 1815 to 1848."

4. B. Johnson, "Taking Care of Labor," and Walker, *A Critical History of Police Reform*, pp. 8–19. Monkkonen, *Police in Urban America*, p. 185, appears to agree with them when he refers in a footnote to Daniel Walkowitz (*Worker City, Company Town*) on the "subtleties of police-labor relations" and cites Sam Walker's case study of the Scranton police ("The Police and the Community: Scranton, Pennsylvania, 1866–1884, A Test Case") as a critique of my approach. Walker was heavily influenced by Gutman, but Monkkonen evidently does not see (nor does Walker) that Scranton more resembled Gutman's small company towns in a largely preindustrial period than it did the middle- and large-sized industrial cities.

5. See the following works by Gutman: "An Iron Workers' Strike"; "The Braidwood Lockout"; "The Buena Vista Affair"; "Two Lockouts in Pennsylvania"; "Class, Status, and Community Power"; "The Tompkins Square 'Riot' in New York City on January 13, 1874: A Re-examination of Its Causes and Its Aftermath." See also James Osborne, "The IWW and the Paterson Strike of 1913: An Ethnic Perspective" (paper presented at Organization of American Historians, Annual Meeting, 1978), and Paul Faler, "Working Class Historiography," *Radical America* 3 (March–April 1969): 63–79.

6. The seminal work on the process of Taylorization is Harry Braverman, *Labor and Monopoly Capital*. The major historical study of the process as it affected workers is David Montgomery, *Workers' Control in America*.

7. For example, Alan Dawley's *Class and Community* is an excellent study of working-class politics in Lynn, Massachusetts, America's leading shoe manufacturing center. Dawley clearly shows that the police force was expanded in 1863 (while opposing workers were off fighting the Civil War) largely as a result of the manufacturers' need to control strike activity. See also Thernstrom, *Poverty and Progress*, chap. 2.

8. Joseph A. Dacus, *Annals of the Great Strikes in the United States*. Phillip S. Foner, *The Great Labor Uprising of 1877* (New York: Monad Press, 1978), p. 119, describes the New York situation.

9. P. Foner, *Great Labor Uprising*, chaps. 8, 9; David T. Burbank, *City of Little Bread: The St. Louis General Strike of 1877* (St. Louis, 1957).

10. The most detailed account of Chicago police action during the 1877 strike is found in chapters 9 and 10 of Flinn and Wilkie, *Chicago Police*. The work is primarily Flinn's, who was a police reporter with access to a great deal of information. See also Allan Pinkerton, *Strikers, Communists, Tramps, and Detectives* (1878; rpr. New York: Arno Press, 1969), also by a participant in the strike activity. Both are strongly pro-police and anti-working class.

11. Flinn and Wilkie, *Chicago Police*, p. 202.

12. James F. Caye, "Pittsburgh Police and the Roundhouse Riot"; Mann, *Our Police*, chap. 9; Robert Bruce, *1877: Year of Violence* (Chicago:

Quadrangle, 1970). The cut in the police force and the McCall incident are described in Mann, pp. 101, 104.

13. This description is from Mann, *Our Police,* pp. 102–116.

14. The reorganization of the Pittsburgh police in 1887 is described in ibid., pp. 139–157. See also the *First Annual Report* of the Department of Public Safety, Pittsburgh (1888).

15. Buffalo Police Department, *Annual Report* (1884), p. 9.

16. Ibid., p. 8.

17. Ibid., p. 6.

18. See the discussions of police protection of scabs in the Chicago strikes of 1900–1915 and the Oshkosh woodworking strike of 1898 later in this chapter.

19. Robert Ozanne, *A Century of Labor-Management Relations at McCormick and International Harvester* (Madison: University of Wisconsin Press, 1967), pp. 9–25.

20. Flinn and Wilkie, *Chicago Police,* pp. 271–278; *Chicago Tribune,* May 1–5, 1886.

21. See Bessie Pierce, *A History of Chicago,* 3: chaps. 7 and 8. On Chicago politics of the period, see ibid., 3: chap. 10.

22. Flinn and Wilkie, *Chicago Police,* pp. 235–237.

23. Ibid., p. 239.

24. Ibid., pp. 240–246.

25. Gavett, *Development of the Labor Movement in Milwaukee,* p. 61; Simon, "The Bay View Incident," p. 9.

26. *Buffalo Express,* August 13–17, 1892.

27. *Buffalo Express,* August 13–15, 1892.

28. *Buffalo Express,* August 19–21, 1892.

29. *Buffalo Express,* August 17–18, 1892. Phillip Foner, *History of the Labor Movement in the United States,* vol. 2 (New York: International Publishers, 1955), pp. 253–254, asserts that special deputies and militia deserted but not that the police did; hence, we are not in disagreement on this point.

30. See generally Almont Lindsay, *Pullman* (Chicago: University of Chicago Press, 1964); Howard Myers, "The Policing of Labor Disputes in Chicago: A Case Study," pp. 247–248.

31. Forrest McDonald, "Street Cars and Politics in Milwaukee, 1896–1901"; Clay McShane, *Technology and Reform: Street Railways and the Growth of Milwaukee, 1850–1910* (Madison: Wisconsin State Historical Society Press, 1975).

32. *Milwaukee Sentinel,* May 4, 1896.

33. *Milwaukee Sentinel,* May 5–8, 1896.

34. *Milwaukee Sentinel,* May 11–13, 1896.

35. Phillip Taft and Phillip Ross, "American Labor Violence: Its Causes, Character and Outcome," in Hugh D. Graham and Ted Gurr, *The History*

of Violence in America. On the heightened violence of the early twentieth century, particularly the use of professional strikebreakers and the resulting violence, see Rhodri Jeffreys-Jones, "Violence in American History: Plug Uglies in the Progressive Era," and "Profit Over Class: A Study in American Industrial Espionage." As good as Jeffreys-Jones's studies are concerning professional strikebreaking organizations, he sees their rise as necessarily proving that local police were disloyal, inept, and unfaithful to employers in the class struggle. I see police and private strikebreakers as having substantially different functions in the division of the labor of strikebreaking: the police had more responsibility in the community approaching the strike area, whereas professional scabs took on protection of the plant area, espionage, hired killings and beatings, and the actual day-to-day operation of a strike-bound business. Although some political administrations in Milwaukee and Cleveland threatened to use the police to arrest professional strikebreakers, usually the two forces worked closely together.

36. Myers, "Policing Labor Disputes in Chicago," pp. 540–543.
37. Ibid., pp. 545–546.
38. Ibid., p. 547; *Chicago Tribune,* July 31, 1904.
39. *Chicago Tribune,* April 8–10, 1905; Myers, "Policing Labor Disputes in Chicago," pp. 581–583.
40. *Chicago Tribune,* May 2–3, 1905; Myers "Policing Labor Disputes in Chicago," p. 585.
41. Quoted in Myers, "Policing Labor Disputes in Chicago," pp. 588–589.
42. Ibid., pp. 593–598. Some indication of the national scope of professional strikebreaking activities can be seen from the places the strikebreakers came from: Omaha, St. Louis, Minneapolis, Kansas City, Cincinnati, Milwaukee, Louisville, Grand Rapids, Philadelphia, Pittsburgh, Columbus, New Orleans, and other large cities, in addition to some from southern Illinois.
43. Myers, "Policing Labor Disputes in Chicago," pp. 597, 599.
44. Ibid., p. 599.
45. Ibid., pp. 602–614.
46. Ibid., pp. 799, 650. Lincoln Steffens describes a virtually parallel situation in New York City; see *The Autobiography of Lincoln Steffens,* pt. 2, chap. 5.
47. Myers, "Policing Labor Disputes in Chicago," pp. 797–810, 708–709; Robert Dvorak, "The Fighting Garment Workers," *International Socialist Review* 11, no. 7 (January 1911): 385–393.
48. Myers, "Policing Labor Disputes in Chicago," pp. 816–818, 711.
49. Ibid., pp. 711–712.
50. Ibid., pp. 820–821.
51. U.S. Bureau of the Census, *Statistics of Cities* (1905), pp. 322–323; *Eleventh Decennial Census of the United States* (1900), vol. 8, *Manufactures:*

956; Lee Baxendall, "Fur, Logs, and Human Lives: The Great Oshkosh Woodworker Strike of 1898," *Green Mountain Quarterly* 3 (May 1976): 3–33.

52. Baxendall, "Fur, Logs, and Human Lives," pp. 20–21, 23–24.
53. *Oshkosh Daily Northwestern*, August 4–5, 1898; Baxendall, "Fur, Logs, and Human Lives," p. 26.
54. *Oshkosh Daily Northwestern*, August 5–7, 1898; Baxendall, "Fur, Logs, and Human Lives," pp. 27–30.
55. Steven Rosswurm, "A Strike in the Rubber City: Rubber Workers, Akron, and the IWW, 1913"; Harold S. Roberts, *The Rubber Workers* (New York: Harper & Row, 1944), chap. 3; Leslie Marcy, "800 Per Cent and the Akron Strike," *International Socialist Review* 13, no. 10 (April 1913): 711–724; *Beacon Journal*, March 8, 1913, quoted in Rosswurm, p. 78. This incident is described in Rosswurm, pp. 77–78.
56. Rosswurm, "A Strike in the Rubber City," pp. 79–82.
57. Marcy, "800 Per Cent," p. 713; Roberts, *Rubber Workers*, pp. 66–68; Rosswurm, "A Strike in the Rubber City," pp. 82–83.
58. This listing is my own and is not necessarily complete. The major source is the *Chicago Tribune*.
59. Sam Bass Warner, *Streetcar Suburbs: The Process of Growth in Boston* (Cambridge, Mass.: Harvard University Press, 1962); McShane, *Technology and Reform*.
60. *Grand Rapids Eagle*, May 11, 17, 1891.
61. *Grand Rapids Democrat*, May 13–17, 1891.
62. *Grand Rapids Eagle*, May 31, 1891.
63. *Grand Rapids Eagle*, June 5, 1891.
64. *Duluth News Tribune*, September 10–12, 1912.
65. *Duluth News Tribune*, September 20, 15, 13, 1912.
66. *Duluth News Tribune*, September 13, 16, 1912.
67. *Duluth News Tribune*, September 20, 19, 23, 1912.
68. Donald G. Bahna, "The Pope-Toledo Strike of 1907," *Northwest Ohio Quarterly* 35 (Summer 1963): 109–110, and (Autumn 1963): 172–187; C. E. Ruthenberg, "The Cleveland Garment Workers Strike," *International Socialist Review* 12, no. 3 (September 1911): 136–140; Robert H. Bremner, "The Civil Revival in Ohio: Police, Penal and Parole Policies in Cleveland and Toledo," *American Journal of Economics and Sociology* 14, (July 1955): 387–403.
69. *Buffalo Express*, August 16, 18, 1892; *Chicago Times*, July 6–7, 1894; *Cleveland Plain Dealer*, August 7, 14, 1896.
70. *Ohio State Journal*, July 24, 1910, August 13, 14, 15, 1910) Eber Heston, "The Street Car Strike at Columbus," *International Socialist Review* 11, no. 2 (August 1910): 133–138; R. E. Porter, "No Beans and Rice for Columbus," *International Socialist Review* 10, no. 11 (May 1910): 1069–1071.

71. *Ohio State Journal,* August 13, 1910; Heston, "Street Car Strike at Columbus," pp. 133–134.
72. *Ohio State Journal,* August 13, 1910.
73. *Ohio State Journal,* August 14, 16, 30, 1910.
74. *Indianapolis News,* November 1–3, 1913; Bruce Rodgers, "The Street Car War in Indianapolis," *International Socialist Review* 14, no. 4 (October 1913): 328–331.
75. *Indianapolis News,* November 4, 1913; *Indianapolis Star,* November 4, 1913.
76. *Indianapolis News,* November 7–8, 1913.
77. *Indianapolis News,* November 22–24, 1913; *Indianapolis Star,* November 22–25, 1913.
78. *Indianapolis News,* November 26, 1913.
79. Buffalo salaries were about average. See Walker, *A Critical History of Police Reform,* pp. 9–10; Myers, "Policing Labor Disputes in Chicago," p. 717. Only one systematic study of police residential patterns has been done; see Eugene Watts, "The Police in Atlanta, 1890–1905," *Journal of Southern History* 39 (May 1973): 165–182. Caye, "Pittsburgh Police and the Roundhouse Riot," studied the mobility patterns of Pittsburgh police in the 1880s and found equal numbers leaving for unskilled and skilled posts. However, I think that if Caye's study had been extended to the 1890s and early 1900s there would have been much less mobility into unskilled occupations.
80. Myers, "Policing Labor Disputes in Chicago," emphasizes these ethnic differences in Chicago strikes but fails to look for the sources of these animosities beyond the prejudices of individual police officers. The Buffalo information is from Harring, "The Buffalo Police," chap. 4.
81. Harring, "The Buffalo Police," pp. 100–108; Myers, "Policing Labor Disputes in Chicago," 247–248, 281; *Buffalo Express,* August 14–15, 1892.
82. Haller, "Historical Roots of Police Behavior," pp. 303–324; Flinn and Wilkie, *Chicago Police,* p. 241.
83. John Flinn and John Wilkie provide textbook examples of this kind of identification of striking workers throughout their *History of the Chicago Police.* The bourgeois press characterized the Great Strikes of 1877, the Haymarket affair and the events leading up to it, and the Pullman strike in these terms. See the *Chicago Tribune, Milwaukee Sentinel, Buffalo Express, Cleveland Plain Dealer,* and *Pittsburgh Gazette,* for example.
84. Myers, "Policing Labor Disputes in Chicago," pp. 715, 825–826; Ozanne, *A Century of Labor-Management Relations.*
85. Simon, "The Bay View Incident"; Henry David, *The History of the Haymarket Affair* (New York: Farrar and Reinhart, 1936).
86. John Kager, "A History of Socialism in Buffalo" (M.A. thesis, Canisus College, 1951), pp. 80–82; Daniel Hoan, *City Government* (New York: Harcourt, Brace, 1936), pp. 197–204.

87. Francis O'Neill, "Anarchy and Anarchists," International Association of Chiefs of Police, *Proceedings of the Annual Meeting* (Louisville, 1902), p. 42.
88. John D. Stevens, "Wobblies in Milwaukee," *Historical Messenger* 24 (March 1968): 23–27; Jacob Margolis, "The Streets of Pittsburgh," *International Socialist Review* 13, no. 4 (October 1912): 313–319; Fred Merrick, "Justice in Pittsburgh," *International Socialist Review* 12, no. 3 (September 1911): 158–163; Patrick Lynch, "The Pittsburgh Stogy Industry in Transition and the IWW, 1906–1920" (unpublished seminar paper, University of Pittsburgh, Department of History, 1977).
89. Lawrence Goodwyn, *Democratic Promise: The Populist Moment in America* (New York: Oxford University Press, 1976), pt. 2, "The Tide Receding."
90. James Weinstein, *The Decline of Socialism in America, 1912–1925* (New York: Vintage, 1969), clearly shows that state repression in 1919 was one factor in the weakening of the American socialist movement. Similarly, Melvyn Dubofsky, *We Shall Be All: A History of the IWW* (New York: Quadrangle, 1969), shows that police repression of the IWW even exceeded that against the socialist party.
91. U.S. Department of Labor, Bureau of Labor Statistics, *Strikes and Lockouts in the United States, 1880–1936*, Bulletin 651 (Washington, D.C., 1938), p. 29. There are no official statistics for the period 1905–1914, but Howard and Ralph Wolf, *Rubber: A Story of Glory and Greed* (New York: Covici, Friede, 1936), p. 503, make an estimate of 15,000, which is reasonable, considering the high level of strike activity of the period.
92. Unfortunately, the best source on the United States Army in labor disputes remains unpublished. See John M. Cooper, "The Army and Civil Disorder: Federal Military Intervention in American Labor Disputes, 1877–1900" (Ph.D. diss., University of Wisconsin, 1971). On the national guard, see Robert Reinders, "Militia and Public Order in Nineteenth Century America," *Journal of American Studies* 11 (April 1977): 81–102; Martha Derthick, *The National Guard in Politics* (Cambridge, Mass.: Harvard University Press, 1965); Charles Peckham, "The Ohio National Guard and Its Police Duties, 1894," *Ohio History* 83 (Winter 1974): 51–67; Joseph J. Holmes, "The National Guard of Pennsylvania: Policeman of Industry, 1865–1905" (Ph.D. diss., University of Connecticut, 1970); William H. Riker, *Soldiers of the State: The Role of the National Guard in American Democracy* (Washington, D.C.: Public Affairs Press, 1957); Ronald M. Gephart, "Politicians, Soldiers and Strikes: The Reorganization of the Nebraska Militia and the Omaha Strike of 1882," *Nebraska History* 46 (June 1965): 89–120.
93. The mine wars in Colorado and West Virginia probably mark the high point of professional strikebreaking activity, with other mining strikes not far behind. In rural areas employers had to rely exclusively on these pri-

vate forces. This is not to say that there was not substantial professional strikebreaking activity in all the cities in the Midwest and Great Lakes region, but almost always the private organizations worked in concert with municipal police.

CHAPTER 7. LIQUOR AND THE SALOON QUESTION

1. The concept "policed society" as used here is taken from Allan Silver, "The Demand for Order in Civil Society."
2. See for example, Walker, *Popular Justice*, p. 56.
3. Ibid., p. 104.
4. Brian Harrison, *Drink and the Victorians: The Temperance Question in England 1815–1872* (Pittsburgh: University of Pittsburgh Press, 1971); R. W. Malcolmson, *Popular Recreations in English Society, 1700–1850* (Cambridge: Cambridge University Press, 1973); and Gareth Stedman-Jones, "Class Expression versus Social Control? A Critique of Recent Trends in the Social History of Leisure," pp. 162–170.
5. David Brody, *Steelworkers in America;* John Koren, *Economic Aspects of the Liquor Problem,* 12th Annual Report of the Commissioner of Labor (Washington, D.C., 1898).
6. Sennett, *Families Against the City.*
7. Norman H. Clark, *Deliver Us From Evil: An Interpretation of American Prohibition* (New York: W. W. Norton Co., 1976); James H. Timberlake, *Prohibition and the Progressive Movement* (Cambridge, Mass.: Harvard University Press, 1963).
8. U.S. Bureau of the Census, *Statistics of Cities* (1905), p. 328; Bureau of the Census, *11th Decennial Census, Social Statistics of Cities* (1900), pp. 41–42.
9. For an analysis of the class basis of the movement in one city, see Roy Rosenzweig, "The Conflict over the Saloon: Working Class Drinking and the Legal Order in Worcester, Massachusetts, 1870–1900" (unpublished paper, 1979).
10. Patricia Simpson, "The Drunk and the Teetotaler: Two Phases of Temperance Reform among the Irish Working Class of Pittsburgh" (seminar paper, History Department, University of Pittsburgh), is a good study of working-class temperance reform. See also Rosenzweig, "The Conflict over the Saloon."
11. John E. George, "The Saloon Question in Chicago," *Economic Studies* 2, no. 2 (April 1897): 67–95; George M. Hammell, *The Passing of the Saloon* (Cincinnati: F. L. Rowe, 1908).
12. Jon M. Kingsdale, "The Poor Man's Club: Social Functions of the Urban Working Class Saloon"; Perry Duis, "The Saloon in a Changing Chicago."

13. Raymond Calkins, *Substitutes for the Saloon* (Boston: Houghton Mifflin, 1901), chap. 1. See also Kingsdale, "The Poor Man's Club," and Duis, "The Saloon in a Changing Chicago."

14. Koren, *Economic Aspects of the Liquor Problem*, p. 78.

15. Kingsdale, "The Poor Man's Club," p. 483; Duis, "The Saloon in a Changing Chicago," pp. 218, 220; George K. Turner, "The City of Chicago," *McClure's Magazine* 28, no. 6 (April 1907): 579.

16. During the "high license" fight of 1906, the Chicago police made regular arrests of saloonkeepers for such offenses as selling liquor to minors. These were few in relation to the 8,000 or more saloons in the city, but most violations were doubtlessly overlooked.

17. *New York Evening Post*, June 18, 1931.

18. Duis, "The Saloon in a Changing Chicago," pp. 214–224.

19. Milwaukee City Documents, *Annual Message of the Mayor* (1884); *Milwaukee Sentinel*, September 16–17, 1885.

20. George, "The Saloon Question in Chicago," pp. 73–74; Duis, "The Saloon in a Changing Chicago," p. 218.

21. Daniel F. Ring, "Some Reform Elements in Milwaukee Politics, 1872–1890" (M.S. thesis, University of Wisconsin, Milwaukee, 1971), pp. 37–42.

22. Ibid., pp. 44–45; *Milwaukee Sentinel*, June 5, 1885; Milwaukee City Documents, *Annual Message of the Mayor* (1884).

23. Ring, "Some Reform Elements in Milwaukee Politics," pp. 45–49; *Milwaukee Sentinel*, September 10–16, 1885.

24. Duis, "The Saloon in a Changing Chicago," 217–218.

25. *Chicago Tribune*, December 18, 1903.

26. Ibid.

27. Ibid.

28. *Chicago Tribune*, December 29, 1903.

29. *Chicago Tribune*, January 15, 1906. The demand was first raised by the clergy and amplified immediately by other groups. See the *Chicago Tribune*, January 16–22, 1906.

30. The role of the mass media in generating "crime waves" for political purposes is carefully analyzed in Stuart Hall, Chas Critcher, Tony Jefferson, John Clarke, and Brian Roberts, *Policing the Crisis: Mugging, the State, and Law and Order*. It should be noted here that the *Tribune's* political leanings were conservative Republican, and it is generally considered the organ of Chicago's bourgeoisie.

31. *Chicago Tribune*, February 15, 1906.

32. Ibid. The photograph Wendling refers to appeared in the *Tribune* on February 13, 1906.

33. *Chicago Tribune*, February 15, 1906.

34. *Chicago Tribune*, February 15, 8, 1906.

35. *Chicago Tribune,* February 15, 1906.

36. The measure passed on March 5, 1906, and a detailed account of this action is contained in the *Chicago Tribune* for March 6; see the *Tribune*'s front-page cartoons for February 14, 24, and 27, March 2 and 5, 1906. An account of Mayor Dunne's signing of the ordinance on March 6 is in the March 7 *Tribune.* The campaign can be followed in the *Tribune,* where it was front-page news from February 16 through March 6.

37. *Chicago Tribune,* February 15, 1906.

38. *Milwaukee Journal,* May 1, 1906.

39. *Milwaukee Sentinel,* June 23, 1906.

40. *Milwaukee Journal,* May 1, 1906.

41. *Milwaukee News,* June 30, 1906; *Milwaukee Press,* July 3, 1906.

42. *Milwaukee News,* July 10, 1906; *Milwaukee Sentinel,* July 10, 11, 21, 1910; *Evening Wisconsin,* July 3, 13, 1906.

43. *Chicago Tribune,* February 13, 1906.

44. The *Chicago Tribune* regularly reported disciplinary measures against police officers. There is an especially long listing of violations during the high-license activity of January–March 1906, suggesting that the police department at least sometimes punished violators of departmental liquor regulations to head off public criticism.

45. August Piper, *Report of an Investigation of the Discipline and Administration of the Police Department of the City of Chicago,* (Chicago: City Club of Chicago, 1906), pp. 6–7. Piper patrolled the streets for about one month and found 174 derelictions of duty, largely saloon related.

46. Ibid., pp. 8–9.

47. *Chicago Tribune,* March 25, 1904.

48. Chicago Police Department, *Annual Reports* (1890–1915).

49. "Socialists, Police Courts, and Juries," *International Socialist Review* 14, no. 5 (November 1913): 302–303.

50. Milwaukee Police Department, *Annual Reports* (1890–1905).

51. Milwaukee Police Department, *Annual Reports* (1890–1900).

52. U.S. Bureau of the Census, *Special Census of Cities* (1905), p. 328; Daniel F. Ring, "The Temperance Movement in Milwaukee: 1872–1884," *Historical Messenger* 31, no. 4 (Winter 1975): 98–105; Mary Clare Fabishak, "The Rhetoric of Urban Reform: Milwaukee during the Progressive Era" (M.A. thesis, University of Wisconsin, Milwaukee, 1974), chap. 4.

53. U.S. Bureau of the Census, *Special Census of Cities* (1905), p. 328.

54. Allegheny Department of Public Safety, *Report of the Bureau of Police* (1891), p. 46.

55. Allegheny City, population about 125,000 in 1900, was on the north bank of the Allegheny River, opposite Pittsburgh. It was annexed to Pittsburgh in 1907.

56. Allegheny Department of Public Safety, *Annual Report* (1892).
57. Pittsburgh Department of Public Safety, *Report of Superintendent, Bureau of Police* (1890), p. 560.
58. Ibid., pp. 515–516.
59. Ibid., p. 301; New York Bureau of Municipal Research, *Report on the Bureau of Police* (1913), p. 513, reprinted in abridged form in Paul U. Kellogg, *Wage Earning Pittsburgh*, vol. 6 of *The Pittsburgh Survey*, pp. 516–526.
60. Adams, "Machine Politics in Action," pp. 10–13; Allen Humphreys Kerr, *The Mayors and Recorders of Pittsburgh 1816–1951* (Pittsburgh, 1952), p. 227.
61. John Bodner, *Immigration and Industrialization: Ethnicity in an American Mill Town, 1870–1940* (Pittsburgh: University of Pittsburgh Press, 1977), pp. 79–81.
62. Pittsburgh Department of Public Safety, *Report of the Assistant Superintendent of Police* (1889), p. 283, and (1890), p. 361.
63. Bodner, *Immigration and Industrialization*, p. 99.
64. Allegheny Department of Public Safety, *Annual Report* (March 31, 1893), pp. 76–77.
65. Virginia Yans McLaughlin, "Like the Fingers on the Hand: Family and Community Life of First Generation Italian Americans in Buffalo, New York, 1880–1930" (Ph.D. diss., State University of New York, Buffalo, 1971), p. 165; Bodner, *Immigration and Industrialization*, p. 94.
66. Harvey S. Ford, "The Life and Times of Golden Rule Jones," p. 338; Cleveland Department of Public Safety, *Annual Report of the Chief of Police* (1908), pp. 13–15. Kohler further discusses his "Golden Rule" program in succeeding annual reports; see (1909), pp. 13–14, (1910), pp. 13–15. Fred Kohler's provocative address to the International Association of Chiefs of Police, "Common Sense: A Golden Rule" was widely reprinted and can be found in the minutes of the 1908 IACP meeting and in the Cleveland Public Library. On the Golden Rule program, see Bremner, "The Civil Revival in Ohio," pp. 387–398; William J. Norton, "Chief Kohler of Cleveland and His Golden Rule Policy," *The Outlook* 92 (November 6, 1909): 537–542; and Frederick C. Howe, "A Golden Rule Chief of Police," *Everybodies* 22 (June 1910): 814–823. A biography of Kohler that illustrates much about the career of nineteenth- and early-twentieth-century police officers and of the police institution in that period is N. R. Howard, "I, Fred Kohler," which appeared as a lengthy series in the *Cleveland Plain Dealer* beginning June 23, 1934. A copy is in the Cleveland Public Library. Chapters 15 and 16 deal with the Golden Rule. On Toledo, the best source is Ford's biography of Jones, which contains extensive discussion of the police and justice.

67. Cleveland Department of Public Safety, *Annual Report* (1908), pp. 13–15; Hoyt Landon Warner, *Progressivism in Ohio, 1897–1917* (Columbus: Ohio State University Press, 1964), chap. 3.

68. Howard, "I, Fred Kohler," chaps. 15, 16, 20–26; Grand Rapids *Annual Report* (1909–1910); Ford, "The Life and Times of Golden Rule Jones," pp. 151–158.

CHAPTER 8. OTHER RECREATIONAL BEHAVIOR

1. Roy Lubove, "The Progressives and the Prostitute"; Egal Feldman, "Prostitution, the Alien Woman, and the Progressive Imagination, 1905–1910," *American Quarterly* 29 (Summer 1967): 192–206; David J. Pivar, *Purity Crusade: Sexual Morality and Social Control 1868–1900.*

2. *Milwaukee Journal,* August 24, 1912. All these incidents are reported in the "Dance Hall" scrapbook in the Milwaukee Municipal Reference Bureau.

3. *Milwaukee Journal,* August 24, 1912.

4. *Milwaukee Journal,* August 24, 1912.

5. *Milwaukee Sentinel,* October 29, November 12, 1912.

6. *Milwaukee Leader,* January 22, 1914.

7. *Milwaukee Free Press,* November 30, 1913.

8. *Chicago Tribune,* February 12, 1906.

9. *Chicago Tribune,* February 12, 1906. After trouble from the Chicago police, the America dance hall changed its name to the United States; *Chicago Tribune,* February 19, 1906.

10. *Chicago Tribune,* February 19, 21–22, 1906.

11. *Chicago Tribune,* December 11, 1906.

12. *Chicago Tribune,* February 13, 19, 1906.

13. *Chicago Tribune,* February 19, 22, 1906.

14. *Chicago Tribune,* March 2, 10, 1906.

15. On the Levee district and the political machine that controlled it, see Lloyd Wendt and Herman Kogan, *Lords of the Levee: The Story of Bathhouse John and Hinky Dink* (Indianapolis and New York: Bobbs-Merrill, 1943). Chicago Commission of Vice, *The Social Evil in Chicago* (1911), links saloons to the prostitution business.

16. Duane Mowry, "The Reign of Graft in Milwaukee," *Arena* 34 (December 1905): 193; Carlin, "Chief Janssen," chap. 4; *Milwaukee Sentinel,* October 1–2, 1905; Mary Clare Fabishak, "The Rhetoric of Urban Reform: Milwaukee during the Progressive Era" (M.A. thesis, University of Wisconsin, Milwaukee, 1974), chap. 3.

17. Harvey Wachtman, "History of the Social Democratic Party of Milwaukee, 1897–1910," *Illinois Studies in the Social Sciences* 28, no. 1 (1945): 80; *Milwaukee Sentinel,* August 28, 1908.

18. Fabishak, "Rhetoric of Urban Reform," chap. 3; Wachtman, "Social Democratic Party of Milwaukee," p. 80.
19. Carlin, "Chief Janssen," chap. 6. The best source on Milwaukee vice is a series of scrapbooks available in the Milwaukee Municipal Reference Bureau under "Licensing," "Gambling," and "Prostitution."
20. *Social Democratic Herald,* July 2, 1906.
21. Illinois State Senate, *The Chicago Police System* (Springfield, 1898), pp. 13–14; Wendt and Kogan, *Lords of the Levee;* Chicago Commission on the Liquor Problem, *Preliminary Report* (1916); Chicago Tribune, April 21, 28, 1907.
22. August Piper, *Report of an Investigation of the Discipline and Administration of the Police Department of the City of Chicago* (Chicago: City Club of Chicago, 1906), p. 14.
23. Ibid., pp. 14–15.
24. Ibid., pp. 44–45.
25. *Indianapolis News,* January 14, 1902.
26. *Chicago Tribune,* March 24, 1904.
27. *Buffalo Express,* June 8, 1907, quoted in Virginia Yans McLaughlin, *Family and Community: Italian Immigrants in Buffalo, 1880–1930,* (Ithaca: Cornell University Press, 1976), p. 112.

CHAPTER 9. THE TRAMP ACTS

1. On the class basis of vagrancy and tramp legislation see William A. Chambliss, "A Sociological Analysis of the Law of Vagrancy," p. 69; and Caleb Foote, "Vagrancy-type Law and Its Administration." For a discussion of the concept of "class legislation," see David Dixon, "Class Law: The Street Betting Act of 1906." For an analysis of the content of the tramp acts in the United States and how these acts differed from pre-existing vagrancy laws see my "Class Conflict and the Enforcement of the Tramp Acts in Buffalo during the Depression of 1893–1894," p. 873; and Peter T. Ringenbach, *Tramps and Reformers,* chaps. 1 and 2.
2. Henry Vincent, *The Story of the Commonweal;* Donald L. MacMurray, *Coxey's Army: A Study of the Industrial Army Movement of 1894;* Peter Carlin, "Social Outcasts: The Tramp in American Society, 1873–1910," (paper read at the annual meeting of the American Historical Association, New York, December 28, 1979).
3. *Detroit Free Press,* April 19–26, 1894; *Detroit News,* April 18, 26, 1894; *Toledo Blade,* June 16, 20, 28, 1894; *Cleveland Plain Dealer,* May 1–6, 1894; *Buffalo Express,* August 14–27, 1894.
4. Biographical information on Rybakowski is sketchy, with different newspapers giving conflicting spellings of his name and facts about his background. The most detailed reporting of this information is found in the

Buffalo Express during late August 1894, and it is these accounts that I primarily follow.

5. *Toledo Blade,* July, 17, 19, 1894.
6. *Toledo Blade,* July 27, 1894; Toledo Police Department, *Annual Reports* (1892, 1894). The East Toledo tramp room is one example of a widespread police practice of the period, the provision of lodging for tramps and others who were homeless. Historian Eric Monkkonen has termed this practice and a similar one, caring for lost children, examples of "class management" (Monkkonen, *Police in Urban America,* chap. 3). I cannot be sure of the exact relationship between what Monkkonen calls "class management" and what I call "class struggle," but I assume that he is generally referring to the same process. However, his emphasis on the lodging function obscures a much more complex relationship. The core of the police function when dealing with tramps was fundamentally violent, as exemplified by all the arrests and beatings that victimized tramps. The provision of lodging, in a prewelfare period, allowed a much more complete measure of control, linking the functions of violent repression and welfare in a total pattern of class domination (Monkkonen's "class management"?). But, at the same time, this relationship never fooled the tramps—most of them stayed as far away from the police stations as they could under ordinary circumstances. Most of the police lodging statistics represent the local homeless—unemployed locals, widows and orphans, immigrants looking for lost families, rejects from various institutions—all banded together as "tramps." Although this is perhaps irrelevant, I also do not understand why Monkkonen links the function of returning lost children with the function of tramp lodging. As far as I know, the police still do the former with great regularity as part of their general service function, right down to the customary ice cream cone.
7. *Cleveland Plain Dealer,* July 21, 1894; *Sandusky Register,* July 24, 1894.
8. *Cleveland Plain Dealer,* July 25, 26, 1894.
9. *Cleveland Plain Dealer,* July 26, 27, 1894.
10. *Cleveland Plain Dealer,* July 28, 1894.
11. *Cleveland Plain Dealer,* July 29, 30, 1894.
12. *Cleveland Plain Dealer,* July 31, August 1–3, 1894.
13. *Buffalo Express,* August 11, 1894.
14. All arrest data are from the Buffalo Police Department *Annual Reports* for the relevant years.
15. *Buffalo Express,* August 21, 1892.
16. Ibid.
17. *Buffalo Express,* August 16, 1892. Grand Master McSweeney's statement blaming the strike violence on tramps must be understood in the context of the period. Unions were not strongly established. They were treading a fine line between the need to organize strong mass actions to fight for their members' livelihoods and the class-collaborationist AFL policy of

seeking respect and recognition from employers. Thus, while the strike was on, the union actively encouraged mass support by the Buffalo working class, and the working class turned out in great numbers. Since a large number of railroad workers were unemployed, there is no reason to doubt that substantial numbers of tramps were involved in this and other strikes. Thus, the characterization of militant workers as "tramps" probably had an element of truth in it, but it concealed the real issue: tramps were unemployed workers, and this use of the term criminalizes militant workers and delegitimates class struggle.

18. *Buffalo Express*, May 14, June 30, 1894.
19. Jack London was 18 when he was imprisoned in the Erie County Penitentiary. He had left Oakland in April 1894, trailing Kelley's Army toward Washington. London caught up with Kelley near Omaha, marched with it to Hannibal, Missouri, and then deserted on May 24. By his own account, he refused to accept discipline and often roamed ahead, begging for food on behalf of the army and keeping the best for himself. After deserting, he "hoboed" to New York City, where he slept, read, and drank ice-cold milk in City Hall Park until he was attacked from behind by a club-swinging policeman. He fled to Niagara Falls to view the sights and clumsily ran into a policeman. He was indignant over getting a thirty-day sentence without even a chance to speak at his trial and without the judge going through the formality of finding him guilty. In prison London quickly became a trusty and, like all other trusties, used the position to exploit other inmates, engaging in graft for extra food, tobacco, and other minor privileges, such as mailing letters. This required using substantial brute force, since 13 trusties had to maintain their privileged positions over 500 inmates in the cell block: "We could not permit the slightest infraction of the rules, the slightest insolence. If we did we were lost. Our own rule was to hit a man as soon as he opened his mouth—hit him hard, hit him with anything." Jack London, *The Road* (Santa Barbara: Peregrine Publishers, 1978), pp. 102–112; Phillip S. Foner, *Jack London: American Rebel* (Secaucus, N.J.: Citadel Press, 1969).
20. London, *The Road*, pp. 74–121.
21. *Buffalo Express*, May 31, 1894.
22. *Buffalo Express*, July 22, 1894.
23. *Buffalo Express*, July 24, 1894.
24. *Buffalo Express*, July 23, 26, 1894.
25. *Buffalo Express*, August 20, 21, 1894; *Buffalo Courier*, August 20, 1894; *Buffalo Evening News*, August 21, 1894.
26. *Buffalo Courier*, June 20, 1894; *Buffalo Express*, June 20, 1894.
27. *Buffalo Courier*, August 21, 22, 1894.
28. *Buffalo Evening News*, August 21, 22, 1894.
29. *Buffalo Express*, August 22, 1894; *Buffalo Courier*, August 22, 1894.
30. *Buffalo Express*, August 25, 1894; *Buffalo Commercial*, August 23, 1894; *Buffalo Evening News*, August 24, 25, 1894; *Buffalo Courier*, August 25,

1894. The three captains were Frank Killeen, George Kress, and Frank Koehler.

31. *Buffalo Evening News,* August 19, 24, 25, 1894.
32. *Buffalo Evening News,* August 24, 25, 1894; *Buffalo Express,* August 25, 1894.
33. *Buffalo Express,* August 25, 1894.
34. *Buffalo Evening News,* August 25, 1894.
35. *Buffalo Express,* August 28, 1894.
36. *Buffalo Express,* August 27, 1894.
37. *Buffalo Courier,* August 27, 1894; *Buffalo Express,* August 27, 1894.
38. *Buffalo Express,* September 10, 1894.
39. Chicago Police Department, *Annual Reports* (1890–1908).
40. Chicago Municipal Lodging House, *Annual Report* (1903), p. 12, (1904), p. 17.
41. *Chicago Tribune,* March 10, 1907.
42. Chicago Police Department, *Annual Reports* (1906–1907).
43. Chicago Police Department, *Annual Report* (1903), p. 11.

CHAPTER 10. POLICING FELONY CRIME

1. Bittner, *The Functions of the Police.* This is a central theme of Bittner's analysis of the police; it is made most clearly in his chapter "Florence Nightingale in Pursuit of Willie Sutton."
2. David Johnson, *Policing the Urban Underworld: The Impact of Crime on the Development of the American Police, 1800–1887.*
3. Roger Lane, "Urbanization and Criminal Violence in the Nineteenth Century," p. 163.
4. Richardson, *The New York Police,* pp. 24–25; Richardson, *Urban Police in the United States,* pp. 19–20.
5. Louis Wirth, *On Cities and Social Life* (Chicago: University of Chicago Press, 1971).
6. O'Connor, *Fiscal Crisis of the State.*
7. Roger Lane, "Crime and Criminal Statistics in Nineteenth Century Massachusetts," *Journal of Social History* (Winter 1968): 156–163.
8. George Kelling et al., *The Kansas City Preventive Patrol Experiment* (Washington, D.C.: The Police Foundation, 1974).
9. Buffalo Police Department, *Annual Report* (1906), p. 22.
10. We do not have enough research on the class basis of crime waves. A model study of a crime wave in Britain is Hall et al., *Policing the Crisis.* A recent historical analysis of a bourgeoisie-manufactured "crime wave" is Jennifer Davis, "The London Garotting Panic of 1862: Moral Panic and the Creation of a Criminal Class in Mid-Victorian England."
11. *Chicago Tribune,* November 17, 1903, pp. 1–2.
12. *Chicago Tribune,* November 28, 1903, p. 3.

13. *Chicago Tribune,* December 10, 1903, p. 1; November 30, 1903, p. 2; December 6, 1903, pp. 1–2; December 9, 1903, p. 1.
14. *Chicago Tribune,* December 6, 1903, pp. 1–2; December 4, 1903, p. 1.
15. *Chicago Tribune,* November 17, 1903. The Committee of Twenty-five, composed of business and civic leaders, is listed in the December 21, 1903, edition.
16. This issue is graphically presented in Jill Nelson, "The Dope Kids of 115th Street," *Village Voice* 25, no. 27 (July 2, 1980). Harlem teenagers, facing a 75 percent unemployment rate and no hope for a better job than "stocking shelves in supermarkets," sometimes choose careers as professional dope pushers, which feature up to $500 a week (tax-free), better hours, and no bosses. Young people faced similar choices a hundred years ago.
17. Charles Loring Brace, *The Dangerous Classes of New York, and Twenty Years Work Among Them* (New York: Wynkoop and Hallenbeck, 1872). Three modern studies employing the concept "dangerous class" as distinct from the lumpenproletariat are Eric Monkkonen, *The Dangerous Class: Crime and Poverty in Columbus, Ohio, 1860–1885;* Louis Chevalier, *Laboring Classes and Dangerous Classes in Paris during the First Half of the Nineteenth Century* (New York: Howard Fertig, 1973); and Robert Tombs, "Crime and the Security of the State: The 'Dangerous Classes' and Insurrection in Nineteenth-Century Paris." Only Tombs uses the term in its correct sense—nothing more than a bourgeois label for parts of the working class and the lumpenproletariat. Monkkonen uses official arrest statistics and poor house admissions to prove that a "dangerous class" existed in Columbus, Ohio. Needless to say, even if those official statistics represent what Monkkonen thinks they do (that is, crime and poverty), the end product is not a "dangerous class." Since almost all of the poor avoided the poorhouse and many criminals avoided getting arrested, it is doubtful that this remains anything more than a computer exercise.
18. *Chicago Tribune,* November 28, 1903, p. 3.
19. *Chicago Tribune,* December 6, 1903.
20. Allan Pinkerton, "The Yeggman," *Proceedings of the Annual Meeting of the International Association of Chiefs of Police* (1905), pp. 55–59.
21. Pittsburgh Bureau of Public Safety, *Annual Report* (1898), p. 477.
22. Michael Feldberg, "Policemen as Social Workers: The 19th Century Experience" (paper presented at the annual meeting of the American Historical Association, 1978).
23. Pittsburgh Department of Public Safety, *Third Annual Report* (1890), p. 381.
24. Ibid., p. 562.
25. James Forbes, "The Reverse Side," p. 368.
26. Ibid., p. 309.

27. Ibid., pp. 321–322.
28. Ibid., p. 319.
29. Ibid., pp. 327–329, 334.
30. Ibid., p. 374.
31. City Council of Pittsburgh, *Report on the Bureau of Police* (1913), reprinted in abbreviated form in Kellogg, *Wage Earning Pittsburgh,* pp. 523–524.
32. Haller, "Historical Roots of Police Behavior."
33. *Milwaukee Daily News,* August 23, 1905; Forbes, "The Reverse Side," pp. 314–315.
34. Milwaukee Police Department, *Annual Reports* (1888, 1890–1900).
35. Ibid.
36. Donald C. Dillworth, *The Blue and the Brass: American Policing 1890–1910* (Gaithersburg, Md.: International Association of Chiefs of Police, 1976), chap. 4; Pittsburgh Department of Public Safety, *Annual Report* (1894), pp. 299–301.
37. "You May Be Arrested for Murder Today," *Chicago Tribune,* February 18, 1906. The issue of police brutality, the "third degree," was vigorously denied by the police, but the charge that the police routinely used brutality against criminals remained common throughout American cities. For a discussion of the issue among police chiefs, see *Proceedings of the Annual Meeting of the International Association of Chiefs of Police* (1910), pp. 61–76.
38. Friedrich Engels, "Results," in *The Condition of the Working Class in England,* pp. 141–142, 154–155, 168–169. We still have a long way to go in research on the class basis of criminal activity. Engels's initial hypothesis is sufficiently proved, however; see John Braithwaite, *Inequality, Crime and Public Policy* (London: Routledge and Kegan Paul, 1979). Data presented in Marshall B. Clinard and Daniel J. Abbott, *Crime in Developing Countries* (New York: Wiley-Interscience, 1973), show that the emergence of a class system in developing countries tends to lead to higher crime rates.

CHAPTER 11. CONCLUSION

1. Lenin, *State and Revolution.* The essence of Lenin's argument is that democracy is the best "shell" for capitalism because of its capacity to obscure class exploitation and to legitimate class society.
2. Edward P. Thompson, *Whigs and Hunters: The Origin of the Black Act,* chap. 10.
3. Bittner, *The Functions of the Police,* chap. 17.
4. Here, perhaps, it is appropriate to say a few words about Sam Walker's theory that it is the public popularity of the American criminal justice system that accounts both for the best and the worst features of the system—

that is, his notion of "popular justice." Besides my reluctance to label specific features as either "best" or "worst"—an ahistorical attempt to apply some 1980s value judgments to very complex social phenomena—I think the whole issue of popularity or unpopularity is not very important. Obviously, various aspects of the criminal justice system are highly popular, but they are also highly unpopular—depending on who is making the judgment and what the issue is. Walker mistakenly reads backward from the popularity that much of the criminal justice system enjoyed in the late 1960s and early 1970s. The overall record runs from bad to good, with stops virtually every place in between—hardly evidence for a theory of popular justice.

5. This example will be familiar to students of labor history as the "Battle of the Running Bulls," where General Motors workers staged an elaborate maneuver to capture several GM plants from GM police and the Flint, Michigan, municipal police in 1937. Irving Bernstein, *Turbulent Years* (Boston: Houghton Mifflin, 1969), pp. 529–530. For those unused to slang terms of the 1930s, the term "bulls" refers to the police.

SELECTED BIBLIOGRAPHY

Adams, Graham. *Age of Industrial Violence*. New York: Columbia University Press, 1966.

Billington, Ray Allen. *The Protestant Crusade, 1800–1860*. New York: Macmillan, 1938.

Bittner, Egon. *The Functions of the Police in Modern Society*. Cambridge: Oelgeschlager, Gunn & Hain, 1980.

Bowles, Samuel, and Gintis, Herbert. *Schooling in Capitalist America*. New York: Basic Books, 1976.

Braverman, Harry. *Labor and Monopoly Capital*. New York: Monthly Review Press, 1976.

Bremner, Robert H. "The Civil Revival in Ohio: Police, Penal, and Parole Policies in Cleveland and Toledo." *American Journal of Economics and Sociology* 14 (July 1955): 387–398.

Brody, David. *Steelworkers in America: The Non-Union Era*. New York: Harper & Row, 1969.

Byington, Margaret. *Homestead: The Households of a Mill Town*. New York: Russell Sage Foundation, 1910. (Volume 6 of Kellogg, *The Pittsburgh Survey.)*

Cain, Maureen. "Trends in the Sociology of Police Work." *International Journal of the Sociology of Law* 7 (1979): 212–229.

Cain, Maureen, and Hunt, Alan. *Marx and Engels on Law*. New York: Academic Press, 1979.

Carlin, Kathleen M. "Chief Janssen and the Thirty-Three Year War: Law Enforcement in an Urban Society: The Concepts of Police Chief Janssen." M.S. thesis, University of Wisconsin, Milwaukee, 1961.

Castells, Manuel. *The Urban Question: A Marxist Approach*. Cambridge, Mass.: MIT Press, 1976.

Caye, James, F. "Pittsburgh Police and the Roundhouse Riot." M.A. thesis, University of Pittsburgh, 1970.

Chambliss, William A. "A Sociological Analysis of the Law of Vagrancy." *Social Problems* 12, no. 1 (Summer 1964): 67–78.

Commons, John R. *History of Labor in the United States.* Vol. 2. New York: Macmillan, 1926.

Cumbler, John T. *Working Class Community in Industrial America.* Westport, Conn.: Greenwood Press, 1979.

Dacus, Joseph A. *Annals of the Great Strikes in the United States.* St. Louis: Scamnel and Company, 1877.

Davis, Jennifer. "The London Garotting Panic of 1862: Moral Panic and the Creation of a Criminal Class in Mid-Victorian England." In V.A.C. Gatrell et al., eds., *Crime and the Law: The Social History of Crime in Western Europe since 1500.* London: Europa Publications, 1980.

Davis, Mike. "Why the U.S. Working Class is Different." *New Left Review* 123 (September/October 1980): 3–44.

Dawley, Alan. *Class and Community: The Industrial Revolution in Lynn.* Cambridge, Mass.: Harvard University Press, 1976.

Diamond, Stanley. "The Rule of Law Versus the Order of Custom." In Robert Paul Wolf, ed., *The Rule of Law.* New York: Simon and Schuster, 1972.

Dixon, David. "Class Law: The Street Betting Act of 1906." *International Journal of the Sociology of Law* 8 (1980): 101–128.

Duis, Perry. "The Saloon in a Changing Chicago." *Chicago History* 4 (Winter 1975): 214–24.

Engels, Friedrich. *The Condition of the Working Class in England.* Moscow: Progress Publishers, 1973. Reprint of authorized English edition of 1892, translated by Mrs. F. Kelley-Wischnewetzky.

Esping-Anderson, Gosta; Friedland, Roger; and Wright, Erik Olin. "Modes of Class Struggle and the Capitalist State." *Kapitalistate* 4/5 (1976): 186–220.

Ewen, Lynda. *Corporate Power and Urban Crisis in Detroit.* Princeton: Princeton University Press, 1978.

Fink, Leon. "The Figure and the Phantom: Class Conflict in the Gilded Age." *Radical History Review* 3, no. 2 (Fall-Winter 1975): 56–69.

———. "Workingmen's Democracy: The Knights of Labor in Local Politics, 1886–1896." Ph.D. diss. University of Rochester, 1977.

Flinn, John, and Wilkie, John. *A History of the Chicago Police.* 1887; rpr. New York: Arno Press, 1971.

Fogelson, Robert. *Big City Police.* Cambridge, Mass.: Harvard University Press, 1977.

Foner, Eric. *Politics and Ideology in the Age of the Civil War.* New York: Oxford University Press, 1980.

Foner, Phillip S. *History of the Labor Movement in the United States.* 5 vols. New York: International Publishers, 1947–1980.

Foote, Caleb. "Vagrancy-type Law and Its Administration." *University of Pennsylvania Law Review* 104 (March 1956): 603–650.

Ford, Harvey S. "The Life and Times of Golden Rule Jones." Ph.D. diss. University of Michigan, 1953.

Foster, John T. *Class Struggle and the Industrial Revolution.* London: Weidenfeld & Nicholson, 1974.

Friedman, Lawrence, and Percival, Robert. *The Roots of Justice: Crime and Punishment in Alameda County, California, 1870–1910.* Chapel Hill: University of North Carolina Press, 1981.

Gavett, Thomas. *The Development of the Labor Movement in Milwaukee.* Madison: University of Wisconsin Press, 1965.

Gold, David; Lo, Clarence; and Wright, Erik Olin. "Recent Developments in Marxist Theories of the Capitalist State." *Monthly Review* 27 (October 1975): 29–43; (November 1975): 36–51.

Goldstein, Herman. *Policing a Free Society.* Cambridge, Mass.: Ballinger, 1977.

Gordon, David. "Capitalist Development and the History of American Cities." In William Tabb and Larry Sawers, eds., *Marxism and the Metropolis.* New York: Oxford University Press, 1978.

Graham, Hugh D., and Gurr, Ted. *The History of Violence in America.* New York: Praeger Publishers, 1969.

Gutman, Herbert. "Work, Culture and Society in Industrializing America, 1815–1919," *American Historical Review* 78 (June 1973): 531–588.

———. "Class, Status, and Community Power in Nineteenth Century Industrial Cities—Paterson, New Jersey: A Case Study." In Frederick Cople Jaher, ed., *The Age of Industrialism in America.* New York: Free Press, 1968.

———. "The Tompkins Square 'Riot' in New York City on January 13, 1874: A Re-examination of Its Causes and Its Aftermath." *Labor History* 6 (Spring 1965): 44–70.

———. "The Buena Vista Affair, 1874–1875." *Pennsylvania Magazine of History and Biography* 88 (July 1964): 251–293.

———. "The Braidwood Lockout of 1874." *Journal of the Illinois State Historical Society* 52 (Spring 1960): 5–28.

———. "An Iron Workers' Strike in the Ohio Valley, 1873–1874." *Ohio Historical Quarterly* 68 (October 1959): 353–370.

———. "Two Lockouts in Pennsylvania: 1873–1874," *Pennsylvania Magazine of History and Biography* 83 (July 1959): 307–326.

Hall, Stuart, et al. *Policing the Crisis: Mugging, the State, and Law and Order.* New York: Holmes and Meier, 1978.

Haller, Mark. "Historical Roots of Police Behavior: Chicago, 1890–1925." *Law and Society Review* 10 (Winter 1976): 303–324.

Harring, Sidney L. "Class Conflict and the Enforcement of the Tramp Acts in Buffalo during the Depression of 1893–1894." *Law and Society Review* 11 (Summer 1977): 873–911.

———. "The Buffalo Police—1872–1915: Industrialization, Social Unrest, and the Development of the Police Institution." Ph.D. diss., University of Wisconsin, Madison, 1976.

Hay, Douglas. "Crime and Justice in Eighteenth- and Nineteenth-Century England." In Norval Morris and Michael Tonry, eds., *Crime and Justice: An Annual Review of Research.* Vol. 2. Chicago: University of Chicago Press, 1980.

———. "Property, Authority, and Criminal Law." In Douglas Hay et al., eds., *Albion's Fatal Tree: Crime and Society in Eighteenth-Century England.* New York: Pantheon, 1975.

Hays, Samuel. "The Politics of Reform in Municipal Government in the Progressive Era." *Pacific Northwest Quarterly* 55, no. 4 (October 1964): 157–169.

———. *The Response to Industrialism, 1885–1914.* Chicago: University of Chicago Press, 1957.

Hough, Leslie Seldon. "The Turbulent Spirit: Violence and Coaction Among Cleveland Workers, 1877–1899." Ph.D. diss., University of Virginia, 1977.

Howard, N. R. "I, Fred Kohler." Series of newspaper articles in pamphlet form. Cleveland Public Library.

Hubbell, Mark S. *Our Police and Our City.* Buffalo: Bensler and Wesley, 1893.

International Association of Chiefs of Police. *Proceedings of the Annual Convention, 1893–1915.* Vols. 1 and 2. New York: Arno Press, 1974.

Jeffreys-Jones, Rhodri. *Violence and Reform in American History.* New York: New Viewpoints, 1978.

———. " Violence in American History: Plug Uglies in the Progressive Era." *Perspectives in American History* 8 (1973): 465–583.

———. "Profit Over Class: A Study in American Industrial Espionage." *Journal of American Studies* 6 (December 1972): 233–248.

Johnson, Bruce. "Taking Care of Labor: The Police in American Politics." *Theory and Society* 3 (Spring 1976): 89–117.

Johnson, David R. *American Law Enforcement: A History.* St. Louis: Forum Press, 1981.

———. *Policing the Urban Underworld: The Impact of Crime on the Development of the American Police, 1800–1887.* Philadelphia: Temple University Press, 1979.

Kellogg, Paul, ed. *The Pittsburgh Survey.* 6 vols. New York: Russell Sage Foundation, 1910.

Ketchum, George. "Municipal Police Reform: A Comparative Study of Law Enforcement in Cincinnati, Chicago, New Orleans, New York, St. Louis, 1844–1877." Ph.D. diss., University of Missouri, Columbia, 1967.

Kingsdale, Jon M. "The Poor Man's Club: Social Functions of the Urban Working Class Saloon." *American Quarterly* 25 (October 1973): 472–489.

Kolko, Gabriel. *Main Currents in Modern American History.* New York: Harper & Row, 1976.

Koren, John. *Economic Aspects of the Liquor Problem.* Twelfth Annual Report of the U.S. Commissioner of Labor. Washington, D.C., 1898.

Lane, Roger. "Urban Police and Crime in Nineteenth Century America." In Michael Tonry and Norval Morris, eds., *Crime and Justice: An Annual Review of Research,* vol. 2. Chicago: University of Chicago Press, 1980.

———. *Violent Death in the City: Suicide, Accident, and Murder in Nineteenth-Century Philadelphia.* Cambridge, Mass.: Harvard University Press, 1979.

———. "Urbanization and Criminal Violence in the Nineteenth Century." *Journal of Social History* 2, no. 2 (December 1968): 156–163.

———. *Policing the City: Boston, 1822–1885.* Cambridge, Mass.: Harvard University Press, 1967.

Lefebvre, Henri. *The Sociology of Marx.* New York: Random House, 1968.

Lenin, V. I. *State and Revolution.* New York: International Publishers, 1971. Originally published in 1918.

Liebman, Robert, and Polen, Michael. "Perspectives on Policing in Nineteenth-Century America." *Social Science History* 2, no. 3 (Spring 1978): 349–351.

Lubove, Roy. "The Progressives and the Prostitute." *Historian* 24 (Summer 1962): 300–330.

Ludtke, Alf. "The Role of State Violence in the Period of Transition to Industrial Capitalism: The Example of Prussia from 1815 to 1848." *Social History* 4 (May 1979): 175–221.

McDonald, Forrest. "Streetcars and Politics in Milwaukee, 1896–1901," *Wisconsin Magazine of History* 29 (Spring 1956): 256–267; (Summer 1956): 384–398.

MacMurray, Donald L. *Coxey's Army: A Study of the Industrial Army Movement of 1894.* New York: Arno Press, 1970.

Mann, Henry. *Our Police: A History of the Pittsburgh Police Force Under Town and City.* Pittsburgh: City of Pittsburgh, 1889.

Marx, Karl. *Das Kapital.* Trans. Samuel Moore and Edward Aveling. New York: International Publishers, 1949. Originally published in English in 1887.

Marx, Karl, and Engels, Friedrich. *The Communist Manifesto.* New York: International Publishers, 1948.

Miliband, Ralph. *Marxism and Politics.* New York: Oxford University Press, 1977.

Miller, Wilbur. *Cops and Bobbies: Police Authority in New York and London, 1830–1870.* Chicago: University of Chicago Press, 1977.

Monkkonen, Eric. *Police in Urban America, 1860–1920*. New York: Cambridge University Press, 1981.

———. *The Dangerous Class: Crime and Poverty in Columbus, Ohio, 1860–1885*. Cambridge, Mass.: Harvard University Press, 1975.

Montgomery, David. *Workers' Control in America*. New York: Cambridge University Press, 1980.

———. "To Study the People: The American Working Class." *Labor History* 21 (Fall 1980): 485–512.

———. "Labor, Radicalism, and the State in Late Nineteenth-Century America." *Journal of Social History* 13 (Spring 1980): 219–247.

———. "Strikes in Nineteenth-Century America." *Social Science History* 4, no. 1 (February 1980): 81–104.

———. "Gutman's Nineteenth-Century America." *Labor History* 19 (Summer 1978): 416–429.

Morris, R. J. *Class and Class Consciousness in the Industrial Revolution, 1780–1850*. London: Macmillan, 1979.

Myers, Howard B. "The Policing of Labor Disputes in Chicago: A Case Study." Ph.D. diss., University of Chicago, 1929.

O'Connor, James. *The Fiscal Crisis of the State*. New York: St. Martins Press, 1973.

O'Donnell, Patrick. "Industrial Capitalism and the Rise of Modern American Cities." *Kapitalistate* 6 (Fall 1977): 91–128.

Pierce, Bessie. *A History of Chicago*. 3 vols. New York: Alfred Knopf, 1937–1957.

Piper, August. "Report of an Investigation of the Discipline and Administration of the Police Department of the City of Chicago." Chicago: City Club of Chicago, 1906.

Pivar, David J. *Purity Crusade: Sexual Morality and Social Control 1868–1900*, Westport, Conn.: Greenwood Press, 1973.

Ramirez, Bruno. *When Workers Fight: The Politics of Industrial Relations in the Progressive Era, 1898–1916*. Westport, Conn.: Greenwood Press, 1978.

Richardson, James. *Urban Police in the United States*. Port Washington, Conn.: Kennikat Press, 1974.

———. *The New York Police: Colonial Times to 1901*. New York: Oxford University Press, 1970.

Ringenbach, Peter T. *Tramps and Reformers*. Westport, Conn.: Greenwood Press, 1973.

Roe, George M. *Our Police: A History of the Cincinnati Police Force, from the Earliest Period Until the Present Day*. 1890; rpr. New York: A.M.S., 1976.

Rosswurm, Steven. "A Strike in the Rubber City: Rubber Workers, Akron, and the IWW, 1913." M.A. thesis, Kent State University, 1975.

Rubinstein, Jonathan. *City Police*. New York: Ballantine Books, 1974.

Samuel, Raphael. *People's History and Socialist Theory*. London: Routledge & Kegan Paul, 1981.

Sennett, Richard. *Families Against the City: Middle Class Homes of Industrial Chicago, 1872–1890*. New York: Vintage Books, 1974.

Shelton, Brenda. *Reformers in Search of Yesterday: Buffalo in the 1890s*. Albany: State University of New York Press, 1976.

————. "The Grain Shovellers' Strike of 1899." *Labor History* 9, no. 2 (1968): 210–238.

Silver, Allan. "The Demand for Order in Civil Society." In David Bordua, ed., *The Police: Six Sociological Essays*. New York: John Wiley & Sons, 1967.

Simon, Roger. "The Bay View Incident and the People's Party in Milwaukee." Seminar Paper, Department of History, University of Wisconsin, 1967.

Skolnick, Jerome. *Justice Without Trial*. New York: John Wiley & Sons, 1966.

Spitzer, Steven. "The Political Economy of Policing." In David Greenberg, ed., *Crime and Capitalism*. Palo Alto, Calif.: Mayfield Press, 1981.

————. "The Rationalization of Crime Control in Capitalist Society." *Contemporary Crises* 3 (April 1979): 187–206.

Sprogle, Howard C. *The Philadelphia Police: Past and Present*. New York: Arno Press, 1974.

Stark, Evan. "Gangs and Progress: The Contribution of Delinquency to Progressive Reform." In David Greenberg, ed., *Crime and Capitalism*. Palo Alto, Calif.: Mayfield Press, 1981.

Stedman-Jones, Gareth. "Class Expression versus Social Control? A Critique of Recent Trends in the Social History of Leisure." *History Workshop* 4 (Spring 1978): 162–170.

Steffens, Lincoln. *The Autobiography of Lincoln Steffens*. 2 vols. New York: Harcourt, Brace and World, 1931.

————. *The Shame of the Cities*. New York: S. S. McClure, 1904.

Tabb, William and Sawers, Larry. *Marxism and the Metropolis*. New York: Oxford University Press, 1976.

Thernstrom, Stephen. *Poverty and Progress: Social Mobility in a Nineteenth Century City*. Cambridge: Harvard University Press.

Thompson, Edward P. *Whigs and Hunters: The Origin of the Black Act*. New York: Pantheon, 1975.

————. "The Crime of Anonymity." In Douglas Hay, et al., eds., *Albion's Fatal Tree: Crime and Society in Eighteenth-Century England*. New York: Pantheon Books, 1975.

————. "Time, Work Discipline and Industrial Capitalism." *Past and Present* 38 (December 1967): 56–97.

————. *The Making of the English Working Class*. New York: Pantheon Books, 1963.

Thrasher, Eugene O. "The Magee-Flinn Political Machine, 1895–1903." M.A. thesis, University of Pittsburgh, 1951.

Tombs, Robert. "Crime and the Security of the State: The 'Dangerous Classes' and Insurrection in Nineteenth-Century Paris." In V.A.C. Gatrell, et al., eds., *Crime and the Law: The Social History of Crime in Western Europe Since 1500*. London: Europa Publications, 1980.

Vincent, Henry. *The Story of the Commonweal*. Chicago: W. B. Conkey Company, 1894.

Walker, Samuel. *Popular Justice: A History of American Criminal Justice*. New York: Oxford University Press, 1980.

———. "The Police and the Community: Scranton, Pennsylvania, 1866–1884, A Test Case." *American Studies* (Spring 1978): 79–90.

———. *A Critical History of Police Reform*. Lexington: D. C. Heath & Co., 1977.

Walkowitz, Daniel J. *Worker City, Company Town: Iron and Cotton-Worker Protest in Troy and Cohoes, New York, 1855–1884*. Urbana: University of Illinois Press, 1978.

Whitaker, John C. *History of the Police Department of Dayton, Ohio*. Dayton: Dayton Police Department, 1907.

Wolfe, Alan. *The Limits of Legitimacy*. New York: The Free Press, 1977.

INDEX

Akron, policing the rubber strike of
1913, 130–131
Allegheny City (Pennsylvania): patrol
wagon and signal system, 53; police
protection of fake cripples, 241; po-
lice regulation of saloons, 174–175
Anarchists, 145
Anti-spitting ordinances: in Chicago,
196–197; in Indianapolis, 196
Arrests, for calling out "scab," 133
Arrests, public order, 198, 206–207, in
Allegheny City, 175; in Chicago,
172; in Milwaukee, 173–174; in
Pittsburgh, 175–176
Arrests, tramps, 206–209

Baltimore, police in: initial creation,
31; patrol wagon and signal system,
53
"Battle of Hobo Run," 215–217
Beck, William, 86–87
Bittner, Egon: on police crime fighting
role, 224; on social services function
of police, 16, 255
Bonfield, John: administrative apparatus
for patrol wagon and signal system,
51; in streetcar strike of 1885,
115–116

Broadway market riot, 79, 213
Brooklyn police, and civil service, 36
Brown, Thomas, 56–57
Buell, Jonathan, 62
Buffalo: mayors, 66–67, politics,
65–67, 68, 71
Buffalo, crime in, 46, 64, 227
Buffalo, police in: Broadway market riot, 79–80; captains, 69; commissioners, 67; creation of uniformed force,
31–33; crowd and strike control, 54;
and free speech, 145, 214; Italian
community and the police, 72–80;
organized along ethnic group lines,
78–80, 142; origins, 61–63; patrol
wagon and signal system, 52–57; and
Polish community, 77–78; reorganization, 64–65; size of force, 34,
75–77; socialization of immigrants,
72, 199, 252; and tramp armies,
212–219, 260, 268–276, 282; turnover, 38; working conditions, 69, 70, 72
Buffalo, strikes in: Erie railroad, 61;
longshoremen's, 74–75; scoopers',
77; switchmen's, 117–119
Bull, William: Buffalo Chief of Police,
71–72; police discipline, 57; repression of tramps, 211–215

Cain, Maureen, 1
"Can-rushing," campaign to outlaw,
    161–162
Capitalist class, defined, 5
"Car barn bandits," 230, 234
Chicago, crime in, 230–234; dance
    halls, 187–190; middle-class isolation
    in, 11; saloons, 154–158; vice,
    193–195
Chicago, police in: corruption,
    193–195; creation of, 31–32; crime
    control, 229–232, 234–235; drinking
    on duty, 169–171; and gambling and
    prostitution, 193–195; patrol wagon
    and signal system, 50–52; Piper re-
    port, 41–42; "police brutality," 189;
    public order arrests, 46, 172; size of
    force, 34; size reduced in recession,
    34–35; and tramps, 219–222
Chicago, strikes and riots in: garment
    workers', 125–127; "Great Strike of
    1877," 107–109; Haymarket,
    113–114; Lager beer riots, 33; Mac-
    Cormick Reaper Works, 113–114;
    Pullman, 119; stockyards, 122–123;
    streetcar, 115–116; teamsters',
    123–125
Chicago "school," 224
Cincinnati, police in: arrest rates, 46;
    creation of uniformed force, 32; and
    Know-Nothings, 33; patrol wagon
    and signal system, 52; in riots of
    1853, 33
City, capitalist: characteristics, 9–12
Civil service and the police: in Brook-
    lyn, 36; and increased job stability,
    42; in Milwaukee, 36
Class conflict: and the police function,
    4, 13–17; and the tramp acts, 201
Class society, defined, 4–5
Cleveland, police in: arrest rates, 46;
    and "Golden Rule" arrest policy, 40,
    180–181; and Jeffries's tramp army,
    204–205; and Rybakowski's tramp
    army, 205, 206, 258, 259

Collins, John M.: on dance halls,
    189–190; on tramps and crime, 222
Columbus, police in, in street railroad
    strike, 137–139
Coxey, Jacob, 202
Crime: arrests for "suspicion,"
    244–245; crime waves and anti-sa-
    loon drive in Chicago, 163; felony
    crime, 224–226; and social class,
    228–233; statistics, 227; thieves,
    235; "waves," 229–232; "yeggs,"
    235–236; and youth, 230, 234–235
Crime control, technological improve-
    ments in, 244–245

Dance halls, 183–194; regulation as
    class legislation, 188–190; and sa-
    loons, 183–184; and sexual activity,
    184–186, 188
Dayton, police in: creation of uni-
    formed force, 32; patrol wagon and
    signal system, 53
Detroit, police in: arrests rates, 46; cre-
    ation of a uniformed force, 31; patrol
    wagon and signal system, 53
Diamond, Stanley, 15
Duluth, Minnesota, street railroad
    strike, 133–135

Engels, Friedrich, 13, 246
Erie County (New York) Penitentiary:
    Jack London's description of,
    210–211

"Free speech," police suppression of,
    144–145, 205, 214
Fogelson, Robert, 27, 38

Gambling and the police, 191–192; in
    Chicago, 193–196; in Milwaukee,
    191–193
Gamewell Signal Company, 53
Golden Rule police arrest policy, 40;
    adopted in Grand Rapids, 181; in
    Cleveland, 180–181; in Toledo, 180

Goldman, Emma, 145
Grand Army of the Republic Encampment, police co-operation during, 244–245
Grand Rapids, police in: and Golden Rule, 181; patrol wagon and signal system, 57–58; street railroad strike, 132–133
Great Lakes region, 22–26
Gutman, Herbert, 104–105, 135

Haller, Mark, 17, 242
Harrison, Carter H., 39, 114–117
Hay, Douglas, 16
"High license" fight: in Chicago, 160–165; to finance police expansion, 165; in Milwaukee, 159–160, 166–168
Hoan, Daniel, 145

Immigrants: divisions within the working class, 6; in Know-Nothing riots, 33; police socialization of, 152–153, 199; Rybakowski's industrial army, 202–206; unemployment, 201–202
Indianapolis, police in: anti-spitting ordinance, 196; street railroad strike, 139–141
Industrial Workers of the World and police: in Arkon, 129–130; free speech fights, 146; in Milwaukee, 146; in Pittsburgh, 146

Janssen, John: career, 89–90; departmental discipline, 57, 93; regulation of dance halls, 187; relations with socialists, 90–91; and small size of force, 36; in street railroad strike, 119–121; vice, 90, 191
Jeffries's army, 205, 211
Jones, Samuel: "Golden Rule" arrest policy, 40; support for strikers, 136
Johnson, Bruce, 104
Johnson, David, 244

Johnson, Tom: "Golden Rule" police arrest policy, 40; support for strikers, 136

Kansas City Preventive Patrol Experiment, 227
Kohler, Fred, 180–181
Know-Nothings: and the creation of a uniformed police, 31, 33–34; riots, 34

Lane, Roger, 224, 227
Legitimacy and the police, 16–17
Lenin, Nikolai, on the capitalist state, 7
Liquor: effect on work, 152; regulation of, 149–154
Liquor Question: Allegheny City, 174–175; Chicago, 154–158; Milwaukee, 158–159; Pittsburgh, 175–177; Steelton, 178–179
London, Jack, arrested for trampling, 210–211
Lumpenproletariat: and the police, 226; and the working class, 234–235

McCormick, Cyrus: and the police, 114–117; and reaper strike, 39
McGarigle, William, 56, 59
McKelvey, William, 27
Marx, Karl: analysis of crime, 224–226; analysis of the police, 13–15; analysis of social class, 4–5
Miller, Wilbur, 16
Milwaukee: economy, 81; politics, 81–86; saloons, 158–159; 167, Social Democratic party, 85, 96–98
Milwaukee, police in: arrest rates of, 23; arrests for "suspicion," 244–245; civil service, 36, 93; dance halls, 184–187; gambling, 167–168; 191–194; origins, 86, 93; police and fire commission, 91; public order arrests, 173; size of force, 36, 86, 93; vice district, 191–193

Milwaukee, strikes in: "Great Upheaval
of 1886," 94–96; streetcar strike,
119–121
Minneapolis, police in: patrol wagon
and signal system, 53
Monkkonnen, Eric, 28
Montgomery, David, 11, 19, 38
Morganstern, Daniel, 71, 206–208
Municipal lodging houses, in Chicago,
221–222
Muth, Henry, 175, 179

National Guard, in Oshkosh woodwork-
ers' strike, 128–129
National Police Chiefs' Association, 43
Newark, police in, creation of, 31
New Orleans, police in: creation of, 31;
patrol wagon and signal system, 53
New York, police in, creation of,
30–31
Niagara Frontier Police Force, 63–64
Niagara Falls (New York), tramps in,
210

O'Meara, Roger, 178
O'Neil, Francis: on electric technology
and police work, 27; on police surveillance of anarchists, 145; on street
crime, 230
Oshkosh (Wisconsin), woodworkers'
strike, 128–130

Parsons, Louisa, 145
Patrol wagon and signal system: administration, 50–51; arrests, 54–55; civilian use, 51; crime control, 54–55;
design, 50–52; effect on police institution, 58–60; expansion of, 52–53;
manpower for, 59; origins of, 47–51;
police assigned to, 56; use in strikes,
53–55, 116–117
Philadelphia, police in: creation of, 31;
patrol wagon and signal system, 53
Piper, August: 41, 167–171; 194–195;
232

Piper report. See Piper, August.
Pittsburgh, police in: and liquor question, 174–179; patrol wagon and signal system, 55; street crime,
237–239
Police and strikes. See individual strikes
Police brutality, 189, 216, 245
Police corruption, 40–41, 70
Police expenditure, 28
Police institution: arrest rates, 46; control of gambling, 191–194; control of
prostitution, 191–194; detectives,
243–245; development of, 26–30;
function under capitalism, 14–18;
initial creation of, 30–34; military
training, 65; police/citizen ratio,
198–199; police criminal activity,
239–243; political surveillance, 145;
professionalization, 44–45; size increases, 28, 29, 34, 76; size of individual forces, 34–36; and social services, 236–239; and state violence,
13–14
Police rank and file: arrests per man,
46; class position of, 141–143; discipline, 44–45, 57–59, 92–93; membership turnover, 38; "mutiny" in
Columbus, 137; "mutiny" in Indianapolis, 139–141; refusing to do antistrike work, 137–141; salary of,
42, 141, 180; work hours, 42; working conditions, 41–43; 45–46
Policed society, 13–16, 149–150
Polish workers, 79, 213–214
Political machines and the police,
11–12, 39, 65–66, 69–71
Population growth in Great Lakes region, 23–24
Prison conditions: in Buffalo, 210–211;
in Pittsburgh, 146
Private police, 47, 123–127
Prostitution, 191–195

Raitz, Benjamin, 203
Regan, Michael, 72, 80, 199

Reitman, Ben, 221
Richardson, James, 224
Riots, and the creation of urban police, 33–34
"Roundhouse riots," 34
Rybakowski, Joseph, 202–205; 212–218

St. Louis, police in: creation of, 31; in Know-Nothing riots, 33–34; patrol wagon and signal system, 53
St. Paul, police in, and patrol wagon and signal system, 52
Saloons: blacklist in Milwaukee, 167; reform movement in Chicago, 159–164; social functions of, 156–158; statistics, 156–158
Schneider, John, 33–34
Seidel, Emil, 82–83, 90–91, 97
Sennett, Richard, 11, 152
Social Democratic Party and the police, 39–40, 82–84, 96–99, 167, 184–185, 192–193
State, capitalist, 7–9
Stedman-Jones, Gareth, 151
Steelton (Pennsylvania), 178–179
Strikes: crime and, 235–236; policy, 101–106, 131–132; statistics, 102
Strikes and the police: Akron rubber strike, 130–131; Buffalo longshoremen's, 74–75; Buffalo scoopers', 77; Buffalo switchmen's 117–119; Chicago garmentworkers', 125–126; Chicago stockyards, 122–123; Chicago streetcar (1885), 115–116; Chicago streetcar (1903), 229; Chicago teamsters', 123–126; Cleveland garmentworkers', 136; Columbus street-car, 137–139; Duluth streetcar, 133–134; Erie railroad, 61; Grand Rapids streetcar, 132–133; Great Strike of 1877, 74, 106–110; "Great Upheaval" (1886), 94–95; Indianapolis streetcar, 139–141; McCormick reaper works, 113–114; Milwaukee streetcar strike (1896), 119–121; Oshkosh woodworkers', 128–129; Pope-Toledo Motorcar Company, 136; Pullman, 119, 137

Temperance movement, 152–154
Thompson, Edward P., 5, 251
Toledo, police in: and Golden Rule, 40, 180; Jeffries's army, 256–257; patrol wagon and signal system, 53; Rybakowski's army, 202–203
Tramp acts, 201
Tramping and crime, 201–202, 235–236

Vigilantism, 130–131

Walber, Emil, 87, 94–95
Walker, Sam, 104
Withey, Lewis, 57–58
Wilkie, John, 50, 51
Working class: arrests for criminal activity, 45–47; ethnic conflict, 6, 142; politics, 36; 144–146; recreational activity, 149–151; 183–189; social conditions, 10–11

"Yeggs," 235–236

Zabel, Winfred, 192–193